6044764

WITHDRAWN

Thing Knowledge

A Philosophy of Scientific Instruments

DAVIS BAIRD

University of California Press

BERKELEY   LOS ANGELES   LONDON

University of California Press
Berkeley and Los Angeles, California

University of California Press, Ltd.
London, England

© 2004 by the Regents of the University of California

The epigraph to chapter 1 is taken from *Daylight: A Daybook
of Spiritual Guidance,* published by Threshold books; reprinted
with permission.

Library of Congress Cataloging-in-Publication Data

Baird, Davis.
  Thing knowledge : a philosophy of scientific instruments / Davis
Baird.
      p.   cm.
  Includes bibliographical references and index.
  ISBN 0-520-23249-6 (cloth : alk. paper)
    1. Scientific apparatus and instruments.   2. Science—Philosophy.
  3. Science—Technological innovations.   I. Title.
  Q185.B24 2004
  502'.8'4—dc21   2003005683

Manufactured in the United States of America

12 11 10 09 08 07 06 05 04
10 9 8 7 6 5 4 3 2 1

The paper used in this publication meets the minimum requirements
of ANSI /NISO z39.48-1992 (R 1997) (*Permanence of Paper*).

For Deanna

That the history of physical science is largely the history of instruments and their intelligent use is well known. The broad generalizations and theories which have arisen from time to time have stood or fallen on the basis of accurate measurement, and in several instances new instruments have had to be devised for the purpose. There is little evidence to show that the mind of modern man is superior to that of the ancients, his tools are incomparably better. . . . Although the modern scientist accepts and welcomes new instruments, he is less tolerant of instrumentation. He is likely to regard preoccupation with instruments and their design as "gadgeteering" and distinctly inferior to the mere use of instruments in pure research. Thus, Lord Rutherford once said of Callender, the father of recording potentiometers, "He seems to be more interested in devising a new instrument than in discovering a fundamental truth." . . .

Fortunately, there is a great body of earnest workers, oblivious to these jibes, devoted to these pursuits, whose handiwork we may examine. They are providing means with which the "Olympians" may continue to study nature.

RALPH MÜLLER, "American Apparatus,
Instruments, and Instrumentation" (1940)

Contents

List of Illustrations and Tables

TABLES

Preface

Contrary to what Ralph Müller writes in the epigraph I have chosen for this book, it is not well known "that the history of physical science is largely the history of instruments and their intelligent use." This is a pity, because instruments, always central to science, have become central to everyday life as well. We rely on instruments to keep weapons off commercial airlines. We rely on instruments to diagnose and treat illness. Instruments scan bar codes as we check out of the grocery store and even open the door for us as they sense our approach to the exit. Scientists could not have mapped the human genome without automatic DNA sequencers. Nanotechnology and nanoscience have been made possible by the development of powerful new microscopes. That the history of science and increasingly the history of modern culture is indeed a history of instruments and their intelligent—and sometimes not so intelligent—use should be well known. We need to take notice.

Part of the reason instruments have largely escaped the notice of scholars and others interested in our modern techno-scientific culture is language, or rather its lack. Instruments are developed and used in a context where mathematical, scientific, and ordinary language is neither the exclusive vehicle of communication nor, in many cases, the primary vehicle of communication. Instruments are crafted artifacts, and visual and tactile thinking and communication are central to their development and use. Herein lies a big problem and a primary reason why instruments have been ignored by those who write about science and technology. Writers, reasonably enough, understand language to be the primary vehicle of communication. Other modes of communication either are not recognized or, if they are, are not well understood. In his discussion of nineteenth-century mechanics, Anthony F. C. Wallace makes this point vividly:

Thinking visually and tactilely has an inherent disadvantage, however, in comparison with thinking in language. Those who think in words—on subjects which are thought about effectively in words—can think a sentence and then utter it for others to hear. If one visualizes a piece of machinery, however, and wishes to communicate that vision to others, there is an immediate problem. Speech (and writing) will provide only a garbled and incomplete translation of the visual image. One must make the thing—or a model, or at the least a drawing—in order to ensure that one's companion has approximately the same visual experience as oneself.

In the Western world, an effect of this special problem in communicating technological information has tended to be the growing isolation of those who think in mental pictures. . . . Indeed, it has become conventional to assume that thought itself is merely a kind of internal speech and to disregard almost completely those kinds of cognitive processes that are conducted without language, as though they were somehow more primitive, and less worthy of intellectual attention. (Wallace 1978, pp. 238–39)

Instruments are a kind of machinery, and what Wallace says here applies to instruments as well. The need for visual and tactile thinking in the development and use of instruments has reduced our perception of instruments to the realm of the "more primitive and less worthy of intellectual attention."

Both to upend instrumentation's place in the intellectual's basement and to make progress understanding the development and use of instrumentation, we need better concepts with which to consider instruments. These concepts have to be accommodated to the fact that an essential dimension of instrumentation lives outside of language. In his lovely "new media" internet publication, Mike Mahoney describes confronting this problem when designing a course on the history of technology:

As an historian of science I had been accustomed to teaching from primary sources, that is, the works of the scientists of the period under study. Hence, in drawing up a syllabus I cast about for the primary sources of technology since the Renaissance. I had great difficulty finding them. Indeed, I never did find them. I stopped looking when it dawned on me that I was looking for the wrong thing in the wrong place. What I needed for my students was not a library, but a museum. They shouldn't be reading great books, but examining great things. Or, to put that last point another way, the great ideas we were seeking did not lie in books. They lay in objects. Understanding those ideas meant learning to "read" in a new way. (Mahoney 1999)

Care must be taken with the use of literary metaphors. We read books. Perhaps one might better say we "examine" instruments—and technological objects more generally. But we want a richer notion than "examine" might suggest, a notion that has the same interpretive and conceptual depth as does "reading." In reading, interpreting, and writing about texts, we can call on a vast arsenal of interpretive techniques, from logical analysis to hermeneutic deconstruction, to help us understand them and advance our literary grasp. We need an equally powerful arsenal of techniques to understand and advance instrumentation and its place in culture.

There are two theaters where these techniques may be used to advance our understanding. There is a literary theater where we produce a textual record of our literary attempts to understand the world and our place in it, and there is a material theater where instruments and other technologies are built, deployed, and insinuated deeply into our lives. Lacking a powerful arsenal of techniques to understand and advance instrumentation and technology and its place in culture leaves us with an intractable and deeply dangerous version of C. P. Snow's "two cultures" (Snow 1963). In the literary theater, lacking any arsenal of techniques to understand and advance instrumentation, textual analysis will have free play, while in the instrumental and technological theater, humanists will be relegated to the sidelines, carping at the ethical, social and—following the Heideggerian line of criticism—metaphysical problems of modern science and technology. But all these legitimate concerns about our "instrumentalized culture" have been and will continue to be impotent. Lacking any genuine understanding of instrumentation and technology in their material nontextual reality, such literary criticism will fail to engage this reality.

In this book I aim to contribute techniques for understanding the material products of technology and science. I do so by articulating a materialist epistemology for instrumentation. I argue for a material counterpart to our language-centered understanding of knowledge. Instruments, on par with theory, bear knowledge. Instruments are not in the intellectual basement; they occupy the same floor as our greatest theoretical contributions to understanding the world. Developing this idea in detail is the project of the first six chapters of the book. The last four chapters deploy the conceptual techniques developed as part of this materialist epistemology to examine several important issues concerning the history and development of science and technology and its deployment in our contemporary culture. I hope that this examination will be more fruitful for its understanding of material knowledge. I don't offer a better word for "reading" instruments, but

I hope I have provided some new, genuinely materialist, dimensions to understanding instrumentation, and, more generally, technological science—or scientific technology.

Thing Knowledge is the product of a long period of research. This means two things. First, I have incurred a lengthy list of debts to people who have helped in many different ways with making this book. And, second, much of the material in *Thing Knowledge* has appeared in journal articles and chapters in other books, although in many instances, this previously published material has been substantially revised and rearranged here. Appended to this preface is a brief discussion of the sources for the chapters that make up *Thing Knowledge.* First, however, I would like to express my thanks to the many people who helped me with this book, knowing, unfortunately, that I shall have forgotten some of them—to whom I apologize.

I have incorporated material into *Thing Knowledge* from three articles that were collaboratively written. With my student Thomas Faust I wrote "Scientific Instruments, Scientific Progress and the Cyclotron" (*British Journal for the Philosophy of Science* 41: 147–75), and with my colleague Alfred Nordmann I wrote "Facts-Well-Put" (ibid., 45: 37–77). Chapter 3 draws on both of these publications, and I must here give thanks and credit to both of my co-authors. Each, in different ways, has had a significant impact on the development of my thinking. Alfred has been my colleague for nearly the entire time I have been working on *Thing Knowledge.* He deserves special additional thanks for reading and commenting on most of the work at its various stages. Chapter 10 draws on my article "Why Trade?" (*Perspectives on Science* 7: 231–54), written with Mark Cohen. Mark specializes in the development and use of magnetic resonance imaging instrumentation for brain research. The sections of chapter 10 that convey stories about MRI instrumentation all come from Mark's expertise.

During all but one year of the dozen years I have been working on *Thing Knowledge,* I have been a faculty member in the Philosophy Department at the University of South Carolina, which has proved to be an extraordinarily helpful posting for me. I can single out a large number of my colleagues here for thanks—for giving of their time and knowledge. R. I. G. Hughes and George Khushf, who specialize in different aspects of the philosophy of science, were tremendously helpful. But I have also been helped with specific questions and problems by colleagues with specializations far from the philosophy of science, especially by Anne Bezuidenhout, Martin Donougho, Jerry Hackett, Christopher Preston, Chris Tollefsen, and Jerry Wallulis. All of my colleagues at USC have, however, been supportive and helpful.

In recent years, I have been active in the Society for Philosophy and

Technology and the International Society for the Philosophy of Chemistry. I have presented work that has gone into the book at the meetings of these societies and I have benefited from the many insightful and critical comments I have received. I thank all for their insights, but I would like to single out Michael Akeroyd, Nalini Bhushan, Larry Bucciarelli, Joe Early, Peter Kroes, Anthonie Meijers, Paul Needham, Joe Pitt, and Eric Scerri. Joe Pitt, in particular, has been extraordinarily generous with his time, thought, and support. He read an early version of the complete manuscript and had many helpful suggestions. Many thanks.

Several chapters follow bits and pieces of the history of the instrumentation company my father, Walter S. Baird, founded in 1936, Baird Associates (BA), which figures in chapters 4, 5, 7, 9, and 10, either prominently or in the background. I have also drawn extensively on my father's posthumous memorabilia (diaries, letters, etc.). Of course, I owe my father a universe of thanks, but I would like to thank him here for pursuing such an interesting dream, one that I have deeply enjoyed seeing a tiny piece of, sixty years later, through the keyhole provided by the memorabilia he left. I also have benefited from help given me by several of the people who worked at Baird Associates. John Sterner co-founded the company with my father, and I have had the privilege of being able to interview him twice about early times at the company. Jason Saunderson was the designer of the direct-reading spectrometer that figures in chapter 4. He did this work while employed at the Dow Chemical Company, but he subsequently came to work for BA and there developed "Spectromet," which figures in chapter 7. I have both been able to interview him and engaged in a lively exchange of letters with him. He taught me much of what I know about the art of spectrometry, c. 1945. There have in addition been many other BA employees who have helped, and to all of them I am very thankful.

I was fortunate to be able to spend a year as a fellow at MIT's Dibner Institute for the History of Science and Technology. It was during this year, which was also supported by a sabbatical leave from USC—for which I am very thankful—that I was able to put all of the pieces of previous work together into a coherent whole, *Thing Knowledge*. The Dibner Institute was a wonderful place to spend a year doing research, and I thank all the staff and fellows there for making my time so memorable and productive. I would like to single out five of my fellow fellows for their particular help with my project: Babak Ashrafi, Ken Caneva, Yves Gingras, Jutta Schickore and Klaus Staubermann. Many thanks to each of them.

Hans Radder organized a conference on the philosophy of experiment in June 2000. His comments and those of several of my fellow conference participants, notably Henk van den Belt, who commented on my paper, Michael Heidelberger, Hans-Jörg Rheinberger, Margaret Morrison, and Mary Morgan, were very helpful.

I was also fortunate to be invited to speak at another conference, co-organized by Leo Slater, Carsten Reinhardt, and Peter Morris. I thank them for this opportunity to present my work, but especially for providing a context for meeting Terry Shinn, whose interests and work are very close to my own, and whose recent edited volume, *Instrumentation: Between Science, State and Industry* (Shinn and Joerges 2001), complements my own work here.

There are others who don't fall into any of these particular categories whose help I am happy to acknowledge. Even the most minimally attentive reader will recognize my debt to Ian Hacking. Many thanks. I also have learned much from discussions with Peter Galison and Andy Pickering. Michael Schiffer was very helpful and provided much valuable feedback and support as I developed the early chapters of the book. And I would especially like to thank Ann Johnson for many useful and enjoyable discussions—and for pointing me to Anthony Wallace and Mike Mahoney, both quoted above.

I have learned much from the various stages of the publication process. I have appreciated the thought-provoking criticisms of the several anonymous readers of the manuscript. I don't know who you are, but thanks. Eric Smoodin and subsequently Kate Toll and Dore Brown have been my editors at the University of California Press All have helped in various ways, but particular thanks to Eric for his unfailing encouragement. I would also like to thank Peter Dreyer, my copy editor, for his superb, fine-toothed reading, catching many errors and straightening out many confusions.

Finally, I have my family to thank, my wife, Deanna, my older step-daughter, Hilary, and my son, Ian, whose entire life so far has more or less spanned the gestation of this book. All have borne with grace all the time I've had to take from them to put into this project. For this I am very grateful. I must, however, single out my wife, Deanna, who has encouraged me, inspired me, supported me, taught me, and cleared the way to make finishing this book possible. Among other things, she taught me of the limits of language as a medium of communication. Her drawings transcend words. Could I draw, I would make a drawing here to express my thanks, for words are insufficient. The book is dedicated to you.

Here, in detail, are the previously published sources for the various chapters:

Part of chapter 1 is taken from my 1995 "Meaning in a Material Medium," in D. Hull, M. Forbes, and R. Burian, eds., *PSA 1994* 2: 441–51.

Part of chapter 3 is taken from my 1994 joint article with Alfred Nordmann, "Facts-Well-Put," *British Journal for the Philosophy of Science* 45: 37–77, and part is taken from my 1990 joint article with Thomas Faust, "Scientific Instruments, Scientific Progress and the Cyclotron," *British Journal for the Philosophy of Science* 41: 147–75. "Facts-Well-Put" also appeared in J. Pitt and E. Lugo, eds., *The Technology of Discovery and the Discovery of Technology: Proceedings of the 1991 Annual Conference of the Society for Philosophy and Technology*, pp. 413–56.

Part of chapter 4 is taken from my 2000 "Encapsulating Knowledge: The Direct Reading Spectrometer," *Foundations of Chemistry* 2: 5–46. A severely condensed version of this article appeared in *Techné: Electronic Journal of the Society for Philosophy and Technology* 3: 1–9 (http://borg.lib.vt .edu/ejournals/SPT/spt.html).

Chapter 5 is a revised version of my 1993 "Analytical Chemistry and the 'Big' Scientific Instrumentation Revolution," *Annals of Science* 50: 267–90.

Part of chapter 6 is taken from my 2000 "Encapsulating Knowledge: The Direct Reading Spectrometer," *Foundations of Chemistry* 2: 5–46, and part is taken from my 1995 "Meaning in a Material Medium," in D. Hull, M. Forbes, and R. Burian, eds., *PSA 1994* 2: 441–51.

Chapter 7 is a revised version of my "The Thing-y-ness of Things: Materiality and Design, Lessons from Spectrochemical Instrumentation," in P. A. Kroes and A. W. M. Meijers, eds., *The Empirical Turn in the Philosophy of Technology*, vol. 20 of Research in Philosophy and Technology, ser. ed. C. Mitcham, pp. 99–117 (Amsterdam: JAI-Elsevier, 2001).

Chapter 8 is a revised version of my 1989 "Instruments on the Cusp of Science and Technology: The Indicator Diagram," *Knowledge and Society: Studies in the Sociology of Science Past and Present* 8: 107–22.

Part of chapter 9 is taken from my "Analytical Instrumentation and Instrumental Objectivity," in N. Bhushan and S. Rosenfeld, eds., *Of Minds and Molecules: New Philosophical Perspectives on Chemistry*, pp. 90–113 (New York: Oxford University Press, 2000).

Part of chapter 10 is taken from my 1999 joint article with Mark Cohen "Why Trade?" *Perspectives on Science* 7: 231–54, and part is from my 1997 "Scientific Instrument Making, Epistemology and the Conflict between Gift and Commodity Economies," *Techné: Electronic Journal of the Society for Philosophy and Technology* 2: 1–16 (http://borg.lib.vt.edu/ ejournals/SPT/spt.html). The *Techné* article also appeared in *Ludus Vitalis*, supp. 2 (1997): 1–16.

1 Instrument Epistemology

> If your knowledge of fire has been turned
>   to certainty by words alone,
> then seek to be cooked by the fire itself.
> Don't abide in borrowed certainty.
> There is no real certainty until you burn;
> if you wish for this, sit down in the fire.
>
> JALAL AL-DIN RUMI,
> *Daylight: A Daybook of
> Spiritual Guidance*

Knowledge has been understood to be an affair of the mind. To know is to think, and in particular, to think thoughts expressible in words. Nonverbal creations—from diagrams to densitometers—are excluded as merely "instrumental"; they are pragmatic crutches that help thinking—in the form of theory construction and interpretation. In this book I urge a different view. I argue for a materialist conception of knowledge. Along with theories, the material products of science and technology constitute knowledge. I focus on scientific instruments, such as cyclotrons and spectrometers, but I would also include recombinant DNA enzymes, "wonder" drugs and robots, among other things, as other material products of science and technology that constitute our knowledge. These material products are constitutive of scientific knowledge in a manner different from theory, and not simply "instrumental to" theory. An example will help fix my meaning.

1. MICHAEL FARADAY'S FIRST ELECTRIC MOTOR

On September 3 and 4, 1821, Michael Faraday, then aged thirty, performed a series of experiments that ultimately produced what were called "electromagnetic rotations." Faraday showed how an appropriately organized combination of electric and magnetic elements would produce rotary motion. He invented the first electromagnetic motor.

Faraday's work resulted in several "products." He published several papers describing his discovery (1821b; 1821a; 1822c; 1822d). He wrote letters

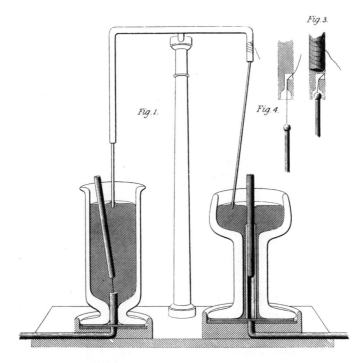

FIGURE 1.1 Michael Faraday's 1821 electric motor (from Faraday 1844).

to many scientific colleagues (1971, pp. 122–39). He built, or had built, several copies of an apparatus that, requiring no experimental knowledge or dexterity on the part of its user, would display the notable rotations, and he shipped these to his scientific colleagues (1822b; 1822a; 1971, pp. 128–29).

A permanent magnet is cemented vertically in the center of a mercury bath. A wire, with one end immersed a little into the mercury, is suspended over the magnet in such a way as to allow for free motion around the magnet. The suspension of the wire is such that contact can be made with it and one pole of a battery. The other pole of the battery is connected to the magnet that carries the current to the mercury bath, and thence to the other end of the wire, completing the circuit (see fig. 1.1).

The apparatus produces a striking phenomenon: when an electric current is run through the wire, via the magnet and the mercury bath, the wire spins around the magnet. The observed behavior of Faraday's apparatus requires no interpretation. While there was considerable disagreement over the explanation for this phenomenon, no one contested what the apparatus did: it exhibited (still does) rotary motion as a consequence of a suitable combination of electric and magnetic elements.

2. DEVICE EPISTEMOLOGY

How should we understand Faraday's device? One could say that it justifies assertions such as, "A current-carrying wire will rotate around a magnet in a mercury bath as shown in figure 1.1." One could say, and Faraday did say, that the phenomenon exhibited by the device articulates Hans Christian Oersted's 1820 discovery of the magnetic effects of an electric current (Faraday 1844, p. 129). One could speculate—and several did—that the device shows that all forces are convertible (Williams 1964, p. 157). Are such theoretical moves all that is important about the device? Why did Faraday think it necessary to ship ready-made versions of this motor to his colleagues?

Moving immediately from the device to its importance for these various theoretical issues misses its immediate importance. When Faraday made the device, there was considerable disagreement over how it worked. Today, many people still do not know the physics that explains how it works. Both then and now, however, no one denies *that* it works. When Faraday built it, this phenomenon was striking and proved to be very important for the future development of science and technology. Whatever explanations would be offered for the device, and more generally for the nature of "electromagnetical motions," would have to recognize the motions Faraday produced. We don't need a load of theory (or indeed any "real" theory) to learn something from the construction and demonstration of Faraday's device. Or to put it another way, we learn by interacting with bits of the world even when our words for how these bits work are inadequate.

This point is more persuasive when one is confronted with the actual device. Unfortunately, I cannot build a Faraday motor into this book; the reader's imagination will have to suffice. But it is significant that Faraday did not depend on the imaginations of his readers. He made and shipped "pocket editions" of his newly created phenomenon to his colleagues. He knew from his own experience how difficult it is to interpret descriptions of experimental discoveries. He also knew how difficult it is to fashion even a simple device like his motor and have it work reliably. The material product Faraday sent his colleagues encapsulated his considerable manipulative skill—his "fingertip knowledge"—in such a way that someone without the requisite skill could still experience the new phenomenon firsthand. He did not have to depend either on the skills of his colleagues or on their ability to interpret a verbal description of his device. He could depend on the ability of the device itself to communicate the fact of the phenomenon it exhibited.

3. INSTRUMENT EPISTEMOLOGY

I conclude from this that there is something in the device itself that is epistemologically important, something that a purely literary description misses. The epistemological products of science and technology must include such stuff, not simply words and equations. In particular, they must include instruments such as Faraday's motor.

Understanding instruments as bearers of knowledge conflicts with any of the more-or-less standard views that take knowledge as a subspecies of belief (Bonjour 1985; Goldman 1986; Audi 1998). Instruments, whatever they may be, are not beliefs. A different approach to epistemology, characterized under the heading "growth of scientific knowledge," also does not accommodate instruments; such work inevitably concentrates on *theory* change (Lakatos 1970; Lakatos and Musgrave 1970; Popper 1972; Laudan 1977). While I examine some instruments that might be understood in terms similar to theories (e.g., models in chapter 2), instruments generally speaking cannot be understood in such terms. Even recent work on the philosophy of experiment that has focused on the literally material aspects of science either has adopted a standard proposition-based epistemology or has not addressed epistemology.[1] This book aims to correct this failure and to present instruments epistemologically.

This project raises a variety of problems at the outset. There are conceptual difficulties that, for many, seem immediately to refute the very possibility that instruments are a kind of scientific knowledge. We are strongly wedded to connections between the concepts of knowledge, truth, and justification. It is hard to fit concepts such as truth and justification around instruments. Even work that drops these connections finds substitutes. Work on the growth of scientific knowledge does not require truth—

---

1. Anderson and Silverman 1995; Baird and Faust 1990; Baird and Nordmann 1994; Buchwald 1994; Franklin 1986, 1990; Galison 1997; Gooding 1990; Hacking 1983; Hankins and Silverman 1995; Ihde 1991; Pickering 1995; Price 1980, 1984; Radder 1988; Shapin and Schaffer 1985; van Helden and Hankins 1994; and Wise 1995 are among recent writings on the philosophy of experiment that have tended to focus on the literally material aspects of science.

"every theory is born refuted." Instead, we have "growth of scientific knowledge" expressed in terms of verisimilitude (Popper 1972), progressive research programs (Lakatos 1970), and the increasing problem-solving effectiveness of research traditions (Laudan 1974). In chapter 6, I develop substitutes for truth and justification that work with instruments.

Prior to these philosophical problems are difficulties arising from the very concept of a scientific instrument. At the most basic level, this is not a unitary concept. There are many different kinds of scientific instrument. What is worse, the different kinds work differently epistemologically. Models, such as Watson and Crick's ball-and-stick model of DNA, clearly have a representative function. Yet devices such as Faraday's motor do not; they perform. Measuring instruments, such as thermometers, are in many ways hybrids; they perform to produce representations. Consequently, before I take on the philosophical issues of truth and justification, I consider these three types of instrument: models (chapter 2); devices that create a phenomenon (chapter 3); and measuring instruments (chapter 4). I do not claim that this is a philosophically exhaustive or fully articulated typology of instruments or instrumental functions. I do claim significant epistemological differences for each type, differences requiring special treatment.

These categories have histories. Indeed, the very category of scientific instrument has its own history (Warner 1994). The self-conscious adoption of instruments as a form of scientific knowledge has a history. I thus argue in chapter 5 that a major epistemological event of the mid twentieth century has been the recognition by the scientific community of the centrality of instruments to the epistemological project of technology and science. My arguments for understanding instruments as scientific knowledge have, then, to be understood historically. While I use examples scattered through history, my goal is neither to provide a history of scientific instruments nor to argue for the timeless significance of this category. To understand technology and science *now*, however, we need to construct an epistemology capable of including instruments.

4. TEXT BIAS

Instrument epistemology confronts a long history of what I call text bias, dating back at least to Plato, with what is commonly taken as his definition of knowledge in terms of justified true belief. To do proper epistemology, we have to "ascend" from the material world to the "Platonic world" of thought. This may reflect Plato's concern with the impermanence of the

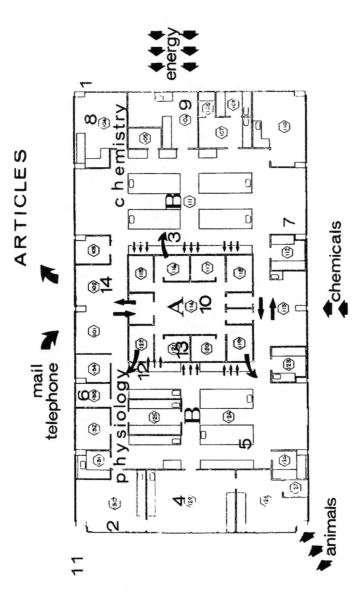

FIGURE 1.2 Laboratory blueprint (from Latour and Woolgar 1979). Reprinted by permission of Sage Publications.

material world and what he saw as the unchanging eternal perfection of the realm of forms. If knowledge is timeless, it cannot exist in the corruptible material realm.

This strikes me simply as prejudice. "It is unfortunate that so many historians of science and virtually all of the philosophers of science are born-again theoreticians instead of bench scientists," Derek de Solla Price writes (1980, p. 75), which is my reaction exactly. Philosophers and historians express themselves in words, not things, and so it is not surprising that those who hold a virtual monopoly over saying (words!) what scientific knowledge is, characterize it in terms of the kind of knowledge with which they are familiar—words.

Prejudice it may be, but powerfully entrenched it is too. The logical positivists were obsessed with "the languages of science" (Suppe 1977). But text bias did not die with them. Consider figure 1.2, taken from Bruno Latour and Steve Woolgar's seminal postpositivist book *Laboratory Life* (1979). Here is the function of the laboratory. Animals, chemicals, mail, telephone, and energy go in; articles go out. The picture Latour and Woolgar present of science is thoroughly literary. "Nature," with the help of "inscription devices" (i.e., instruments), produces literary outputs for scientists; scientists use these outputs, plus other literary resources (mail, telephone, preprints, etc.), to produce their own literary outputs. The material product the scientists happened to be investigating in Latour and Woolgar's study—a substance called "TRF"—becomes, on their reading, merely an instrumental good, "just one more of the many tools utilized as part of long research programmes" (Latour and Woolgar 1979, p. 148).

This picture of the function of a laboratory is a travesty. There is a long history of scientists sharing material other than words. William Thompson sent electric coils to colleagues as part of his measurement of the ohm. Henry Rowland's fame rests on the gratings he ruled and sent to colleagues. Chemists share chemicals. Biologists share biologically active chemicals—enzymes, etc.—as well as prepared animals for experiments. When it is hard to share devices, scientists with the relevant expertise are shared; such is the manner in which E. O. Lawrence's cyclotron moved beyond Berkeley. Laboratories do not simply produce words.

There is much to learn from Latour and Woolgar's *Laboratory Life*, as well as from the subsequent work of these authors. Indeed, Latour and Woolgar are important because they do attend to the material context of laboratory life. But, continuing a long tradition of text bias, they misdescribe the telos of science and technology exclusively in literary terms. Although the rhetoric with which they introduce their "literary" framework for analysis seems new, even "postmodern," it is very old. Once again scholars—wordsmiths—have reduced science to the mode with which they are most familiar, words.

5. SEMANTIC ASCENT

A considerable portion of David Gooding's *Experiment and the Making of Meaning* (1990) focuses on Michael Faraday's experimental production of electromagnetic rotations—the motor I started with. Given this focus, one might suspect that Gooding would see the making of phenomena—such as that exhibited by Faraday's motor—as one of the key epistemological *ends* of science, but he does not. The first sentences of his book are instructive:

> It is inevitable that language has, as Ian Hacking put it, mattered to philosophy. It is not inevitable that practices—especially extra-linguistic practices—have mattered so little. Philosophy has not yet addressed an issue that is central to any theory of the *language* of observation and, therefore, to any theory of science: how do observers *ascend* from the world to talk, thought and argument about the world. (p. 3; emphasis added)

Scientists "ascend" from the world to talk about the world, from instruments to words, from the material realm to the literary realm, according to Gooding. Semantic ascent is the key move in experimental science. Words are above things.

As with Latour and Woolgar, I do not mention Gooding's use of "semantic ascent" to criticize him, for the problem of how words get tied to new bits of the world is important and Gooding has much of great interest and value to say about it. But thinking in terms of the metaphor of ascent implies a hierarchy of ultimate values. It turns our attention away from other aspects of science and technology that are equally important.

It is instructive to see how Gooding discusses Faraday's literary and material products. Faraday accomplished two feats. He built a reliable device and he described its operation. Gooding writes: "[T]he literary account places phenomena in an objective relationship to theories just as the material embodiment of the skills places phenomena in an objective relation to human experience" (p. 177). Faraday's descriptions—his literary "ascent"—"places phenomena in an objective relationship to theories." Analogously, his material work—his device—"places phenomena in an objective relation to human experience."

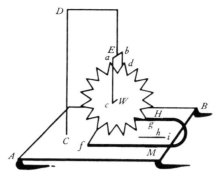

FIGURE 1.3 Peter Barlow's 1821 star electric motor (from Faraday 1971). Reprinted by permission of the Cambridge University Press.

But "human experience" is the wrong concept. Faraday's descriptions could speak to theory. In doing so, they could call on the power of logic and contribute to knowledge. We need an analogously detailed articulation of how Faraday's material work could contribute to knowledge. "Human experience" ducks this responsibility. We can and should say more, and in more detail, about what the material work had "objective relations" with. Avoiding doing so is a symptom of the disease of semantic ascent.

Faraday's device had a good bit to "say." The apparatus "spoke" objectively about the potential for producing rotary motion from electromagnetism, which could be developed through material manipulations, starting with the apparatus as a material given. Six months after Faraday made his device, Peter Barlow produced a variant (fig. 1.3) using a star-shaped wheel.

Current runs from one "voltaic pole" to the star's suspension [*abcd*] through the star to the mercury bath [*fg*] and thence to the other voltaic pole. A strong horseshoe magnet [*HM*] surrounds the mercury bath and, as Barlow put it in a letter to Faraday, "the wheel begins to rotate, with an astonishing velocity, and thus exhibits a very pretty appearance" (Faraday 1971, p. 133, letter dated March 14, 1822).

It is another step to figure out how to create such rotary motion without the use of mercury. Then we might have something useful. There is a significant story here, a story not primarily about the evolution of our words and equations but about material manipulations. The story involves many players and a full telling would not serve much purpose here (see King 1963; Gee 1991). It involves the invention of the electromagnet—

developed by William Sturgeon, among others, and considerably improved by the early American physicist Joseph Henry. From the electromagnet to the electric motor is another step, one taken by several people independently (King 1963, pp. 260–71).

The story of one of the claimants to inventing the electric motor, Thomas Davenport, a Vermont blacksmith, is instructive (see Davenport 1929; Schiffer 1994). In 1834, Davenport was intrigued by news of a powerful electromagnet built by Professor Henry that was capable of lifting a common blacksmith's anvil. Davenport traveled some distance from his home in Vermont to Rennselaer in Troy, New York, to see a demonstration of the electromagnet. He was amazed and entranced with its possibilities. A year later, Davenport succeeded in building a motor capable of driving a seven-inch-diameter wheel at thirty revolutions per minute (see fig. 1.4).

The motor works by switching the polarity of four electromagnets in synchronicity with the motion of the wheel so that the wheel is always drawn forward. (A similar technique is used to make the cyclotron work; see chapter 3.) All of this was accomplished despite the fact that Davenport did not know electromagnetic theory. When he first saw Henry's electromagnet, he had never heard of any of the main contributors to the science of electromagnetism. But he did have an appreciation for the phenomenon exhibited by the electromagnet, and he was able to use this knowledge— presented by the device itself—to make other devices. Davenport was interested in developing devices that would have practical utility, and he did succeed in using his motor to drive a printing press (Schiffer 1994, p. 64). But Davenport's motor also expresses a further articulation of knowledge of electromagnetic phenomena.

Semantic "ascent" prevents us from attending to those pieces of the history of science and technology that do not immediately speak to theory. Yet, as is clear from several of the examples discussed in this book, maneuvers in the material realm are central to the progress of science and technology. The more basic point here is that the material realm provides a space within which work can be done. Exactly what is done in this space frequently—although not always—depends on available theory. But that theory also frequently turns out to be erroneous. This does not bring work to a halt. On the contrary, work can go forward independent of theory or with controversial and/or erroneous theory. Many new instrumental— and subsequently valuable—technological developments have resulted from work based on erroneous theory. Furthermore, theoretical advance frequently follows on instrumental advance.

FIGURE 1.4 Thomas Davenport's electric motor, patented in 1837 (from Davenport 1929). Reprinted by permission of the Vermont Historical Society.

6. MULTIPLE EPISTEMOLOGIES

A primary consequence of the epistemological picture I am presenting here is that no single unified account of knowledge will serve science and technology. In advancing a materialist account of epistemology—thing knowledge—I do not also argue negatively that propositional and/or mentalistic accounts of knowledge are wrong. On their own, however, they do not provide a sufficient framework for an adequate epistemology of technology and science. More is needed, and a critical part of this is an articulation of how the material dimensions of science and technology do epistemological work. Things and theory can both constitute our knowledge of the world. But I deny that there is a unified epistemological treatment for both. Even within my materialist epistemology, different kinds of instruments constitute knowledge in fundamentally different ways.

Models, which I discuss in chapter 2, work epistemologically in ways that are very similar to theory. They provide representations, and in so doing, they can be assessed in terms of the virtues and vices that are used to assess theoretical representations: explanatory and predictive power, simplicity, accuracy, and so on.

Instruments that create phenomena, such as Faraday's motor, are different and constitute knowledge in a different, nonrepresentational way. Such instruments work epistemologically in a manner that draws on pragmatist conceptions of knowledge as effective action. A fundamental difference, however, is that with instruments, the action has been separated from human agency and built into the reliable behavior of an artifact. I call this kind of knowledge "working knowledge." When we have made an instrument to do something in a particular way and it does it successfully and reliably, we say the instrument works. It is *working knowledge,* and this knowledge is different from the knowledge constituted by models—model knowledge. Working knowledge is the subject of chapter 3.[2]

Measuring instruments, the subject of chapter 4, present a third kind of material knowledge that is a hybrid of the representational and effective action senses of knowledge. Measurement presupposes representation, for measuring something locates it in an ordered space of possible measurement outcomes. A representation—or model—of this ordered space has to be built into a measuring instrument. This can be as simple as a scale on a thermometer. At the same time, a measuring instrument has to do something and do it reliably. It has to work. Presented with the same object for measurement, the instrument must yield outcomes that are the same or can be understood to be the same given an analysis of error. That is, the instrument has to present a phenomenon in the sense of constituting "working knowledge" as discussed in chapter 3.[3] Measuring instruments integrate the two epistemological modes I detail in chapters 2 and 3, model knowledge and working knowledge. I describe this integration as "encap-

---

2. In coining this neologism, I call on our use of "working" to describe an instrument or machine that performs regularly and reliably. I also draw on the phrase "to have a working knowledge." Someone with a working knowledge of something has knowledge that is sufficient to do something. My neologism "working knowledge" draws attention to the connection between knowledge and effective action.

3. On this point, see Hacking 1983, ch. 14.

sulated knowledge," where effective action and accurate representation work together in a material instrument to provide measurement.

7. SUBJECTIVE AND OBJECTIVE

Louis Bucciarelli begins his book *Designing Engineers* (1994) with a question raised at a conference he attended on technological literacy: Do you know how your telephone works? A speaker at the conference noted with alarm that fewer than 20 percent of Americans knew how their telephones worked. But, Bucciarelli notes, the question is ambiguous. Some people (although perhaps less than 20 percent) may have an inkling of how sound waves can move a diaphragm and drive a coil back and forth in a magnetic field to create an electric current. But there is more to telephony than such simple physics. Bucciarelli wonders whether the conference speaker knows how his phone works:

> Does he know about the heuristics used to achieve optimum routing for long-distance calls? Does he know about the intricacies of the algorithms used for echo and noise suppression? Does he know how a signal is transmitted to and retrieved from a satellite in orbit? Does he know how AT&T, MCI, and the local phone companies are able to use the same network simultaneously? Does he know how many operators are needed to keep the system working, or what these repair people actually do when they climb a telephone pole? Does he know about corporate financing, capital investment strategies, or the role of regulation in the functioning of this expansive and sophisticated communication system? (Bucciarelli 1994, p. 3)

Indeed, Bucciarelli concludes, "Does *anyone* know how their telephone works?" (ibid.; emphasis in the original).

Here, following the conference speaker, Bucciarelli uses "know" in a subjective sense. He makes a persuasive case that, in this sense, no one knows how his or her phone works. In the first place, the phone system is too big to be comprehended by a single "subjective knower." In the second place, the people who developed pieces of the hardware and software that constitute the phone system may have moved on to other concerns and forgotten the hows and whys of the pieces they developed. Their "subjective knowledge" may thus be lost. In the third place, complicated systems with many interacting parts do not always behave in ways we can predict in detail. Despite having created them, programmers cannot always predict, and in this sense do not "subjectively know," how their complicated computer programs will behave.

It is, of course, well and proper to engage in what might be called sub-jective epistemology. This is the attempt to understand that aspect of knowledge that is a species of subjective belief. But if we want to under-stand technological and scientific knowledge, this is the wrong place to look. This is true for several reasons, the first of which is made clear by Bucciarelli's telephones. If no one—subjectively—knows how the phone system works, the situation with all scientific and technological knowledge is radically worse. The epistemological world of technology and science is too big for a single person to comprehend. People change the focus of their research and forget. Expert knowledge systems transcend their makers.

There is a second important reason why the epistemology of technology and science should not be sought at the level of individual belief. One of the important defining characteristics of scientific and technological knowledge is that it cannot be private. A scientist may do some research that provides strong evidence—in the scientist's view—for some claim. But the claim is not scientific knowledge until it has been subjected to scrutiny by the relevant scientific community and accepted by that community. Scientific and technological knowledge is public in the sense that the knowledge has passed review by peers. With respect to theoretical knowledge, publication in a book or journal article (or preprint, etc.) is the significant point when knowledge claims pass into the public realm of scientific and technological knowledge. In addition to these literary domains of scientific and techno-logical knowledge, there are material domains. When Faraday sent copies of his motor to his colleagues, he was making it available for peer review.

We may be interested, for example, in what Faraday knew—subjec-tively—when he sent around copies of his motor. This can be important for understanding the history of electromagnetism. We can uncover evidence concerning the papers Faraday read. We can read Faraday's own notes. We thereby can develop an appreciation of his subjective theoretical knowl-edge. But we also can uncover evidence about Faraday's tactile and visual skills in eliciting the phenomenon that he ultimately built into his motor (see Gooding 1990). We thereby develop an appreciation for Faraday's em-bodied skills, his know-how and tacit knowledge. Taken together, we come to understand Faraday's subjective knowledge that went into both the writ-ing of his articles and the making of his motor.

Once out of his hands and subject to review by his peers, the articles *and* the motor both pass into the public domain of objective knowledge. An ad-equate epistemology of science and technology has to include such public objective knowledge. Here are the epistemological products of the subjec-tive engagements of scientists, engineers, and others. These products include theories and the like, written products that occupy the pages of professional journals. But they also include the material artifacts that I consider under the headings of model knowledge, working knowledge, and encapsulated knowledge, in short, thing knowledge.

8. ARGUMENTS AND ORGANIZATION

The multiple material epistemologies that I articulate as thing knowledge rest on several interconnected and mutually supporting arguments. There are four types of argument that run through the various chapters, arguments from analogy, arguments from cognitive autonomy, arguments from history, and, finally, what I call arguments by articulation. The specific instances of each type of argument are different from one another in detail, inasmuch as they serve different epistemological conceptions, and while all the arguments stand as integral parts of the overall picture I present of thing knowledge, it is useful to disentangle the strands and explain how each fits into the organization of the book as a whole.

I present a series of arguments by analogy that the material products of science bear knowledge. In chapter 2, I show how, in several epistemologically important respects, material models function analogously to theoretical contributions to science and technology. Material models can provide explanations and predictions. They can be confirmed or refuted by empirical evidence. I develop these points by appeal to a version of the semantic account of theories where a theory is identified with a class of abstract structures called models. I argue that the material models that are the focus of chapter 2 satisfy all the requirements for abstract models in the sense of the semantic view of theories.

In chapter 3, I present a distinct argument from analogy that deals with "working knowledge." My discussion of Faraday's motor in this chapter foreshadows this argument. We say someone knows how to ride a bicycle when he or she can consistently and successfully accomplish the task. A phenomenon such as that exhibited by Faraday's motor shares these features of consistency and success with what usually is called know-how or skill knowledge. One might say that Faraday's motor "knows how to make rotations," but that overanthropomorphizes the motor. I prefer to say that the motor bears knowledge of a kind of material agency, and I call such knowledge "working knowledge." The analogy runs deeper. We are frequently unable to put into words our knowledge of how to do something like ride a bicycle; it is tacit knowledge. We find a similar situation with instruments such as Faraday's motor, and from two points of view. From an anthropomorphic point of view, the motor articulates nothing in words. But from the point of view of its maker—Faraday, in this case—it was also difficult to articulate how the phenomenon came about. Yet, as in the case of bicycle riding, it is clear that the instrument presents a phenomenon, that it works. The action is effective in a general sense, even lacking a verbal articulation for it. The knowledge resides in the regular controlled action of the instrument. The instrument bears this tacit "working knowledge."

A different collection of arguments that runs through *Thing Knowledge* turns on what can be called the cognitive autonomy of instruments. Davenport learned something from his examination of Henry's electromagnet. He then took what he learned and turned it into another, potentially commercially useful, device. He did this while ignorant of theory and unable to express in words either what Henry's electromagnet had taught him or what he was doing with this knowledge. In chapter 2, I present a variant of this argument. Here we see how James Watson's ability to physically manipulate cardboard models of DNA base pairs led to his discovery of base-pair bonding. Watson employed a distinct "cognitive channel" from the consideration and manipulation of theoretical or propositional material. Variants of this argument appear in other guises in chapters 3, 4, 7, and 8. In a nutshell, the point is that making is different from saying, and yet we learn from made things and from the act of making. Cognitive content is not exhausted by theory, and for the same reason, epistemic content should not be exhausted by theory either. This is, perhaps, the core meaning of the epigraph to chapter 6, by Richard Feynman, "What I cannot create I do not understand." Feynman subjectively knew something through his efforts to create it, after which it carried the objective content of this knowledge in a way that might be subjectively recovered by someone else, just as Henry's electromagnet had meaning for Davenport.

A lot of *Thing Knowledge* is historical and my use of history serves a third collection of arguments for the epistemological standing of instruments. There is, in the first place, the argument that we miss a tremendous amount of what is epistemologically significant in the history of science and technology if we limit our examination to the history of theory. Carnot cycles in thermodynamics are the cycles that were being traced out by steam engine indicators in the twenty years preceding Sadi Carnot's and Émile Clapeyron's work on thermodynamics (see chapter 8 for details). The examples in the rest of the text all aim to show how significant the development of instrumentation has been and how this development proceeds in partial (and sometimes nearly complete) independence of theory.[4] In chapter 5, I discuss a specific transformation in the history of analytical chemistry during the middle years of the twentieth century. Here scientists came to understand that the development of instruments was a central component to the progress in our knowledge of the world. This was the time when Ralph Müller wrote the lines that serve as the epigraph for this book: "the history of physical science is largely the history of instruments" (Müller 1940, p. 571).

At the end of the day, the fundamental argument for the epistemological place of instruments is my articulation of how instruments do epistemological work. This concern drives the organization of the book.

I start with three chapters articulating three different ways in which instruments bear knowledge, first as a material mode of representation, then as a material mode of effective action, and finally as a material mode of encapsulated knowledge synthesizing representation and action. Chapter 5 examines the historical evidence of the coming to scientific self-awareness that instruments bear scientific knowledge. These four chapters, together with the introductory first chapter, make the case that instruments need to be understood epistemologically on a par with theory.

Chapter 6 develops a philosophical theory of knowledge that is up to this task. Here I extend and modify Karl Popper's account of objective knowledge to accommodate instruments as elements of a neo-Popperian "world 3" of objective knowledge. This is the most theoretical of the chapters, and as an immediate antidote to the theory of chapter 6, I focus on the specifically material aspects of thing knowledge in chapter 7. The final three chapters examine three different respects in which thing knowledge shifts our understanding of science and technology.

Collectively, the point of the various chapters is to articulate a picture of why and how instruments should be understood epistemologically on a par with theory. While the various arguments aim to persuade readers of this conclusion, it is the overall picture that must seal the deal. Beyond why instruments should be understood as knowledge bearers, I show how they do this and what the consequences are.

9. BEYOND SCIENCE TO TECHNOLOGY

The kind of epistemology that I advocate here brings out relationships that, while of recognized importance, have not found a comfortable place in the

---

4. Here I follow the argument in Galison 1997.

philosophy of science and technology. The idea that engineers and industrialists simply take and materially instantiate the knowledge provided by science cannot stand up to even the most cursory historical study. James Watt's work on steam engine instrumentation—specifically the indicator diagram—made a seminal contribution to the development of thermodynamics (chapter 8). Yet without a broader understanding of epistemology, where instruments themselves express knowledge of the world, alternatives to this notion of "applied science," to the idea of engineering and industry as epistemological hangers-on, are difficult to develop.

"Craft knowledge," "fingertip knowledge," "tacit knowledge," and "know-how" are useful concepts in that they remind us that there is more to knowing than saying. But they tend to render this kind of knowledge ineffable. Instruments have a kind of public existence that allows for more explicit study. My intention is not to downplay the significance of "craft knowledge" and the rest. On the contrary, I believe that an analysis of instruments as knowledge provides insight into this difficult and important epistemological territory.

The most immediate consequence of recognizing instruments as knowledge is that the boundary between science and technology changes. Recent science studies scholarship has recognized a more fluid relationship between science and technology than earlier positivist and postpositivist philosophy of science. Still, it is to theoretical science that one turns to examine *knowledge*. Previously ignored contributions of craftsmen and engineers are now understood to have provided important, and in many cases essential, contributions to the growth of scientific knowledge. But it is theory that is seen to be growing. Davenport's story is a sidebar.

The picture I offer here is different. I see developments of things and of theory as being on a par. In many cases, they interact, sometimes with beneficial results all around, but in many cases, too, they develop independently, again sometimes with beneficial results. Work done in industry, putting together bits of the material world, is as constitutive of knowledge as work done by "theoretical scientists." Some of it is fundamental (John Harrison's seaworthy chronometer, perhaps [Sobel 1995]); some of it is less so (the translucent case for Apple's iMac, perhaps). In this sense, material contributions are not different from theoretical contributions—which run the gamut from Einstein's general theory of relativity to psychotherapeutic notions such as the idea that subliminal exposure to the words "Mommy and I are one" will improve behavior.[5]

5. "Mommy and I Are One," *Science News* 129, no. 10 (March 8, 1986): 156.

There are, however, important differences between work with theory and work with things. Things are not as tidy as ideas. Plato was exactly right on this point. Things are impermanent, impure, and imperfect. Chapter 7 concerns these differences between things and ideas and the epistemological ramifications of these differences. In part, I argue there that many instruments hide the very materiality they are made from. The ideal measuring instrument provides information about the world that can be trusted and acted upon. The instrument performs semantic ascent for us, providing output that is useful in the commerce of ideas. The instrument renders the materiality of the world transparent, and, indeed, it renders the materiality of thing knowledge transparent. In the information age, we like to pretend that we can live entirely in our heads, or, rather, in the data.

Recognizing instruments as bearers of knowledge provides valuable conceptual space within which to fruitfully address vexing problems. The last two chapters concern two such problems.

Chapter 9 focuses on mechanical objectivity, juxtaposing the mechanical grading widely used in aptitude tests (such as the Scholastic Aptitude Test, or SAT) with instrumental approaches to chemical analysis. At issue here is a profound question of what kinds of assessments or measurements deserve our trust, and why. Understanding how knowledge is encapsulated in our instruments provides insight into the allure of mechanical objectivity. By encapsulating knowledge in our measuring instruments, these methods minimize the role of human reflection in judgment. They offer a kind of "push-button objectivity" where we trust a device and not human judgment. How many people check their arithmetic calculations with an electronic calculator?

This has radically changed our world. Putting our faith in "the objectivity" of machines instead of human analysis and judgment has ramifications far and wide. It is a qualitatively different experience to give birth with an array of electronic monitors. It is a qualitatively different experience to teach when student evaluations—"customer satisfaction survey instruments"—are used to evaluate one's teaching. It is a qualitatively different experience to make steel "by the numbers," the numbers being provided by analytical instrumentation.

Chapter 10 examines a different respect in which the appearance of thing knowledge in the mid twentieth century is radically changing our world. Thing knowledge casts into sharp relief a conceptual and cultural problem that fundamentally threatens our "intellectual commons": namely, what the value of knowledge is and how it should be exchanged. Through the middle of the twentieth century, knowledge expressed as ideas was exchanged on fundamentally different terms than commodities. The academic producers of knowledge were paid primarily in terms of recognition, not cash. Recognition is given for knowledge made available in public forums, such as professional journals available in libraries. This can work when the production cost of knowledge is relatively low. Making instruments, however, is expensive, and for this reason they are treated as commodities. This began with the advent of thing knowledge in the middle of the twentieth century, and now we are witnesses to the transformation of all knowledge into commodities. Recognition for important contributions to knowledge is nice, but financial reward in the shape of patent fees and grants has assumed central importance.

2 Models: Representing Things

> Mr. Johnston gave the Society an account of Mr. Tompion's
> curious machine for explaining the motion of the sun,
> moon, and earth, according to the Copernic system.
>> Minutes of the Spalding Gentleman's Society,
>> quoted by SILVIO BEDINI, "In Pursuit of Provenance"

1. A TINKER'S THEORY

We can begin by considering the "curious machines" called orreries. (They were named for Charles Boyle, the fourth earl of Orrery and patron of John Rowley, who built one for him in 1713, although the device had actually been invented a few years earlier by a clockmaker's apprentice named George Graham.) In essence, they are models of our solar system—as well as being amazing demonstrations of the skills of the artisans who made them, predominately during the eighteenth century. In the orrery, knowledge takes a material, although still representational, form, and it is this kind of material knowledge that is the focus of this chapter.

Eighteenth-century sensibilities did not, however, accept orreries as "proper scientific knowledge." Knowledge was supposed to be propositional, and material knowledge, as presented in an orrery, was not. Consider Joseph Wright of Derby's wonderful painting *The Orrery* (c. 1764) (fig. 2.1).

A group of people stand around a demonstration of the movements of the heavenly bodies. All are lighted by the sun, which cannot be seen at the center of the orrery. A natural philosopher (top center) lectures on the scientific lessons of the instrument, but his gaze is directed away from it toward the writing being done by the man at the top left. The third adult male is also focused away from the instrument toward the writing. While the three adult males attend to words, the other figures—a woman and several younger persons—are all transfixed by the orrery. Here we have curiosity, fascination, delight, inspiration, awe, reverence. Forget the words of the philosopher; at a more primitive or fundamental level, the orrery transports our imaginations. Here we are on a small planet orbiting the sun, one among several, the intricate motions of which can be "captured"

FIGURE 2.1 Joseph Wright of Derby, *The Orrery* (c. 1764). Reproduced by permission of Derby Museums and Art Gallery.

mechanically. The device itself is a fantastic display of our ability to represent the details of God's handiwork, while at the same time it allows us to fathom a bit of this handiwork and our place in it.

Newton believed that God played an active role in the workings of the solar system. God supplied the energy necessary to keep the planets on their courses and occasionally intervened to put them back on the right track. Leibniz disagreed. The universe could not lose energy; the clock would run forever, and it required no day-to-day supervision on God's part: "To think otherwise made God a tinker and repairman and detracted from his absolute perfection" (King and Millburn 1978, p. 168).

Here in a nutshell we have the epistemic struggle of the instrument. On the one hand, material models clearly transport the imagination; they carry much of the fundamental message of science. As I document below, they even convey details—allowing for explanation and prediction. But they are the products of instrument makers, who, while perhaps a step above tinkers, are nonetheless stained by the imperfections of their medium, things. Like Newton's universe, material models need day-to-day supervision. They need energy supplied from the outside to keep them on their true courses. Mathematical equations, following Leibniz's vision, do not have these needs. They exist in the unchanging, self-sufficient world of ideas.

2. WHAT ARE MODELS?

Orreries are models. But what are these? The first kinds of things I think of when I think of models are the plastic models of ships and airplanes that I tried to build as a kid. But the term covers a very wide array of other meanings, running the gamut from model as an ideal—"Jill is a model citizen"—to artists' models. "Model theory" in logic is the study, at a very abstract level, of structures of "objects" and their "relations." These objects may be concrete physical objects—the chairs in my office—or, more frequently, abstract objects—the natural numbers. In biology, certain living organisms, specially bred mice, for example, are called "models."

Even within the study of science and technology, the term "model" has a wide variety of meanings, many of which—the majority perhaps—are not material in nature but conceptual (Hesse 1963). The contrast between mechanical models and mathematical models is central to the history of nineteenth-century physics. Mathematical models clearly are conceptual in nature, being specified by sets of mathematical equations. The mechanical models of the nineteenth century usually were not actual physical objects but imagined collections of objects interacting according to the laws of mechanics. On the other hand, it must be noted that nineteenth-century British scientists did contrive some fantastic material mechanical devices to represent electromagnetic phenomena (Wise 1979; Buchwald 1985; Schaffer 1994; Buchwald 1998).

According to the "semantic view of theories," a theory is a collection of models. How this collection is specified is a matter of dispute (van Fraassen 1980; Giere 1988; Morrison 1998). Following twentieth-century developments in logic, the collection might be specified by a set of theoretical postulates. But other approaches have been considered. Nancy Cartwright, for example, has argued that "phenomenological models" are specified by their ability to represent experimentally produced phenomena (1983, ch. 6).

Nelson Goodman, in *Languages of Art* (1968, pp. 171–73), identifies two general kinds of use for "model." In the first case, a model is an instance of what it models; a model home, for example, is a sample of what a developer can provide. In the second case, a model, while not itself an instance, defines and stands for a class of objects that it models: "The car of a certain model belongs to a certain class. . . . What is modeled is the particular case that fits the description" (ibid., p. 172). Goodman advocates restricting the use of the term:

> "Model" might well be . . . reserved for cases where the symbol is neither an instance nor a verbal or mathematical description: the ship model, the miniature bulldozer, the architect's model of a campus, the wood or clay model of an automobile. None of these is a sample—a ship, a bulldozer, a campus, or a car; and none is a description in ordinary or mathematical language. Unlike samples, these models are denotative; unlike descriptions, they are nonverbal. (Goodman 1968, p. 172)

No doubt there are significant reasons why the word has so many and such varied uses. Finding the connections between the seemingly disparate uses could provide significant insight into the way models work. For this reason, I am reluctant to allow Goodman to legislate the proper use of the word. On the other hand, Goodman provides a good place to begin, and I shall, for the most part, follow his usage. The material models I focus on satisfy Goodman's restricted use of the term. They are not verbal—being material—and they are not (usually) instances.

This chapter provides an epistemological discussion of such material models. I examine three cases of models that have historical and scientific significance, the orreries of the early eighteenth century, John Smeaton's model waterwheel from later in that century, and Watson and Crick's mid-twentieth-century model of DNA. I show how these models do much of the same epistemological work as theories, and I provide an analysis of how this work is done.

There is a historical dimension to my epistemological story of models. I do not develop this history in any detail, but my particular examples hint at it. Although models did the work of abstract theory—in some cases better than the available theory itself—there was resistance in the eighteenth century to seeing them as epistemologically on a par with theory. From a theoretician's point of view, they were a tinker's theory. By the mid twentieth century, however, material models of chemicals—"ball and stick" models—were a recognized epistemologically respectable modality. Linus Pauling discovered the α-helical structure of proteins in this modality, and Watson and Crick followed the same path to their discovery of the structure of DNA.

Models are a good place to begin an examination of material epistemologies because they operate epistemologically in ways very similar to theory. Both do their epistemological work by representing their objects. But this is only one kind of material epistemology, and chapter 3 presents a fundamentally different kind.

3. THE ORRERY

In the early eighteenth century, instrument makers put a great deal of effort into making physical models of the solar system. These models showed the motion of the earth around the sun and the moon around the earth. They showed the revolutions of the earth and moon on their axes and the tilt of the earth's axis relative to the plane of its orbit around the sun. Later models incorporated the motions of the other planets and their moons. Numerous modifications were developed for more persuasively presenting the picture of the heavens adopted by the new "mechanistic philosophy." I cannot here do anything like full justice to the intricate history of these devices, and I shall only touch on a few highlights. More detail is available in several good sources (Millburn 1976; King and Millburn 1978; Millburn and King 1988; Bedini 1994; Taub 1998).

Sir Richard Steele wrote about John Rowley's orrery (fig. 2.2) in the October 27–29, 1713, issue of his newspaper *The Englishman:*

> I sit down therefore at present to do Justice, and consequently great Honour, to that worthy and ingenious Artificer Mr. John Rowley; who has lately distinguished himself by the Invention of a Machine which illustrates, I may say demonstrates, a System of Astronomy, as far as it relates to the Motions of the Sun, Moon, and Earth, to the meanest Capacity. (quoted in King and Millburn 1978, p. 54)

But Rowley's was not the first device of this kind. Sometime between 1704 and 1709, George Graham, who was apprenticed to the London instrument maker Thomas Tompion, had made two models of the sun-earth-moon system that exhibit the same motions (King and Millburn 1978, pp. 152–53; Bedini 1994).

That these instruments have a representative function is obvious, although just what is represented is, perhaps, more subtle than first appears. The heavenly bodies are not created to scale, and the metal bars that hold them in place do not denote anything "real." In a curious sense—which we see repeated with the DNA model later in the chapter—what is physically present in the model is just what does not denote anything "real." It is the relative motions of the various model bodies that denote the orbits of the heavenly bodies they represent.

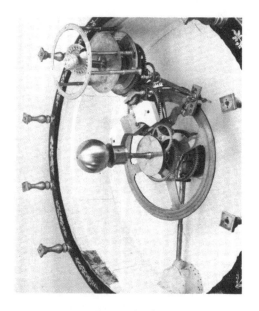

FIGURE 2.2 John Rowley's orrery (c. 1713). Reproduced by permission of the Science Museum, London.

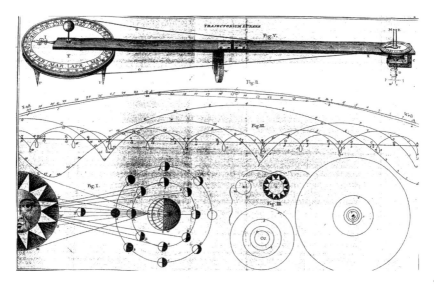

FIGURE 2.3 James Ferguson's solar moon orbit orrery (from Ferguson 1809, pl. 7).

People wrote about orreries in typically theoretical ways. Rowley's orrery, Steele observed, was "a Machine which illustrates, *I may say demonstrates*, a System of Astronomy"; Graham's proto-orrery, the secretary of the Spalding Gentlemen's Society noted, was a "machine for *explaining the motion* of the sun, moon, and earth" (emphases added). Explanation and demonstration are theoretical moves. Orreries were useful for calculation. In 1744, James Ferguson—also a talented instrument maker—developed a modified orrery to demonstrate the complex motion of the moon's orbit around the sun (not its simpler orbit around the Earth). In his device, the earth was on an arm pivoting from the sun, which was kept still. A series of pulleys moved the moon on its orbit around the earth as the earth moved around the sun. Pencils—two small points sticking up in figure 2.3—were put in place of both the earth and the moon. When put into motion, both the earth's and the moon's orbits would be drawn on a sheet of paper held over the device (Millburn and King 1988, pp. 33–37).

Ferguson used another orrery to determine the year of Christ's Crucifixion, when the Passover full moon fell on a Friday:

> To determine this, I went to work with my orrery. . . . I began with the 21st year after the common date of our Saviour's birth; and observing from thence in every year to the 40th, was surprised to find that in the whole course of 20 years so run over, there was but one Passover full

Moon that fell on a Friday; and that one was in the 33 rd year of our
Saviour's age; not including the year of his birth. (quoted in ibid., p. 75)

Significantly, however, Ferguson did not rest with the results of his orrery.
He backed them up with straight calculation:

> But that it might not be said, I trusted to the mechanical performance
> of a machine, I calculated the mean times of all the Passover full Moons
> from astronomical tables for the above twenty years, and found, as a
> thing very remarkable, that the only Passover full Moon which fell on
> a Friday in all that time, was the one above mentioned. (quoted in ibid.,
> p. 75)

At this point, orreries were at best devices for approximating calculations
based directly on theory. They were not theory itself.

Orreries may not have been able to carry the epistemic weight of full astronomical theory at the level of fine calculation displayed in Ferguson's attempt to date Christ's Crucifixion. But they did have a significant theoretical function at the fundamental level of metaphor. Derek de Solla Price has
argued that, far from being mere pedagogic devices, orreries and their pre-
cursors, which can be found well back into antiquity, are fundamental material expressions of a "strong innate urge toward mechanistic explanation"
(Price 1964, p. 10):

> We now suggest that from Ctesibius and Archimedes onward we can
> see the development of a fine mechanical technology, originating in the
> improvement of astronomical simulacra from the simple spinning globe
> to the geared planetarium and anaphoric clock. . . . [T]hey represent . . .
> man's urge to exhibit the depth of his understanding and his sophisti-
> cated skills by playing the role of a do-it-yourself creator of the uni-
> verse. (Price 1964, p. 15)

Price reminds us that our words "theory" and "equation" (although Greek
and Latin respectively in origin) come to us by way of medieval terms that
embraced tangible models of the heavens. He writes:

> These devices [astronomical simulacra] had the status of *theories* in
> the sense in which some philosophers of science have used the term.
> They were tangible models that served the same purpose of geometric
> diagrams or mathematical and other symbolism in later theories. They
> were embodied explanation of the way that things worked. . . . As
> a matter of fact, the medieval terms for planetary simulations were
> Theorik and Equatorie; the brass devices went by the names we now
> use for abstract modeling. (Price 1980, p. 76)

These models were "read" metaphorically. No one expected to find brass
gears in the heavens. But the idea that the motions of the heavenly bodies

were brought about by some kind of mechanical actions, as were the motions in orreries, became current. People did not expect to find cosmic brass gears, but they did expect there to be a mechanical explanation for the motions of the heavenly bodies. So, while these may have been "tinker's theories," they played a pivotal role in establishing the mechanical philosophy of the day.

4. JOHN SMEATON'S MODEL WATERWHEEL

While orreries did not carry the same epistemic weight as theory, there were occasions when the mechanical performance of a machine was more trustworthy than "pure theory." Consider the work of the noted civil engineer John Smeaton in developing a better waterwheel.

In 1751, Smeaton was asked to build a waterwheel (Smiles 1862, vol. 2). Looking at what had been written on the subject, he did not find consistent information on how best to extract power from water with a waterwheel. Among other problems, the theoretical literature did not treat overshot and undershot wheels differently, yet Smeaton's experience strongly suggested that there was a difference. Something was amiss.

Antoine Parent's 1704 theoretical analysis of waterwheel operation was the accepted standard through Smeaton's time (Reynolds 1983, pp. 206–10). I shall pass over the details and simply note that through an early application of differential calculus, Parent had determined those conditions under which, in the terms of his theoretical framework, the operation of a waterwheel would be most efficient. He found that, at best, a waterwheel could extract 15 percent of the available power. Furthermore, this maximum could only be obtained when the load being lifted was $4/9$ of the load that would stop the wheel's motion in the flowing stream, and only when the velocity of the wheel was $1/3$ of the velocity of the stream.

Parent's work suffered from several fundamental errors. There were conceptual errors concerning the proper measure of the work. Several of the assumptions on which he based his calculations were in error. Most important, he treated all waterwheels—overshot and undershot—the same way. This was partly a consequence of the mechanical philosophy of the time. As Richard Westfall put it: "[A]ll the phenomena of nature are caused by particles of matter in motion acting on each other by contact alone" (quoted in Reynolds 1983, p. 212). Hence it wouldn't matter whether these particles hit the waterwheel blades first and then fell with the blade (as in an overshot wheel) or hit the blade after falling on their own (as in an undershot wheel).

FIGURE 2.4 John Smeaton's model waterwheel (from Smeaton 1809a, p. 13).

In order, then, to determine on his own how best to design and build waterwheels, Smeaton built a model (fig. 2.4).[1] Several features of Smeaton's model are worth noting. He contrived a ratchet and pin mechanism in the axle of the wheel. This way he could stop the motion of the wheel reasonably precisely, which allowed him to make more careful measurements of the distance the weight was lifted. When running experiments, he kept

1. On waterwheels, see Smeaton 1809a, 1809b, 1809c; Donkin 1937; E. C. Wright 1938; P. Wilson 1955; Cardwell 1967, 1971; Pacey, 1974; Skempton 1981; Reynolds 1983; Vincenti 1990; Schaffer 1994.

the water level in the reservoir at a constant height—as is the case with "actual" waterwheels. Smeaton could adjust or vary several parameters of his model waterwheel. By means of a stop, he could adjust the size of the sluice opening. He could vary the height of the head of water used in a run. He could vary the load that the wheel lifted. Perhaps most important, he could run tests on both undershot and overshot wheels.

He conducted trials of one minute each, organized into sets. In any given set of trials, he would vary the load—from four pounds to nine pounds—and keep the other parameters of the experiment constant. In this way, he found the load that would allow for the maximum effect. Parent had used the differential calculus to find the point of maximum efficiency; Smeaton used what Walter Vincenti has dubbed "the method of parameter variation" (Vincenti 1990, p. 139) to find this maximum. The theoretical parameters Parent varied, or "maximized over," function the same way as the physical parameters Smeaton maximized over in his model.

Smeaton's model provided a better way to determine waterwheel efficiency than Parent's theory for two reasons. In the first place, the model provided a better representation than the theory. In the second place, it was physically straightforward to vary the point at which the water meets the wheel. The common understanding of the mechanical philosophy and confusion with the concepts of work and power made this operation conceptually difficult.

Parent's theory and Smeaton's model both provided representations of waterwheels. Parent's theory had built-in assumptions about efficiency and work. With Smeaton's model, they were literally built in. Smeaton, unencumbered by misleading theory and well informed by his practical experience with waterwheels, was better able to represent them in a material model than Parent was in equations.

Smeaton's work paid off. Contrary to Parent's theory—where overshot and undershot wheels were treated identically—Smeaton showed that overshot wheels were substantially more efficient than undershot wheels. This finding had an impact on the subsequent construction of waterwheels. Where possible, overshot wheels were built. Sometimes, for lack of sufficient fall in the river, overshot wheels could not be built. Here a compromise was developed, a "breast wheel," where the water met the wheel roughly halfway down its diameter and moved it by a combination of gravity and impact. Smeaton was awarded the 1759 Copley prize by the Royal Society for his work on waterwheels.

Looked at one way, Smeaton's model waterwheel is not a model in Goodman's sense. Smeaton's model waterwheel is itself a waterwheel. It is an instance and thus violates Goodman's requirement that models not be instances. But, seen in a more fundamental sense, Smeaton's model is not "really" a waterwheel. It does no real work: it is not drawing power from a river, but relies instead on a human pushing a pump to fill a reservoir. Smeaton's model is a dynamic representation of real waterwheels. The fact that a fundamental aspect of the forces driving its dynamic behavior is the same as with real waterwheels—namely, water moving a bladed or bucketed wheel—only underwrites its claim to being an accurate representation. Smeaton was interested in his model, not as a waterwheel, but as a representation of waterwheels, a representation that he could materially manipulate in the same way that Parent had conceptually manipulated the equations of his theoretical model of waterwheels.

Historically, another step was necessary for Smeaton's model to be taken as knowledge in itself. Smeaton's model was not the point of the exercise. Smeaton wanted to establish truths about waterwheel efficiency that could then guide him in designing and building waterwheels. The ultimate goal was an efficient waterwheel and the proximate goal was better propositional knowledge about waterwheel efficiency. Smeaton understood his model instrumentally. While it worked much as theory works—representing its object and promoting "calculations" about that object—Smeaton presented to the Royal Society not his waterwheel, but rather the results of experiments with it. The model is an experimental setup for investigating a particular kind of technological artifact. While Smeaton's model has all the ingredients of knowledge, as with the orrery, this was not the conceptual temper of his times. The model was not yet knowledge itself. These concepts began to shift in the twentieth century (see chapter 5).

5. THE DOUBLE HELIX

If we move ahead 200 years to the "ball and stick" model used by James Watson and Francis Crick in their discovery of the structure of DNA, we find that matters have changed. Here the model is knowledge, one species of thing knowledge. Molecular models have a long and fruitful history in chemistry. Rather than discussing the broader history of the widespread use of models in chemistry (see Suckling et al. 1978; Juaristi 1991; Hoffmann 1995, esp. ch. 15; Francoeur 1997), let us take one seminal episode, James Watson and Francis Crick's discovery of the structure of DNA. Watson's own account of this (Watson [1968] 1981) is wonderfully well put and widely known, and there are other excellent sources for it (e.g., Olby 1974; Judson 1979; Crick 1988), so I shall simply make a few observations on the subject here.

Watson and Crick brought several resources to their work on the structure of DNA and appropriated others. They both brought the available background knowledge about the chemical composition of DNA, along with their shared belief that DNA is the material of the gene. They appropriated X-ray diffraction studies by Rosalind Franklin and Maurice Wilkins. Crick developed a mathematical theory for interpreting molecular structure from such diffraction studies, and Watson contributed some biological metaphysics, notably the idea that everything important in biology comes in pairs. But most significant for my purposes, they brought the use of material models to represent the spatial relations of atoms in compounds. The use of models had played a significant role in Linus Pauling's recent discovery of the α-helical structure of proteins. "The α-helix had not been found by only staring at X-ray pictures; the essential trick, instead, was to ask which atoms like to sit next to each other," Watson writes. "In place of pencil and paper, the main working tools were a set of molecular models superficially resembling the toys of preschool children" (Watson 1981, p. 34). Crick confirms this. It was their knowledge of the way models had been used in the discovery of the α-helix that gave them a decisive advantage in working out the structure of—which is to say, a model for—DNA (Crick 1988, pp. 68–69).

The modeling materials provided a space within which to explore ideas about molecular structure. Not infrequently, the models showed Watson and Crick what was wrong with their ideas. "On a few walks our enthusiasm would build up to the point that we fiddled with the models when we got back to our office," Watson says. "But almost immediately Francis saw that the reasoning which had momentarily given us hope led nowhere" (Watson 1981, pp. 91–92).

When Watson and Crick were short of reasons why the atoms "should" be one way or another, the models gave them room to explore possibilities "without reason," which is to say, without propositional reason, but with the reason supplied by the material modeling space. They knew that DNA was made up of a "backbone" and four "bases." The backbone is composed of sugar and phosphate groups joined together in a chain, and they had evidence that it formed a helix. They knew neither how many helical chains were involved nor the relationship between the chains. At a crucial juncture, however, they decided to try putting two backbones on the outside of the model:

"Why not," I said to Jim one evening, "build models with the phosphates on the outside?" "Because," he said, "that would be too easy" (meaning that there were too many models he could build in this way). "Then why not try it?" I said as Jim went up the steps into the night. (Crick 1988, p. 70)

Watson carries on the story:

The next morning, however, as I took apart a particularly repulsive backbone-centered molecule, I decided that no harm could come from spending a few days building backbone-out models. This meant temporarily ignoring the bases, but in any case this had to happen since now another week was required before the shop could hand over the flat tin plates cut in the shapes of purines and pyrimidines [the bases]. (Watson 1981, p. 103)

Their use of two chains was a biologically inspired guess. Putting the backbones on the outside was a shot in the dark.

Watson had no difficulty putting the backbones together. Then he began to worry about how the bases might connect in the middle. He still didn't have the tin plates from the machine shop, so he made cardboard cutout versions and started playing around with them to see how they might connect. After a few false starts, he found the solution. One of the two purine-bases (adenine—"A") hydrogen-bonds with one of the two pyrimidine-bases (thymine—"T"), while the other purine (guanine—"G") hydrogen-bonds with the other pyrimidine (cytosine—"C"), A with T, G with C. The bond distances for the two pairings were the same. The bases could bond on the interior, holding the two-strand backbone together without distortion.

Much as mathematical theories provide a mathematical space for theorists to play in, trying out ideas to see what might work, molecular models provide a similar space to play in. It was in this material space that Watson discovered the manner in which the base pairs bonded.

With this crucial insight, the remaining structure came quickly. They built a complete double helical model—including the tin plates hot off the machine shop's presses. The model was immediately persuasive (fig. 2.5). There is a geometric beauty to the form that is very compelling. It is also worth noting that in this image, in contrast to Wright's painting of the orrery, the attention of both scientists is directed to the model.

Beyond its aesthetic appeal, Watson and Crick's double helix has the standard theoretical virtues. It explained the known evidence about DNA. After seeing Watson and Crick's model, Maurice Wilkins checked the agreement between his lab's X-ray data and the model and found that it provided an excellent explanation for those data. Indeed, Rosalind Franklin, working

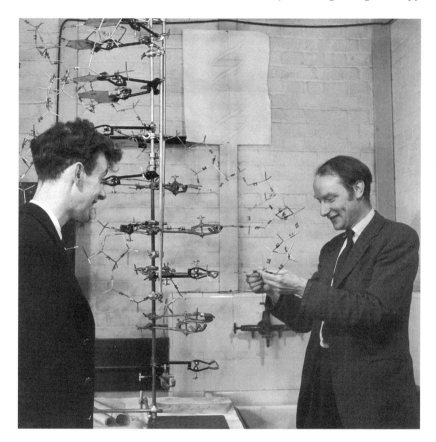

FIGURE 2.5 James Watson, Francis Crick, and their DNA model (1953). Reproduced by permission of A. C. Barrington-Brown, Photo Researchers, Inc.

in Wilkins's lab, had incontrovertible evidence that the DNA backbone was on the outside of the structure, evidence that Watson had not been aware of when he decided to try backbone-out models. The model also explained Erwin Chargaff's finding that DNA always has the same amounts of adenine as thymine and guanine as cytosine; these are the pairs that bond exclusively to each other.

The model made important predictions. Within a week of making the discovery, Watson was confronted with a chemical analysis of some DNA that contained no cytosine. But, what it did contain was a modified type of cytosine that hydrogen-bonded with guanine in the same manner as regular cytosine. Furthermore, there was always the same amount of this modified cytosine as guanine.

The model's most important prediction is wonderfully understated in Watson and Crick's conclusion to their initial announcement of the structure of DNA: "It has not escaped our notice that the specific pairing we have postulated immediately suggests a possible copying mechanism for the genetic material" (Watson and Crick 1953, p. 737). This prediction from their model has proven enormously important and valuable, so much so that the struggle to find the structure almost fades into the background now that the solution seems—after the fact—so obvious:

> In retrospect, the achievement is so lucid that it looks transparent. The helix, made of two matched strands, a unit of thymine always opposite one of adenine, and cytosine always opposite guanine, is so logical and natural that it now seems self-evident. Clearly this is how the dividing cell is able to split its hereditary material in half, and how each of the two daughter cells is able to make a whole again by using one strand of DNA as a template to form the other strand. If we had to design heredity, and were as simple as nature and as clever as Crick and Watson, that is just how we would do it. (Bronowski 1981, p. 202)

6. MODEL AS KNOWLEDGE

Watson and Crick's DNA model provides a two-part argument for understanding models as scientific knowledge. There is a negative part: It makes little sense to think of the Watson/Crick model in other terms. They did not use the model as a pedagogic device. They did not simply extract information from it. The model was not part of some intervention in nature. It was not a part of an experiment.

There also is a positive part: Watson and Crick's model performs theoretical functions with contrived bits of the material world instead of words. Their model has the standard theoretical virtues. It can be used to make explanations and predictions. It was confirmed by X-ray and other evidence, and it could have been refuted by evidence—for example, if DNA had been found with markedly different quantities of adenine and thymine. Although it was made of metal, not words, there can be little doubt that Watson and Crick's model of DNA is knowledge.

There remains the somewhat sticky business of sorting out the relationship between material models, such as Watson and Crick's, and theories understood in the usual propositional terms. This is best done with the semantic view of theories (Suppes 1961, 1962, 1967; van Fraassen 1980;

Giere 1988). I adapt what follows from R. I. G. Hughes's contribution to this approach to understanding theory (Hughes 1997).

According to the semantic view of theories, a theory does not directly describe the world. Instead, it describes or is coextensive with a "model" or class of "models." With a successful theory, the model or one model in the class of models "represents" a portion of the world. This use of "model" is more general than that covering the several cases of specifically material models that have occupied this chapter. On the other hand, Hughes is clear that his use of "model" includes material models (ibid., p. S329).

There is one crucial distinction between the conceptual models that are the usual fare of the semantic view and the material models I am interested in here. Material models are specified directly in their materials. So the relationship between theory and model is different. With conceptual models, the theory specifies a model or class of models. With material models, the models specify or, perhaps better, point to the theory. The theory is the open-ended generalization of the model. How generally could Smeaton's model waterwheel be taken? Given the available resources for building waterwheels in his day, quite generally. But his model could not be extended to the water turbines of today.

The semantic view of theories takes no position on the question of where knowledge claims apply—to a theory, a class of models, or a single model. In conceptual cases, where the theory specifies the class of models, it is more natural to speak of theoretical knowledge. By contrast, in material cases, where the model points to the theory, it is more natural to speak of model knowledge, one species of thing knowledge.

Hughes provides a three-part account for how models represent the world. He calls it the "DDI account," referring to its three parts: denotation, demonstration, and interpretation.

In the first place, models *denote* some part of the world. The motions of the various parts of orreries denoted orbits and revolutions of various planets and moons. A significant feature of denotation is its independence of resemblance. Here Hughes follows Nelson Goodman's discussion in *Languages of Art* (Goodman 1968, pp. 3–6). Goodman and Hughes are concerned with the fact that, with conceptual models, the parts of the model do not resemble the part of the world they denote. Hughes writes:

> To take a more typical example, we may model an actual pendulum, a weight hanging by a cord, as an ideal pendulum. We may even be tempted to say that in both cases the relation between the pendulum's length and its periodic time is approximately the same, and that they

are in that respect similar to each other. But the ideal pendulum has no length, and there is no time in which it completes an oscillation. It is an abstract object, similar to material pendulums in no obvious sense. (Hughes 1997, p. S330)

In a similar vein, Goodman points out that a painting always more closely resembles other paintings than it resembles some depicted object (Goodman 1968, p. 5).

The atypical examples Hughes alludes to in the passage quoted above are material models; here matters can be different. Orrery orbits are themselves orbits about the orrery's artificial sun. Smeaton's model waterwheel was itself a waterwheel, albeit a small one, and the bond geometry in Watson and Crick's DNA model stood in a precise geometric relationship to bond angles and lengths in actual (crystallized) DNA.[2] Thus, while models generally need not resemble their objects, they may do so, and with material models, this is common.

With both material models and conceptual models, to properly understand the model, one must know which parts denote what. Thus, the sticks in Watson and Crick's model denote bond lengths, not rigid metallic connections. An orrery's planets denote appropriate heavenly bodies, and their motions denote the motions of those heavenly bodies. The metal rods that hold the planets and the gears that drive them at appropriate rates do not denote anything specifically. On the other hand, at a more general level, the mechanism of the orrery—taken as a whole—denotes "mechanism," metaphorically speaking, underlying the motions of the heavenly bodies—taken as a whole.

It is the degree of specificity of denotation that marks the difference between metaphor and model. There are obviously no gears in the heavens corresponding to the gears in an orrery, but the solar system is metaphorically viewed as a mechanism. There are, however, orbits in the heavens corresponding to the orbits in orreries. Here, the orrery is a model in the sense of the semantic view of theories.

One important use of models—material or conceptual—is demonstration, the second part of Hughes's DDI account. Thus, James Ferguson used an orrery to demonstrate—in this case to draw—the shape of the moon's orbit relative to the sun. John Smeaton used his model waterwheel to determine the relative efficiency of overshot as opposed to undershot waterwheels. Watson and Crick used their model of DNA to explain genetic re-

---

2. I am indebted to Paul Needham for forcing me to be clear on this point.

production. Demonstration powers a model's ability to explain and predict. With conceptual models, demonstrations proceed conceptually, frequently mathematically. With material models, demonstrations use material relations, which may be causal (Smeaton's waterwheel) or geometric (Watson and Crick's DNA model) or a combination of the two (Ferguson's moon-orbit orrery).

Finally, we interpret the results and simultaneously demonstrate the empirical adequacy of the model. In Smeaton's day, overshot waterwheels were more efficient than undershot wheels. Remarkably, Ferguson's calculation of the year of Christ's Crucifixion by a "mere machine" agreed with a calculation based on astronomical tables. Watson and Crick concluded that adenine forms hydrogen bonds with thymine and cytosine with guanine. DNA must have equal quantities of these substances—a fact that was ascertained in the laboratory.

7. MATERIAL MANIPULATION

So, in the end, material models can be understood as one kind of model embraced by the semantic view of theories. They are one way to develop theory and make the connection between theory and the world. The materials provide the space in which scientists—Ferguson, Smeaton, or Watson and Crick—develop and articulate their subjective knowledge of the bit of the world they are concerned with. The model produced is the objective bearer of this knowledge.

There is, however, one important difference that distinguishes material models from other kinds of models. Material models can be manipulated materially. This can include tactile manipulation—such as Watson's play with cardboard DNA bases. But it can also take the form of chemical, thermal, electrical, hydrodynamic (Smeaton), and other manipulations. This is particularly important when conceptual manipulations are impossible either for lack of a theory or because analytical manipulations would be too difficult. Smeaton used a material model because the available conceptual model was not good. Ferguson was able to find the moon's orbit with his material model when an analytical approach would have exceeded the computational abilities available to him. Watson discovered pair bonding through the manipulation of material objects—cardboard cutout models of the bases—in space when an analytic approach would have taken too long, if, indeed, it would have succeeded at all.

Crick's description of Watson's discovery of pair bonding is particularly revealing. He writes:

> The key discovery was Jim's determination of the exact nature of the two base pairs (A with T, G with C). He did this not by logic but by serendipity. (The logical approach—which we would certainly have used had it proved necessary—would have been: first, to assume Chargaff's rules were correct and thus consider only the pairs suggested by these rules, and second to look for the dyadic symmetry suggested by the C2 space group shown by the fiber patterns. This would have led to the correct base pairs in a very short time.) In a sense Jim's discovery was luck, but then most discoveries have an element of luck in them. The more important point is that Jim was looking for something significant and immediately recognized the significance of the correct pairs when he hit upon them by chance—"chance favors the prepared mind." This episode also demonstrates that play is often important in research. (Crick 1988, pp. 65–66)

It is true, Watson did not use logic in the sense of mathematical manipulations. But it is significant that Crick reserves use of the words "serendipity" and "luck" for material manipulations, as opposed to "logical manipulations." The subtext is that the logical method would have ground out the result with certainty, if without inspiration. This certainly is a mistaken way of looking at these matters. The "logical approach" would have required making the appropriate logical assumptions and moves, just as Watson's "playing" with cardboard models required its own assumptions and moves. Serendipity would have had to play its role, fixing on the appropriate assumptions and space of possible moves (conceptual or material), either way. This much we learn from the fact that logic problems assigned as homework do not simply solve themselves. Crick's application of the terms "serendipity" and "luck" to material manipulations is surely a vestige of Ferguson's concern that people might think he had determined when the Passover full moon fell on a Friday by using a mere machine, a vestige of the notion that models are a tinker's theory.

The ability to manipulate material models by hand, so to speak, is important because it provides a different entry point for our cognitive apparatus. Conceptual manipulation provides one entry, material manipulation a second independent entry. By admitting that models, and instruments more generally, have epistemic status, that they are knowledge, we enlarge our ability to bring our cognitive apparatus to bear on the world.

3 Working Knowledge

... then will something else happen, and shatter the doubts
of skeptics, like the celestial fire upon the altar of Elijah.

CHARLES SANDERS PEIRCE, *Pragmatism and Pragmaticism*

1. THE PULSE GLASS

In a letter to John Winthrop dated July 2, 1768, Benjamin Franklin brought
a new device to the attention of his scientific colleagues, the pulse glass (see
also B. Franklin 1941; 1972, 15: 166–72). This simple device consists of a
narrow tube bent at right angles at either end, with two larger spheres on
the ends. The tube is roughly one-third to one-half filled with water or al-
cohol, evacuated, and sealed (fig. 3.1).

Because of the vacuum, the liquid in the glass can be brought to a boil
by holding it in one's hand. Several toys are now made from pulse glasses,
including the "fever meter" and the "drinking duck." By holding the lower
sphere of the fever meter in one's hand, one can cause violent boiling in the
upper sphere. When the duck is appropriately suspended, it will rock back
and forth, "drinking" from a cup of water virtually indefinitely.

During the late eighteenth and early nineteenth centuries, this simple,
seemingly innocuous, device was a subject of considerable controversy, giving rise to bizarre observations. In his letter to Winthrop, Franklin notes,
for example, that "the instant it begins to boil a sudden coldness is felt in
the ball held; a curious experiment [. . .] similar to the old observation, I
think of Aristotle, that the bottom of the boiling pot is not warm; and may
help to explain that fact, if indeed it is a fact."[1]

---

1. B. Franklin 1972, 15: 171. The editors of Franklin's letters attribute this "observation of Aristotle's" to Aristotle's *Problems* 24.5. In translation this reads:
"Why is it that the bottom of a vessel containing boiling water does not burn, but
one can carry it holding it by the bottom, whereas if the water be removed it burns?
Is it because the heat as it is engendered in the bottom of the vessel is extinguished
by the water? That is also why substances which can be melted do not melt if any
liquid is added to them" (Aristotle 1984). My colleague Rosamond Sprague notes
that the first sentence, if read without the "but one can carry it" clause, is true; pots

FIGURE 3.1 Jules Salleron's pulse glass (from Salleron 1858–64, reprinted in Turner 1983, p. 114, pl. 5).

While the pulse glass led Franklin to question experience with pots of boiling water, it led James Watt to a small concern over his priority in improvements on the steam engine. Writing as if he were perfectly able to explain the phenomenon, Watt notes in his editorial comments on John Robison's 1822 *System of Mechanical Philosophy:* "The invention of the pulse glass is ascribed to Dr. Franklin, its date uncertain, probably subsequent to my improvement of the Steam Engine, at least certainly not known to me at that time. The boiling in vacuo was known long before the pulse glass was invented" (Robison 1822, 2: 14).

Why should Watt have cared whether the pulse glass was invented before or after his improvement on the steam engine? Why did Franklin accept the putative observation of Aristotle that the bottom of a pot of boiling water is not hot?

The pulse glass tapped into important realms of material agency, about which there was much confusion in Watt and Franklin's day. The phenomenon of boiling—or is it evaporation? (see Erasmus Darwin below)—was scientifically and technologically very important, but ill understood. Watt's interest, of course, derived from his interest in steam engines. Watt believed that steam engines derived their motive power from the elasticity of steam, and that the pressure at which the steam was generated affected its ability to produce power. As Watt saw the pulse glass, it demonstrated that

---

burn only when the water in them has boiled off. She speculates that someone misunderstood the sense of "burn"—and gave it a transitive reading, "burn *someone* or *something.*" This may be why the "but one can carry it" clause was added. She also points out that very likely the *Problems* were not by Aristotle, but by the Peripatetic School considerably later (Sprague 1990).

the boiling of water and the generation of power depended on pressure. Indeed, he worried that the pulse glass demonstrated this so strikingly that it threatened to diminish his originality as a steam engine innovator. The pulse glass could have served to pique the divergent interests of Franklin and Watt only if it was itself absolutely convincing.

This is the first and probably most important feature of the pulse glass. It embodies a phenomenon compellingly. Franklin clearly was taken with the pulse glass:

> I placed one of his[2] [pulse] glasses with the elevated end against this hole [from his room to the outside air], and the bubbles from the other end, which was in a warmer situation, were continually passing day and night, to the no small surprise of philosophical spectators. Each bubble discharged is larger than that from which it proceeds, and yet that is not diminished; and by adding itself to the bubble at the other end, that bubble is not increased, which seems very paradoxical. (B. Franklin 1972, 15: 170)

Franklin *enjoyed* the phenomenon and the effects of its display. In the notes appended to his 1791 poem *The Botanic Garden*, Erasmus Darwin writes: "The quick evaporation occasioned in vacuo by a small degree of heat is agreeably seen in what is termed a pulse glass" (Darwin 1978, vol. 1, Additional Notes, p. 67). The instrument engages us immediately. And while it may arouse our curiosity, the phenomenon needs no further explanation to be appreciated. Its instrumental compactness also makes for an ideal philosophical toy, at all times ready for the instantaneous recall of a phenomenon. The drinking duck, like Faraday's motor, provides a pocket edition of a material fact.

Even long after the pulse glass was recognized as a technologically certified phenomenon, its theoretical description and explanation remained unclear. This type of instrument shares this with natural phenomena. Its description and explanation depend on theoretical interests, while *it* persists through theoretical change.

In the passage reproduced above, Benjamin Franklin gives at least two interpretations of the pulse glass: bubbles "were continually passing day and night"—that is, the phenomenon involved a sort of perpetual motion; and the discharged bubbles got larger without diminishing the air from

---

2. He refers to Edward Nairne, a well-known commercial instrument maker in London at the time. Franklin frequented his shop and commissioned several instruments—including several pulse glasses. Nairne suggested several experiments that Franklin describes with the pulse glass.

which they sprang—that is, something appeared to emanate from nothing. He also notes that coldness is felt in one bulb just when the other bulb begins to boil, connecting this with Aristotle's purported observation about boiling pots of water. Erasmus Darwin regarded the process as evaporation, and while boiling and evaporation are today considered equivalent, one can imagine a theoretical context where it might at least be a question whether they designate the same phenomenon.

Watt connected the action of the pulse glass with the ability to generate power with a steam engine. His views on the relationship between heat, work, pressure, and the elasticity of steam are now considered obsolete (see chapter 8), however, and in contemporary theoretical jargon, the phenomenon is said to be a reversible isothermal transformation (but see the discussion of Sadi Carnot's early use of the pulse glass in this line of investigation in Mendoza 1960, p. 66).

William Hyde Wollaston, who was responsible for making the pulse glass a standard demonstration instrument, called the "cryophorus," in the nineteenth century, argued that it demonstrated the transmission of cold (Wollaston 1812, 1813), and A. P. Saunders said that it illustrated the nature of thermal equilibria (Saunders 1908, p. 279).

Notwithstanding the theoretical confusion surrounding the pulse glass, it remained technologically stable, producing its phenomenon reliably. Clearly, it presents one instance of material agency, whether or not we know the explanation for this agency. The instrument became the point of departure for further instrumental developments including J. F. Daniell's dew point hygrometer (Daniell 1820a, 1820b, 1823; see also Reid 1839, p. 699; Middleton 1969, pp. 115–17). Moreover, even though a complete and uncontested theoretical account of the pulse glass is available today, it remains fascinating. The phenomenon cannot be diminished by or reduced to a theoretical explanation.

2. KNOWING MATERIAL AGENCY

The pulse glass thus contributed to science a compact, instrumentally framed fact, a relative technological certainty in a sea of theoretical confusion, and the foundation for further instrumental development. Like Faraday's motor, the pulse glass presents an instance of an instrument—a contrived part of the material world—that creates and exhibits an element of material agency. In both cases, there was at the time no consensus on the right sequence of words to describe this agency. Yet the agency itself could not be denied. Charles Sanders Peirce describes such a situation as follows:

> When an experimentalist speaks of a *phenomenon*, such as "Hall's phenomenon," "Zeeman's phenomenon" . . . he does not mean any particular event that did happen to somebody in the dead past, but what *surely will* happen to everybody in the living future who shall fulfill certain conditions. The phenomenon consists in the fact that when an experimenter shall come to *act* according to a certain scheme that he has in mind, then will something else happen, and shatter the doubts of skeptics, like the celestial fire upon the altar of Elijah. (Peirce 1931–34, vol. 5, para. 425)

Ideally, a phenomenon has the striking and persuasive quality of the divine blaze by which Elijah embarrassed the 450 prophets of Baal, but it must also be constant and reliable, a permanent fixture of the living future.

The ability to make, manipulate, adapt, and develop material agency, as Franklin and his followers did with the pulse glass and as Faraday and his followers did with his motor, is ample proof of knowledge of the agency. In a subjective sense, the people involved possess the necessary know-how to produce a reliable permanent fixture of the living future. In an objective sense, there are devices made by humans that exhibit particular phenomena over which we have substantial material—if not linguistic—control.

I call this kind of knowledge "working knowledge." It is a form of material knowledge distinct from the model knowledge discussed in chapter 2. Subjectively, a person who has "a working knowledge" has knowledge sufficient to do something. Objectively, a device that bears working knowledge works regularly. It presents a phenomenon, which might be used to accomplish something. This form of material knowledge, in contrast to model knowledge, is not representational, but rather appeals to pragmatist notions of knowledge as effective action.

Three important tasks remain to articulate and understand this kind of knowledge. The first concerns the meaning of devices that bear working knowledge. Such devices do not represent as models do, so how do they "speak" to us of the world? The second concerns the instrumental crafting of working knowledge. It is material agency, but corralled, controlled, and purified. The process of making such material knowledge is a process of contriving, arranging, and refining materials. How does this take place? This process is the key to new worlds of phenomena, new domains of knowledge—working knowledge and other forms of knowledge too. Finally, along the way toward making this working knowledge, we devise new techniques that, in themselves, are bits of working knowledge. We collect descriptions of these techniques in what I call "instrument cookbooks," which I discuss at the close of this chapter.

3. THE AIR PUMP AS A STAGE FOR MATERIAL AGENCY

The air pump hosted many different experiments. The early "void-in-the-void" experiments of Robert Boyle (1660) have received considerable attention. Two notable works, one by James Bryant Conant (1950) and one by Steve Shapin and Simon Schaffer (1985), show how important these experiments were for establishing the scientific "experimental life" and the scientific view of the vacuum. In the eighteenth century, however, the air pump was frequently exhibited in public performances. Another painting by Joseph Wright of Derby (whose painting of the orrery is discussed in chapter 2) shows it in action (fig. 3.2).

The experiment in this painting is not a void-in-the-void experiment, and the experimenter—unlike in the painting of the orrery—is not focused on the written word. Here the experimenter gazes out beyond the scene framed in the painting, beyond the air pump receiver with the bird dying of asphyxiation, beyond the social engagement that surrounds him. Here the experimenter sees the material agency—that which is killing the bird—behind the appearances. Nothing appears to intervene between the experiment, the experimenter, the viewers of the painting, and the awesome power at work (Busch 1986; Nordmann 1994).

There is a marked distinction between the two paintings by Wright, and between the experiments they depict. This experiment engages its audience in a radically different way, as suggested in the following passage by Joseph Priestley:

> All true history has a capital advantage over every work of fiction.
> Works of fiction resemble those machines which we contrive to illustrate the principles of philosophy, such as globes or orreries, the use of which extend[s] no further than the views of human ingenuity; whereas real history resembles the experiments with the airpump, condensing engine and electrical machine, which exhibit the operations of nature, and the nature of God himself. (Priestley 1817–31, 24: 27–28)

Here lies the important distinction between the representational knowledge of the orrery and the working knowledge of the air pump. With "works of fiction," we interpose a representation between the world and ourselves. We create a model of the world, a "fiction." With "real history,"

FIGURE 3.2 Joseph Wright of Derby, *Experiment with the Airpump* (1768). Reproduced by permission of the National Gallery, London.

we directly engage the world, but in a technologically controlled way. Material agency is revealed in our mechanical contrivances. The pneumatic mechanism of the air pump enabled material agency to manifest itself, but under artificial control. Much as we control concepts through the exercise of our literary skills, we control material agency through the exercise of our making skills.

The void-in-the-void experiment pales in comparison to the spectacle of the bird flapping helplessly in the air pump's receiver. However, there is nothing ingenious about putting animals in the receiver of an air pump and watching what happens. No theories are refuted; long-familiar physical features of the vacuum and of animal respiration are merely reenacted. What is the point? What accounts for the popularity of this theoretically uninteresting experiment in the eighteenth century? What was spectacular about the spectacle of a bird deprived of air? Or, posing the question in Priestley's terms, how does this experiment resemble not fiction but real history? An obvious answer suggests itself: The experiment with the bird involves life and death, the fate of the bird is simply much more engaging than the relative height of a barometric column. It appeals more directly to human concerns. But a comparison with another experiment serves to show not so much that this explanation is wrong as that it is incomplete.

In Wright's painting, a person is timing just how long it takes for the bird to suffocate. Data are being gathered, which may figure in a larger context. Robert Boyle conducted experiments comparing the "times wherein animals may be killed by drowning, or withdrawing of the air" as early as 1670, noting, for example: "A greenfinch, having his legs and wings tied to a weight, was gently let down into a glass body filled with water; the time of its total immersion being marked." After half a minute, he found the bird "quite dead" (Boyle 1809, p. 487).

Boyle's experiment with the greenfinch is precisely equivalent to the one depicted in Wright's painting. And it equally addresses human concerns with life and death. But by contrast with the bird in the receiver of the air pump, Boyle's second experiment is crude and insipid. It strikes no one as either suspenseful or sublime enough to redeem its pedestrian, distasteful, even revolting, character.

Priestley's question remains. What is it about the experiment with the air pump that makes it resemble not fiction but real history? To quote Priestley again: "By the help of these machines, we are able to put an endless variety of things into an endless variety of situations, [of] which nature herself is the agent that shows the result" (Priestley 1775, 1: xii).

In 1803, John Robison, one of the first historians of eighteenth-century chemistry, explained what was so special about "nature herself" being "the agent that shows the result." In the preface to Joseph Black's *Lectures on the Elements of Chemistry*, Robison lauds Black's discovery of a new gas, "fixed air." With this discovery, he says, we "are now admitted into the laboratory of nature herself, and instructed into some of those great processes by which the author of this fair world makes it a habitable place" (Black 1803, 1: lvi).

With the air pump, we are admitted into the laboratory of nature herself. While we are not guided by human theorizing, it does take technological ingenuity to unlock this laboratory. We know material agency— nature herself—not through our words but through our crafts. We make instruments where material agency is both in our control and engaged, "working." We *make* this working knowledge of material agency. The experiment of the bird and the air pump engages the human family in a sublime experience of the conditions of life and death, with the experimenter him- or herself a God-like authority, perhaps about to turn the valve and revitalize the bird.

4. KEYS TO NEW WORLDS OF PHENOMENA

In our own day, particle accelerators occupy an epistemological space similar to that of the air pump in the eighteenth century. Popular television shows display their phenomena. They allow us to probe some of the deepest secrets of the cosmos. They are a stage on which material agency is engaged but controlled by human artifice. While much is known about the development of E. O. Lawrence's cyclotron, the first really powerful particle accelerator, examining this history once again allows me to present, by way of example, the crafting of working knowledge.

By the 1920s, there was a recognized need for the creation of particle accelerators. They would enable scientists to artificially produce and use energetic particles (Paul 1979, p. 26). Our ability to control more precisely the particles with which we probed the subatomic world would greatly promote its exploration. "The development of methods of nuclear excitation on an extensive scale is thus a problem of great interest; its solution is probably the key to a new world of phenomena, the world of the nucleus," Lawrence and his student and co-worker M. S. Livingston write (Lawrence and Livingston 1932, p. 20). When Lawrence began work on the cyclotron, we were on the verge of being able to harness and deploy a new world of phenomena. This was one of Lawrence's primary interests in developing the cyclotron, and it is one of the reasons why it has been so important. It helps us do new things with nature; it reveals and creates a new part of the world.

The basic idea behind the cyclotron is to use a negative charge in electric potential to accelerate a positive ion. By suitably controlling the path of the ion with an electromagnet, the same potential difference is repeatedly used to accelerate the ion to higher and higher energies. Since the same potential accelerates the ion many times, the magnitude of the accelerating potential can be small relative to the total energy passed on to the ion. It is for the same reason that a series of small but well-timed pushes can get a person on a backyard swing swinging very high. The cyclotron employs a series of small, properly timed pushes to get an ion moving very fast.

Physically, the cyclotron consists of two electrodes that resemble a tuna fish can cut in half through a diameter. The two electrodes (called Ds because of their shape) are connected to a high-frequency alternating current power source. An ion source is placed near the center of the two electrodes, and the entire assembly is enclosed in a good vacuum. The accelerator chamber is mounted between the poles of an electromagnet (fig. 3.3). A positive ion created at the ion source is accelerated into the D at a negative

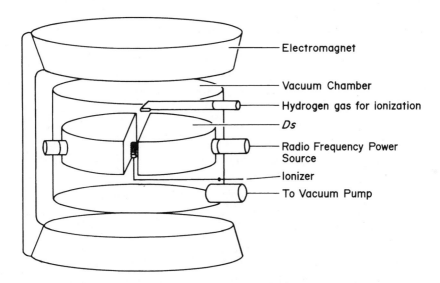

FIGURE 3.3 Cutaway diagram of a cyclotron (from D. Baird and Faust 1990). Reprinted by permission of the British Society for the Philosophy of Science.

potential. Because of the perpendicular magnetic field present in the **D**, the ion follows a semicircular orbit until it appears again at the gap between the two **D**s. The frequency of the oscillator supplying alternating voltage to the **D**s is such that by the time the ion has appeared at the gap between the **D**s, the voltages on the two **D**s will have exchanged. Consequently, the positively charged ion will be accelerated across the gap into the other **D**, which is now at negative potential. Again, the magnetic field will cause the ion to follow a semicircular path—this time with a larger diameter, because the ion has a higher velocity (having been accelerated twice). When the ion reappears at the gap, the potential of the two **D**s will have switched again, and the ion will thus be accelerated (a third time) across the gap into the opposite **D**. Every time this cycle is repeated, the ion is boosted to yet higher energy, ultimately resulting in a very energetic particle (fig. 3.4).

The trick that makes a cyclotron feasible is having the current alternate with the same frequency with which the ion appears at the "acceleration gap." Fortunately, the time it takes an ion (with constant mass) to travel the semicircular orbit in a constant magnetic field, perpendicular to the plane of the ion's motion, is independent of the size of the orbit. The greater distances traveled in larger orbits are exactly compensated for by the increased velocity of the ion. Consequently, an oscillator producing alternating current oscillations at a fixed frequency—tuned to the mass of the ion and the

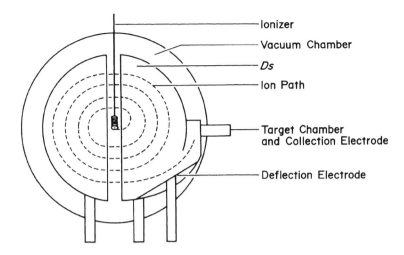

FIGURE 3.4 Top schematic view diagram of a cyclotron (from D. Baird and Faust 1990). Reprinted by permission of the British Society for the Philosophy of Science.

strength of the magnetic field—will oscillate at just the right frequency to accelerate the ion each time it reaches the "acceleration gap." This is called the resonance of the magnetic field with the alternating current, and the cyclotron was originally called a magnetic-resonance accelerator.

5. FROM IDEA TO INSTRUMENT

Lawrence got the idea for the cyclotron during the summer of 1929 from an article by Rolf Wideröe (1928) describing how he had used two straight cylindrical electrodes placed end to end in a vacuum tube to accelerate potassium ions. The lengths of the electrodes and the frequency of the power source they were connected to were such that by the time the ion had traversed the length of the first electrode, the second electrode would have a charge to attract and consequently accelerate the particle. Wideröe applied 25,000 volts to each electrode and succeeded in accelerating the ions to 50,000 volts. Lawrence wanted to accelerate particles to more than 1,000,000 volts. Wideröe's approach was promising, because it employed relatively small applied voltages. In principle, additional electrodes, enough to accelerate ions to 1,000,000 volts, could augment such a setup. Lawrence calculated that it would take several meters of electrodes to succeed with this method—and, with a student, David Sloan, he built such a linear accelerator, with which he accelerated mercury ions to over 200,000 volts (Lawrence and Sloan 1931).

A more economical approach would be to route the ions in a circle so that the same applied voltage could be used over and over again. Lawrence made a "back-of-an-envelope" calculation and found that the time it takes an ion (with constant mass) to complete its circular orbit is independent of the radius of the orbit (although dependent on the charge and mass of the ion and the strength of the magnetic field). This calculation established the resonance principle (Livingston and Blewett 1962, p. 140; Lawrence 1965, p. 431).[3] The idea of the cyclotron was born.

During the spring of 1930, another of Lawrence's students, N. E. Edlefsen, put together a small cyclotron using a magnet with two-inch-diameter pole faces. The vacuum chamber was made of windowpane, scraps of brass, and an overcoat of wax (Pais 1986, p. 408). Edlefsen reported resonance across a very broad band of frequencies. The first cyclotron research publication (Lawrence and Edlefsen 1930) reported no experimental success, but only the method of cyclotron resonance. Privately, Lawrence said of the attempt, "It was a failure, but it did show promise" (McMillan 1979, p. 155; this quotation was provided by M. S. Livingston in a discussion of McMillan's paper).

Edlefsen left Berkeley in the summer of 1930, and Lawrence gave the problem to another student, M. S. Livingston. Livingston first attempted to reconstruct Edlefsen's work. He found it hard to achieve a good vacuum with Edlefsen's materials. In their place, Livingston fashioned a vacuum chamber out of a brass ring and brass cover plates; he used sealing wax to seal the vacuum. He enlarged the diameter on the magnet poles to four inches, and he only used one D-shaped electrode; the other "dummy-D" was formed by a slotted bar (Livingston 1985, p. 256). Hydrogen ions (both protons and hydrogen gas ions) were produced in the center of the chamber by the ionization of hydrogen gas by electrons emitted from a tungsten-wire cathode. This cyclotron succeeded.

---

3. I have just sketched out in qualitative terms the argument for the resonance principle. More precisely, the argument runs as follows: Consider an ion of mass m and charge e moving with velocity v in a magnetic field, B. The magnetic field exerts a force on the ion of magnitude evB. The direction of this force is perpendicular both to the motion of the ion and to the magnetic field. Moreover, this force is balanced with the centrifugal force on the ion, mv^2/r, where r is the radius of the ion's circular motion. Thus we have $mv^2/r = evB$. We can solve this equation for v, $v = eBr/m$. The frequency, f, with which the ion revolves is the ion's velocity divided by the circumference, $f = v/2\pi\rho$. When we plug in the value for v from the previous equation, we get the result that the frequency of revolution, f, is independent of the radius, r, $f = (eBr/m)/2\pi\rho = eB/2\pi\mu$.

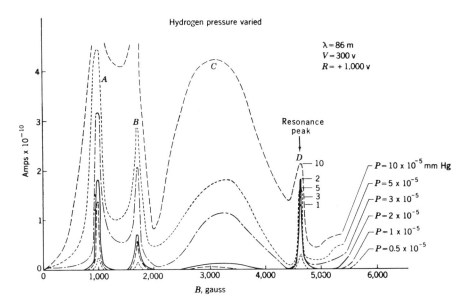

FIGURE 3.5 Cyclotron resonance graph, 1931 (from Livingston and Blewett 1962).

Livingston tuned his four-inch cyclotron by varying the strength of the magnetic field. He plotted the magnetic field strength against the current in the collector electrode. In November 1930, Livingston observed sharp peaks in the collector current as plotted against magnetic field strength (fig. 3.5). These peaks agreed with the predicted field strength for resonance. Livingston also varied the frequency of the applied alternating current electric field on the Ds. He then looked for the magnetic field strength where resonance was achieved as determined by the sharp increase in collector current. This relation, between magnetic field strength and alternating current frequency where resonance is achieved again agreed with theoretically anticipated results. The instrument worked.

There is no doubt that the agreement between Lawrence's theoretical calculation and instrumental behavior was central to Lawrence's and Livingston's confidence that the four-inch cyclotron was working properly. However, the phenomenon itself must not be lost sight of. Livingston observed a sharp, recognizable, and repeatable change in the collector current as he varied the magnetic field strength. The effect is too dramatic to be "noise." Edlefsen produced no such effect. Indeed, much of the theory behind Livingston's four-inch cyclotron required considerable amendment to account for relativistic effects and the deviations of the actual electric and magnetic fields from those assumed to be in place.

6. BIGGER AND BETTER

Livingston's success in demonstrating resonance with the four-inch model showed that the cyclotron idea was sound. In order to obtain the higher energies Lawrence was after, the power of the magnet and the radius of the Ds had to be increased. During the summer and fall of 1931, he designed and built a ten-inch cyclotron that in January 1932 succeeded in producing 1,220,000-volt hydrogen ions (protons) (Lawrence and Livingston 1932). At this point, the ten-inch cyclotron was not set up for experimental studies with the high-energy ions it could produce. During much of the spring of 1932, the necessary targeting and counting apparatus was added. By the fall, the ten-inch model had corroborated and extended the disintegration results that had been performed at the Cavendish Laboratory (Cockcroft and Walton 1932; Lawrence, Livingston et al. 1932). Meanwhile, Lawrence obtained an obsolete large (eighty-ton) magnet from the Federal Telegraph Company. He had the pole faces machined to a 27½-inch diameter. In November, this cyclotron produced a 0.001 microamp current of 4,800,000-volt hydrogen gas ions (Livingston and Lawrence 1933).

Over the next year and a half, Lawrence, Livingston, and their associates added a series of small but significant improvements. For example, the tungsten wires, which provided the source of electrons for ionizing the hydrogen, were surrounded by water-cooling jackets; this allowed a higher output of electrons (and ultimately of ions) without overheating the tungsten. Similarly, the coils for the electromagnets were immersed in oil for cooling. The Ds were supported with copper tubes that served to connect them with the radio-frequency oscillator power source; these were insulated with Pyrex sleeves that also preserved the vacuum as the tubes left the chamber. They were ultimately able to obtain a 0.3 microamp current of 5,000,000-volt deuterium ions (Livingston 1933; Livingston and Lawrence 1933, 1934).

The subsequent history of the cyclotron was one of increasing the diameter and improving a thousand and one construction details. In 1936, a new 27-inch chamber was designed and built (Lawrence and Cooksey 1936). In 1937, the magnet faces of the 27-inch cyclotron were enlarged to 37 inches and a new chamber was built. Improvements came on many

FIGURE 3.6 MIT cyclotron (from Livingston and Blewett 1962).

fronts. The radio-frequency power source was placed inside the vacuum chamber to prevent breakdown of the insulators. The deflected beam was routed into a chamber with an air lock so that targets could be changed while the main vacuum was maintained. Oil- and water-cooling tanks and coils were added to much of the instrument (McMillan 1985, pp. 668–70). There were numerous improvements in the control and focusing of the ion beam, in the initial source for the ions, and in the vacuum technology. In 1939, Lawrence completed the even bigger, 60-inch "Crocker" cyclotron. By now all of the experience gained with smaller instruments could be put together in what Livingston described as "a beautifully engineered and re-liable instrument . . . [which] became the prototype of scores of cyclotrons around the world" (1969, p. 37) (fig. 3.6).

Each step, from Edlefsen's two-inch model to the 60-inch model, im-proved the power, reliability, and usefulness of the instrument. These steps represented palpable progress in our knowledge. Knowledge of what? The cyclotron is not simply a powerful probe for exploring the nuclear realm — although it most certainly is that too. It is a site for the development of ma-terial knowledge on a variety of fronts, including vacuum systems, radio frequency electronics, and ion-beam control, among other things. In all of these cases, it was material work that bore the knowledge. The instrument incorporates all this material knowledge into its finished reliable—working knowledge—form.

7. FOCUSING

"The basic resonance principle applied to an idealized particle moving in an orbit located on the median plane of the cyclotron chamber and crossing the accelerating gaps in perfect synchronism with the electric field. However, essentially all ions being accelerated deviate from these ideal conditions," Livingston and J. P. Blewett observe in their 1962 book *Particle Accelerators* (p. 143). Given only the electric and magnetic forces as Lawrence initially imagined them, virtually all of the ions formed near the center of the instrument would either crash into the top or the bottom of one of the Ds or travel slightly too fast or too slowly and fall out of resonance. Fortunately, both the electric and the magnetic fields in an actual cyclotron differ from the ideal fields as Lawrence first imagined them. These deviations from Lawrence's ideal serve to concentrate the beam of ions essentially in resonance and between the top and bottom of the Ds.[4]

Lawrence wanted to eliminate the electric field from the interior of the two Ds. The only field that he thought should be present there was the magnetic field—with lines of force running perfectly perpendicular to the plane of the Ds. To achieve this end, Lawrence had Livingston build the four-inch model with fine tungsten wires across the opening to the D (Davis 1968, p. 35; Livingston 1969, p. 26). With this arrangement, Livingston got a small amount of current at the anticipated resonance frequency, but much less than hoped for. Livingston guessed that a large number of ions were hitting the tungsten wires, so (when Lawrence was traveling) he removed the wires and obtained a substantial (between 10- and 100-fold) increase in the beam intensity at the anticipated resonance frequency (Livingston 1969, pp. 26–27).

When he returned, Lawrence determined that the increased beam intensity was likely due to the unanticipated focusing action of the electric field. Lawrence and Livingston explained this qualitatively with a figure (fig. 3.7). Because of the direction of the lines of force, the electric field

---

4. There are many different aspects to the development of the cyclotron that I could present. Here and in the next section, because they well serve my philosophical purpose, I discuss focusing the beam and improving the vacuum system. Other details are discussed in D. Baird and Faust 1990.

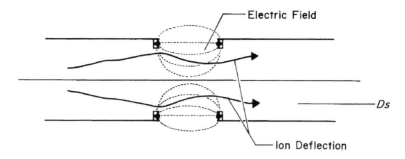

FIGURE 3.7 Cyclotron electrostatic focusing (from D. Baird and Faust 1990). Reprinted by permission of the British Society for the Philosophy of Science.

tends to direct the ion toward the median plane in the first half of its journey across the accelerating gap and away from the median plane in the second half of its journey. But the ion has a higher velocity in the second half of its journey. Consequently, "the outward acceleration during the second half will not quite compensate the inward acceleration of the first, resulting in a gain of an inward component of velocity as well as an inward displacement" (Lawrence and Livingston 1932, p. 29).

Livingston again encountered difficulties when he tried to achieve resonance with the ten-inch model. His first guess was that this might be due to irregularities in the magnetic field. He tried to true the faces of the magnet by remachining them, but this did not help. He then cut pieces of sheet iron as shims and placed them between the faces of the magnet and the vacuum chamber. This improved the output of the instrument. Through successive trial-and-error shimming, Livingston got the ten-inch model running effectively (Livingston 1985, p. 259).

Initially, Livingston added the shims to perfect what he took to be an inhomogeneous magnetic field. By the time he and Lawrence wrote about the ten-inch model, they had come to understand that the shimming caused the magnetic field to decrease with the increasing radius, resulting in a focusing effect (fig. 3.8). The magnetic field imparts a force on a charged particle perpendicular to the magnetic field. Thus, the convex "bulging" in the magnetic lines of force helped to focus the beam by forcing stray ions back toward the median plane (Lawrence and Livingston 1932, p. 29).

Another four years passed before anything like a decent theoretical understanding of cyclotron focusing was available. In the interim, there was considerable confusion about the relative contributions of the magnetic and electric fields to focusing. In 1936, Livingston argued that the electric field was primarily responsible for focusing (Livingston 1936, p. 57). Rose

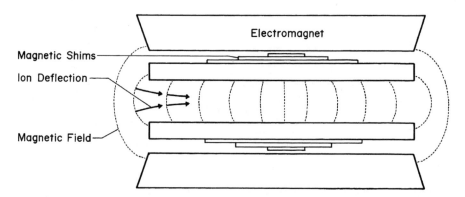

FIGURE 3.8 Cyclotron weak magnetic focusing (from D. Baird and Faust 1990). Reprinted by permission of the British Society for the Philosophy of Science.

and Wilson separately argued that magnetic focusing was most important (Rose 1938; Wilson 1938). In the meantime, better empirical techniques were developed to set up the best magnetic field. Better probes for finding and measuring the beam's width became available. Common rules of thumb evolved, such as: "Those cyclotrons which have achieved high efficiency in acceleration of ions and a high-intensity beam show a consistent shape of magnetic field. This is an approximately linear decrease over most of the pole face. . . . For medium-energy cyclotrons (15 to 20 Mev) the total decrease below the value of the central field out to the exit slit is about 2 per cent" (Livingston and Blewett 1962, p. 145).

Clearly, it is the deviations from the ideal fields that Lawrence initially imagined that serve to focus ions accelerating in the cyclotron. "The feature which makes the method of multiple acceleration practical is the focusing resulting from the shape of the magnetic field" (ibid., p. 143). Almost paradoxically, it was Lawrence's understanding of the action of "pure" magnetic and electric fields that made the cyclotron plausible to begin with, while it was Livingston's empirically developed deviations from these "pure" fields that made the cyclotron work, that made working knowledge, as opposed to the theoretical knowledge of Lawrence's resonance principle.

8. THE AIR PUMP AGAIN

Improvements in the primarily engineering aspects of the cyclotron were also fundamental to its progress. Perhaps the most central of these are improvements in establishing and maintaining a good vacuum in the cyclotron chamber. There are at least four different kinds of improvements to the vacuum: (1) better seals; (2) better means to communicate across the vacuum seal; (3) better and faster pumps; and (4) better ways to detect leaks. Improvements came in all four areas.

The first two-inch cyclotron was put together out of materials found lying around in any physics laboratory: windowpane, brass scraps, and wax. Livingston's need for a very thin chamber made windowpane a poor choice. In the four-inch and ten-inch models, Livingston used a brass ring soldered to brass plates instead. The whole chamber was painted over with a mixture of sealing wax, beeswax, and rosin (Livingston 1985, p. 258). The 27-inch model was also sealed with wax, although a groove was cut in the chamber wall for the top plate to sit in (Lawrence and Livingston 1934, p. 609). Subsequently, in the 37-inch model, this wax "paint" was replaced with pure gum sulfur-free rubber (and, where oil was present, neoprene) gasket seals (Kurie 1938, p. 697).

It was clearly desirable to communicate motion of various sorts across the vacuum barrier. For example, with both the 10-inch and first 27-inch models, targets were mounted on removable stems, which could only be changed when the vacuum chamber was brought up to atmospheric pressure (Livingston 1936, p. 68). A target wheel that could be rotated from the outside by means of a greased ground-glass plug was added to the subsequent 27-inch model. At some point in the development of the 27-inch model, R. R. Wilson devised what has come to be known as the Wilson seal (McMillan 1959, p. 669). Wilson surrounded a metal rod with a rubber gasket cut with an inside diameter considerably smaller than that of the rod. As a result, the gasket would bend out to one side or the other. The surrounding metal flanges ensured that it bent toward the high-pressure side of the barrier (fig. 3.9). The high pressure forced the gasket against the rod to produce a good seal even when the rod was rotated or moved back and forth (Wilson 1941).

Fast pumps were also necessary for successful operation of the cyclotron. Oil-diffusion pumps were the fastest pumps available for use in the 27-inch model, but there was a tendency for the mercury or oil to "backstream" into the vacuum chamber. Livingston developed a series of liquid air traps and other baffles to catch the oil (Livingston 1933, p. 214). Pump speeds were increased. Livingston used a pump with a speed of 6 liters per second in the first 27-inch model. By the time of his 1944 review article on the cyclotron, pump speeds of 1,200 liters per second were common (1944, p. 132).

Means for discovering and locating leaks were also important. One standard technique involved spraying ether over suspected leaks and watching

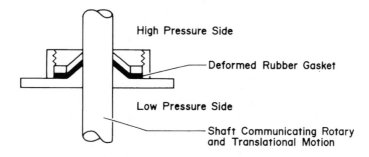

FIGURE 3.9 Wilson seal (from D. Baird and Faust 1990). Reprinted by permission of the British Society for the Philosophy of Science.

for current changes in a test probe. The procedure was developed early on and continued to be a primary means for leak detection, although the resulting "hospital atmosphere" was not perhaps entirely desirable (Livingston 1969). A more expensive technique involved using a concentric pair of gaskets with a tap-hole between them connected to a pump. A leak in one of the gaskets could be detected and controlled by the pump. Even so, leak detection, location, and repair continued to be a headache: "A standard procedure to seal small leaks in metallic joints is to paint with Glyptal, a thick, elastic, slow drying paint of low vapor pressure. The prevalence of red Glyptal patches on essentially all cyclotron chambers is an indication of the seriousness of the vacuum-leak problem" (Livingston 1944, p. 135).

9. MAKING WORKING KNOWLEDGE

It is important to recognize such details, because they are the meat and potatoes of making an instrument; in other words, of crafting material agency and making working knowledge. Successful making of working knowledge depends on solving such problems as how to develop and maintain a vacuum—300 years after the invention of the air pump! Of course, the ability of the cyclotron to serve experiments—for example, to confirm J. D. Cockcroft's disintegration results—depended on the successful solution to such "engineering details." But when I speak of working knowledge here, I am referring not to such experimental work but to the successful operation of the machine itself, our ability to reliably accelerate positive ions to high energies.

At a more general level, I identify eight different activities that went into making the instrument.

1. Experimental idea: Lawrence's idea of using circular motion to repeatedly and economically implement Wideröe's linear scheme for accelerating particles was the beginning of the cyclotron.

2. Theoretical test: Lawrence would not have pursued his idea had he not determined by a theoretical calculation that, under ideal circumstances, an ion would follow a spiral of increasing diameter and energy, with a fixed-frequency power oscillator for resonance.

3. Empirical test: The cyclotron emerged from a series of successively larger models. Lawrence well knew that neither the two-inch nor the four-inch model would produce ions with the energy he sought. These models were built to test the idea empirically and to provide experience with the anticipated unknowns in creating a working material instrument.

4. Functional components: The cyclotron was (and is) conceived of in terms of several functionally understood components (radio-frequency power source, ion source, vacuum system, etc.). Implementing the design and, particularly, improving the performance proceeded by attempts to improve the performance of each individual component.

5. Intuition and trial and error: Bugs in the components and the apparatus as a whole were worked out in many cases by trying something out. Livingston removed Lawrence's tungsten wires on a hunch, and he added shims to the magnet to make the magnetic field more uniform. In both cases, the result was improved performance, whether or not the intuition motivating the idea was right.

6. Tinkering: With almost every component, various physical parameters were fiddled with in order to improve the performance of the instrument as a whole. This is perhaps best illustrated by the "cut and try" shimming of the magnetic field.

7. Adapting devices from other instruments: Livingston adapted an ion source for the cyclotron from direct voltage accelerators. The early radio-frequency power oscillators were adapted and improved by amateur radio techniques.

8. Knowing when an apparatus is working: Two checks were important. Initially, it was important that collector current showed sharp peaks at theoretically anticipated frequencies. Ultimately, the reliability and control exhibited by the instrument argued for its success.

These activities are neither necessary nor sufficient for progress in developing new instruments. The particulars in the development of each different instrument are too varied for such a characterization. But a converse mistake would hold that nothing general and philosophically important can be said about activities promoting the creation of new instruments. I do identify two related general characteristics to making an instrument, emulation and adaptation, and the movement from simple to complex.

Brooke Hindle's work in the history of technology teaches us about emulation and adaptation. His central claim is that invention proceeds by emulating established mechanical devices for new purposes, with whatever adaptations are called for. The uses of the older device and the newer one emulating it need not be closely related. Hindle discusses in detail how Samuel Morse adapted a canvas stretcher—which he used as an artist—for use as a telegraphic message recorder (1981, p. 120). Hindle stresses how visual imagination is central to invention, and why, consequently, it is no surprise that many inventors are also artists (Fulton and Morse being his prime examples). Visual imagination provides one mechanism for adaptation. In a text Hindle wrote with Steven Lubar, there is a description of this mechanism:

> Designing a machine requires good visual or spatial thinking. It requires mental arrangement, rearrangement, and manipulation of projected components and devices. It usually requires a trial construction of the machine, or at least a model of it, and then more mental manipulation of possible changes in order to bring it to an effective working condition. (Hindle and Lubar 1986, p. 75)

It was Lawrence's visual imagination that could turn Wideröe's linear accelerator into a spiral-path cyclotron. Successively larger models were built and improved upon stage by stage.

There is another general aspect to the creation of the cyclotron that both clarifies the operation of the eight activities described above and shows how previously successful instruments are central to the creation of new instruments. Broadly, the story of the cyclotron is a progression from Lawrence's relatively simple idea to the plethora of complexities involved in completing a working cyclotron and improving its performance. This is a very common aspect of making knowledge. The simple idea serves as an overarching guiding and explanatory framework within which to organize the increasing abundance of construction details. Such a framework allows those involved to identify different construction needs in terms of the various functional parts of the instrument. Conversely, such a framework explains the various parts of the instrument.

The simple experimental idea provides an explanatory framework. But it clearly does not consist of true experimental or theoretical assertions. In the first place, the experimental idea is better understood as an annotated figure than as a series of assertions. Indeed, it seems that Lawrence did not understand Wideröe's German very well, but he could follow Wideröe's figures and the equations associated with them. Second, and more important, the experimental idea functions as an idealization. Lawrence imagined particles created exactly between the top and bottom of the Ds, moving according to pure magnetic and electric fields. As the instrument developed into a reality, it became clear that virtually all ions were not created on the median plane and focusing the particles depended on their motion being directed by fields that diverged from Lawrence's ideal.

Still, Lawrence's experimental idea explained the need for each of the parts of the instrument. The electromagnet and the radio-frequency oscillating power source clearly are central to the experimental idea. Even when clear divergences between the experimental idea and experimental reality arise—as with the fine tungsten wires that covered the D—the idea remains as a useful way to conceive of the instrument at a first approximation and to organize the functional components to its operation and construction.

Once the basic design is set, serious detailed work can commence on the different components of the machine. In many cases, this involves "cut and try" material tinkering with the apparatus. In other cases, solutions from other instruments are picked up and adapted. Sometimes improvements in one area solve problems in another. At other times, improvements in one area pose problems for other areas.

The movement from simple idea to complex implementation is epistemologically important. The basic idea of cyclotron resonance is faulty. The pure fields Lawrence had in mind would not produce high-energy particles, because of the focusing requirements. Yet every presentation of the cyclotron starts with this simple idea and adds qualifying complexities later. Such a presentation is certainly good pedagogy, but it is more. Good ideas do more than figure in building a single instrument; they establish an approach. The details of how such an approach is implemented in any of a variety of instruments require adaptation and modification in each separate case. A good idea can father many instruments. Consider McMillan's assessment of Lawrence's inspiration for the cyclotron:

> Lawrence realized the difficulty of applying the linear accelerator to particles as light as protons with the high-frequency techniques available at that time. Then came the "flash of inspiration," the invention of the cyclotron. . . . I consider this to be the single most important invention in the history of accelerators: it brought forth a basic idea of great power, and one capable of later elaborations and variations, such as the

use of phase stability and strong focusing. All the big proton synchro-
tons are really just an extension of the cyclotron principle. (McMillan
1979, pp. 125–26)

Good, simple experimental ideas guide the construction of a particular
instrument, but, more important, they also establish a vital resource for
many future developments. Their simplicity allows for their use in a wide
diversity of cases. This is how progress through emulation and adaptation
occurs: a simple idea is emulated and adapted for the particular case as it
arises.

10. INSTRUMENT COOKBOOKS

Lawrence and his co-workers had little interest in vacuum technology per
se. But the successful operation of the cyclotron depended on their ability
to create and work with a good vacuum. Happily, there are numerous material solutions to the problems that must be tinkered with to make an
instrument. Furthermore, these solutions are an expanding resource; solutions to problems solved on the fly can be preserved for future cases requiring such techniques. Thus, not only do instruments accumulate but,
perhaps more important, instrumental techniques accumulate, and their
accumulation is central to scientific progress, progress in the development
and material articulation of working knowledge.

Consider J. H. Moore, C. C. Davis, and M. A. Coplan's book *Building Scientific Apparatus: A Practical Guide to Design and Construction* (1983).
The authors include chapters on mechanical design, working with glass,
vacuum technology, optics, charged particle optics, and electronics. In the
chapter on laboratory vacuum systems, they recommend the use of materials such as Pyrex: "These glasses are chemically inert and have a low
coefficient of thermal expansion. Because of the plasticity of the material,
complicated shapes are easily formed. Glass vacuum systems can be constructed and modified in situ by a moderately competent glassblower. The
finished product does not have to be cleaned after working" (p. 85).

The authors also describe a means for converting linear motion outside
a vacuum system into circular motion inside the system. This can best be
described by illustration (fig. 3.10). They discuss a problem that arises with
metal bearings in vacuum systems—they become rough very quickly—
and propose a solution:

> The tendency for a bearing to gall is reduced if the two mating bearing
> surfaces are made of different metals. For example, a steel shaft rotat-

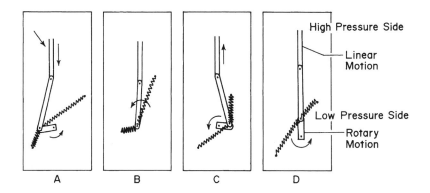

FIGURE 3.10 Mechanism for converting linear to rotary motion across a vacuum seal (from D. Baird and Faust 1990). Reprinted by permission of the British Society for the Philosophy of Science.

ing without lubrication in a brass or bronze journal will hold up better than in a steel bushing. A solid lubricant may be applied to one of the bearing surfaces. Silver, lead indium, and molybdenum disulfide have been used for this purpose. Graphite does not lubricate in a vacuum. MoS_2 is probably best. (ibid., p. 90)

Acetone (as Livingston reported with the cyclotron) is useful for detecting leaks:

A squeeze bottle of acetone or a spray can of liquid Freon cleanser is a useful tool. These liquids will usually cause a very abrupt increase in indicated pressure as they flow through a leak, but sometimes rapid evaporation of a liquid through a leak will cause the liquid to freeze and temporarily plug the leak, causing the pressure to fall. A disadvantage of this method is that the solvent may contaminate O-rings. (ibid., p. 105)

The information in this book and others like it, and, more generally, in the practices that are passed from teacher to apprentice at laboratories such as the Berkeley Radiation Laboratory, constitutes an important resource for making instruments—making working knowledge. Pyrex has proved to be a good material for constructing vacuum systems. Some unrecorded engineer figured out the spring system for converting linear motion into circular motion. Experience has also taught us about the use of moving metal parts in a vacuum, and how to use acetone to detect leaks.

The kind of information preserved in books such as *Building Scientific Apparatus* is different from the kind of information encoded in scientific theories or experimental data. These books, and journals such as the *Re-*

view of Scientific Instruments, record and preserve an array of techniques for accomplishing certain effects, which, as a matter of fact, have been found to be important in making things. They provide a written record of instrumental techniques, descriptions of working knowledge. We do not expect there to be a general theory for converting linear motion into circular motion: instead, there are techniques for doing so. There are fairly general theories about materials such as Pyrex, but no such theory would have as a consequence the fact that Pyrex is commonly a good material for the construction of vacuum systems. Such a consequence depends too directly on the specific contingencies of how experimental practice evolved. Still, the use of Pyrex does serve as an important technique in vacuum system construction.

Perhaps the most important point about instrument cookbooks is that they describe working knowledge; they do not bear it themselves. For a person to learn this kind of information, he or she must work with the materials involved. Instrument cookbooks point to useful ways to begin crafting such working knowledge, but they are not sufficient. There is a parallel with working problems in order to understand theory. One may have the illusion of understanding, but until one tries to solve problems with theory, deep understanding remains at bay. Following this parallel, the materials themselves arranged as necessary to accomplish desired ends stand in the same relation to a person working them as do theories and sample problem solutions. In either case, we can speak of subjective knowledge consisting of the skills necessary to work with symbols or with materials. Objective knowledge is in the organization of the symbols themselves or the materials themselves. In the case of working knowledge—knowledge of material agency—objective knowledge is in the instruments and the materially instantiated techniques that constitute instruments and make their construction and reliable operation possible.

4   Encapsulating Knowledge

The true instrumental method of analysis requires no
reduction of data to normal pressure and temperature, no
corrections or computations, no reference to correction
factors nor interpolation on nomographic charts. It indicates
the desired information directly on a dial or counter and if it
is desired to have the answer printed on paper—that can be
had for the asking. It is strange and difficult to comprehend
why the last few steps have not been taken by the analyst
in bringing his instruments to this stage of perfection. They
are minor details, the absence of which in his motor car,
office equipment, or telephone he would not tolerate for a
moment.

RALPH MÜLLER, "Instrumentation" (January 1947)

1. MEASURING INSTRUMENTS

During the 1940s, innovations in spectrometry brought certain applications of spectrometric instruments to the stage of perfection described above
by Ralph Müller. Through the wedding of photomultiplier tube electronics with commercial emission spectrographs, analysts in several economically important industries, such as magnesium, steel, and aluminum, could
in minutes determine the percentage quantities of various elements in "the
melt." The information was available fast enough to direct the production
of the metal (Saunderson et al. 1945; Hasler et al. 1948).

In a general sense, analytical instruments, such as the spectrometer, tell
us something about a "specimen"; they measure it in some manner by generating a signal through an interaction with it. This signal undergoes a series of transformations that ultimately results in information for those using the instrument.

Measuring instruments, from relatively simple rulers to complex spectrometers, are ubiquitous in science, technology, and, indeed, many aspects of daily life. Measuring instruments present a third kind of thing
knowledge. They are not models, although their operation requires them
to include material representations of the spaces of possible measurement
outcomes—the scale on a rule, for example. Neither are they instances of
working knowledge, although again their operation requires reliable per-

67

formance—working knowledge. A thermometer must produce "the same" phenomenon—the mercury must rise to the same height in its tube when subjected to the same conditions. It is something that "surely will happen to everybody in the living future who shall fulfill certain conditions," in Peirce's words. Measuring instruments are a kind of hybrid, combining model and working knowledge.

It is common to say that measuring instruments "extract information" from a specimen (Sydenham 1979; Taylor et al. 1994; Rothbart and Slayden 1994). I think it more philosophically prudent to say that an instrument interacting with a specimen generates a signal, which, suitably transformed, can then be understood as information about the specimen. There are two reasons for this. The first is methodological. It is vital to recognize that instruments interacting with specimens create phenomena and in so doing, these instruments constitute working knowledge. Putting aside any interpretation of the meaning of an instrument's output, the behavior of the instrument has to be public, regular, and reliable; these are necessary constituents of valid measurement. But these necessary features also are the sufficient features of working knowledge. Measurement requires our ability, as Ian Hacking puts it, "to produce, in laboratory conditions, a stable numerical phenomenon over which one has remarkable control" (1983a, p. 237). The second reason is metaphysical. Information is semantic in nature; it carries meaning and hence eliminates possibilities. To understand the signal as information, it therefore needs to be placed in a field of possibilities. Recognizing such a field of possibilities requires thought, a contribution of the human instrument maker and user.

Instrumentally encapsulated knowledge, the kind of thing knowledge presented in a measuring instrument, consists of the material integration of the two kinds of thing knowledge considered in chapters 2 and 3. At a fundamental level, measurement requires a phenomenon—the working knowledge of chapter 3. Here is the signal generated by the instrument interacting with the specimen. But it is a field of possibilities, typically— although not always—understood theoretically, that drives the choice of signal generated and the transformations that are made to the signal as it is rendered "a measurement." These choices, then, encapsulate in the material form of the instrument a representation of this field of possibilities— model knowledge. When the integration of both forms of material knowledge is done seamlessly, the instrument appears to extract information from nature.

This much is the main message of this chapter. But details of how this kind of encapsulated knowledge can be accomplished puts informative and persuasive flesh on these bare bones. To this end, I describe how the "direct-reading" spectrometer encapsulated knowledge, primarily from spectrochemical analysis and electronics, to make its particular kind of chemical measurement possible.

2. ENCAPSULATING ANALYSIS

Direct-reading spectrometers were developed simultaneously and independently in several places during the mid 1940s. Several academic laboratories looked into the possibility of using photosensitive electron tubes to read spectra (Duffendack and Morris 1942; Rank et al. 1942; Dieke and Crosswhite 1945). Laboratories in two industrial settings produced what ultimately became the two first commercially available direct-reading spectrometers. M. F. Hasler and his co-workers at Applied Research Laboratories (ARL) developed a direct reader they dubbed the "quantometer" (Hasler and Dietert 1944).[1] ARL's quantometer was developed in the mid 1940s with the support of the Aluminum Company of America (ALCOA), where quantometers found their first use. By the late 1940s, ARL was marketing the quantometer for general use in spectrochemical analysis in metals manufacturing (Hasler et al. 1948). Independently and simultaneously, Jason Saunderson and his co-workers at the Dow Chemical Company developed their own direct-reading spectrometer (Saunderson et al. 1945; Saunderson and Hess 1946). Initially developed for internal use in Dow's production of magnesium alloys, the Saunderson direct reader ultimately was licensed to Baird Associates for commercial development, manufacture, and sale (Carpenter et al. 1947).[2]

Direct-reading spectrometers depend on the ability of their makers to put in material form the knowledge and skills necessary for reliably making such analytical measurements. In the language of technology studies, these instruments "de-skill" the job of making these measurements. They do this by encapsulating in the instrument the skills previously employed by the analyst or their functional equivalents. These skills include a knowl-

1. Work on the quantometer was done by a father-and-son team at the University of Pittsburgh: H. V. Churchill, father and chief chemist, worked with Raynor Churchill, son and chief spectroscopist. Maurice Hasler, a California Institute of Technology physicist and owner/founder of ARL, developed the Churchill direct reader into a reliable, commercially viable product. It was manufactured by Henry Dietert of the H. W. Dietert Corporation in Detroit.
2. For more on the Baird Associates connection, see chapter 7.

edge of the "spectral fingerprints" of the elements of interest, and of which of these spectral lines are best used for quantitative measurements. They include the accurate normalizing of the spectral lines involved, as to both place and intensity. They include reading the intensity of the spectral lines and determining percentage concentration from spectral intensities. They include encoding and displaying this information. The instrument is "skilled" as the analyst's job is "de-skilled."

The development of the direct-reading spectrometer is interesting for a variety of reasons. For my purposes here, we can see in it how various kinds of knowledge were integrated into a material medium to produce a measuring instrument. Model knowledge is built into the instrument in several ways, including the material representation of wavelengths of light emitted by important elements in the "exit slits" of the instrument (see below, § 4, esp. fig. 4.5). Working knowledge is built into the instrument, again in several ways, including the use of a diffraction grating to disperse light into constituent wavelengths (see below, § 3, esp. fig. 4.1). Theoretical knowledge is also built into the instrument, of which the theory of condenser discharge is a particularly clear example (see below, § 4, last paragraph). Functional substitutes for human discriminatory skills are built into the instrument too. With a spectrograph, where photographic film is employed instead of photomultiplier tubes, humans have to determine how dark—or "dense"—a "spectral line" is; instruments called densitometers helped to refine this skill. With a direct-reading spectrometer, photomultiplier tubes and electronics are crafted to provide a functional substitute for this skill. The material medium of the instrument encapsulates and integrates all these different kinds of knowledge. All are necessary for the instrument to render information about a specimen.

Yet this description can be misleading. Here I analyze the instrument's unified operation into epistemic parts. But the whole is not simply the sum of the parts. One cannot enumerate so many distinct items of knowledge of these various different kinds. The instrument presents an epistemic synthesis, seamlessly joining representation and action to render information. This synthesis does and must take place in a material medium.

3. THE INSTRUMENTAL BACKGROUND OF THE DIRECT READER

A spectrograph starts out with a light source (which might, for example, be the sun, the discharge of an electric arc, or a candle flame). The light is passed through a narrow slit; the different wavelengths are separated spatially by a dispersing device, such as a prism or a grating; and the dispersed light is then focused on some recording or observing surface. When a pho-to*graphic* record of the dispersed light is made, the instrument is called a spectro*graph*; when the dispersed light is focused on an eyepiece, it is called a spectro*scope*. Direct readers, which produce concentration readouts, are called spectro*meters*.

Passing the light through a slit produces an image of a sharply defined line—the slit. By dispersing this light in two dimensions as a function of wavelength, a spectrometer produces multiple images of the entrance slit, each at a single wavelength. The placement of a slit image is a function of wavelength; one can determine the wavelengths of light present in the light source by noting the placement of the slit images.[3]

The main function of either a prism or a grating is to *disperse* the different wavelengths of light. Within an instrument, dispersion can be measured in terms of the number of angstroms per millimeter into which the element spreads out the light (1 angstrom, Å, is 1×10^{-8} cm). A grating spectrograph with a dispersion of 5 Å per mm spreads light with wavelengths that differ by 5,000 Å across one meter.

For the spectrochemical analysis of metals—among other analytical concerns—grating spectrographs have many advantages over prism spectrographs. There is an interesting story behind the development and acceptance of grating spectrographs (for some of which, see chapter 10). However, for current purposes, I need only note that by the end of the 1930s, commercial grating spectrographs suitable for quantitative analysis—that is, with adequate precision, dispersion, and resolving power—were available (D. Baird 1991). These instruments were modified to make direct readers.

The story behind the development of high-quality gratings is of some interest in the present context. A grating is a surface into which many parallel grooves have been scratched, or "ruled"—more than 30,000 per inch in some gratings. In "transmission gratings," the grooves are, in fact, slits through the grating material. In the more common "reflection gratings," the grooves are grooves on a reflective surface.

A grating separates the different wavelengths of light because of the phenomenon of diffraction. Suppose a beam of light is passed through a screen with a narrow slit and then through a second screen with several

3. There are many good introductions to the theory behind spectroscopy; three I've found particularly helpful for both their clarity and their historical significance are Baly 1927, Sawyer 1944, and Harrison et al. 1948.

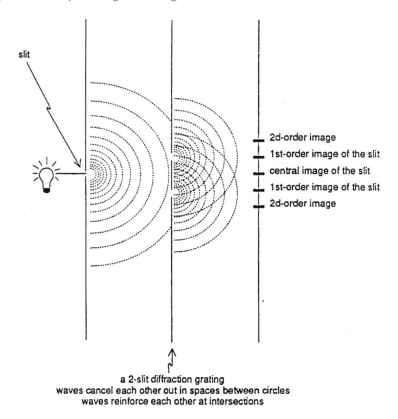

slit

2d-order image
1st-order image of the slit
central image of the slit
1st-order image of the slit
2d-order image

a 2-slit diffraction grating
waves cancel each other out in spaces between circles
waves reinforce each other at intersections

FIGURE 4.1 Diffraction schematic (1991)

closely spaced slits—a transmission grating. A series of images of the original slit can be focused on a target screen. This happens because the light waves emanating from each of the slits in the transmission grating interfere with one another. The "interference pattern" of images of the slit has a central bright line. On either side of this bright line are dark areas where the wave fronts cancel each other out. Then there are two more bright lines—images of the slit where the wave fronts augment each other—called "first-order" images of the slit. On either side of the first-order images, there are second-order images, and then third-order images, and so on. The distance from the central bright line to these other images is a function of wavelength. Given information about the grating, one can determine wavelength by measuring the distance from the central slit image to the first-, second-, third-, etc., order images (see fig. 4.1).

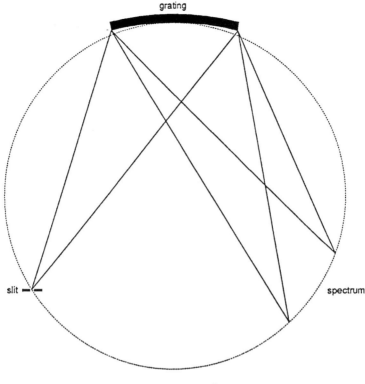

FIGURE 4.2 Rowland circle (1991)

In 1882, Henry A. Rowland developed both a device for making gratings on concave surfaces and the theory of concave grating spectroscopes (Rowland 1882, 1883). By appropriately using a concave grating, one need not have additional mirrors or lenses to focus the light; the concave grating can both disperse and focus the light. This has several advantages. In the first place, it allows for a simpler optical path, with fewer elements to align. It also produces a brighter image, since there are fewer optical elements to absorb or deflect the light. Finally, it cuts down on the amount of scattered light, or "noise." Rowland showed that if a grating were ruled on a surface with a radius of curvature R, then, by placing the slit and the grating on a circle with radius $R/2$—the "Rowland circle"—the spectrum produced would be in focus on the circumference of this circle (fig. 4.2). For many years, Rowland's "ruling engine" was the only source of gratings of high enough quality to compete effectively with prisms for spectral analysis (Rowland 1902, pp. 691–97).

Spectroscopy works as a method for chemical analysis because each element emits its own characteristic wavelengths of light. Thus, by looking at the wavelengths of light emitted, one can analyze the nature of the elements present in the light source. This has been known since the work of Gustav Kirchhoff and Robert Bunsen in the 1860s (Kirchhoff and Bunsen 1860a, 1860b, 1861a, 1861b), and prism spectroscopes had been commercially available since about that time (Bennett 1984). But spectroscopy did not become a common method of chemical analysis until the 1930s.

There were many reasons for this. In his 1941 historical discussion of spectrochemical analysis, Frank Twyman notes that some elements would not produce spectra when excited in a flame; they required the higher energies supplied by an electric arc, but until this century electric current was not a readily available commodity for a research chemist. Photographic methods had to be further developed so that the results of a spectrum analysis could be recorded for later careful study. The maze of spectrum lines produced by any slightly complicated material was such that "wet" methods of analysis seemed easier. Wavelength tables of common spectrum lines for the elements were not available until well into the first quarter of the twentieth century (Twyman 1941, pp. 34–36; Harrison 1939b). Indeed, the spectroscope was primarily a tool of physicists studying optics and was built to be maximally adjustable to allow the greatest amount of optical experimentation. "[S]ummarizing all the mentioned investigations, I come to the conclusion that quantitative spectroscopic analysis has shown itself as impractical," Heinrich Kayser asserted around 1910 in volume 5 of his *Handbuch der Spectroscopie* (8 vols., 1900–1932; quoted in Meggers and Scribner 1938, p. 3).

All of this began to change during the 1920s. Electricity had become readily available, and photography was by then widely used by researchers. Indeed, Eastman Kodak made special emulsions for spectrographic work, on both glass plates and 35 mm film. The quantum theory began to make some sense of the maze of spectrum lines, and the Depression produced a group of workers willing to grind out the MIT wavelength tables of the elements (Harrison 1939a; Twyman 1941, pp. 34–36; Laitinen and Ewing 1977, p. 131). Once analysts began to use and gain experience with spectrographic analysis, the advantages of speed and sensitivity became increasingly apparent.

Metals turned out to be an important proving ground for spectrochemical analysis. Metals are hard to analyze by classical wet methods. Within the metals industry, speed was vital. Wet analyses could take days, whereas spectrographic analyses would take hours. By 1944, direct readers performed in a matter of minutes analyses that had earlier taken weeks (Laitinen and Ewing 1977, pp. 116–17).

4. DIRECT READING

At a general level, quantitative spectroscopic analysis works because the greater the presence of a given element in the sample, the more intense that element's spectral lines will be. Thus, with photographic instruments, an analyst determines the amount of an element in a sample by examining the intensity—or darkness—of the various spectral lines recorded on a photographic plate or film. However, many variable conditions in the production of the light used for a given analysis make this direct use of line intensities problematic for measuring concentrations. The conditions of the arc or spark producing the light can vary enough that line intensities for the same concentration will vary as well. Other sources of variability in the instrument and sample preparation also contribute to variations in line intensity not correlated with variations in concentration.

A significant step came in 1931 with Walther Gerlach and Eugen Schweitzer's "internal standard method" (Gerlach and Schweitzer 1931, ch. 5). Here, instead of directly measuring a line's intensity, one measures the ratio of an unknown's line's intensity to the intensity of a major constituent in the mixture. Thus, to determine the concentration of calcium, say, in magnesium alloy, a magnesium line would be used as the "internal standard;" the intensity of a calcium line would be measured in comparison to the intensity of a magnesium "standard" line. Since all of the exogenous factors affecting line intensity affect both the internal standard line and the line for calcium, the relative intensity of these lines remains unchanged by these exogenous factors. Spectroscopists plot a "working curve" of the logarithms of the ratio of intensities of the unknown's line—I_x—to the internal standard's line—I_o—against the logarithm of the concentration of the unknown. The ratio of the intensities of these lines can then be used to measure—albeit indirectly—the concentration of the unknown (see fig. 4.3).

The significant technical development that made the direct reader possible was the invention of photomultiplier tubes. The initial motivation for

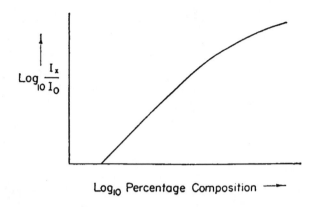

FIGURE 4.3 Spectral analysis working curve (from Harrison et al. 1948). Reprinted by permission of Pearson Education.

developing photosensitive tubes came from the television industry (White 1961, p. 15). By 1940, scientists at RCA had developed a photosensitive tube that would amplify the initial electric response to the light signal 2,000,000 times (Zworykin and Rajchman 1939; Rajchman and Snyder 1940). With the advent of the war, these tubes found a wide variety of uses, from checking for defective fuses in grenades (White 1961, p. 143) to generating jamming signals to counteract enemy radar (Saunderson 1997).

These tubes achieve their amplification through the carefully controlled phenomenon of secondary emission. A light beam striking the initial cathode causes it to emit electrons. These electrons are drawn to (or "electrostatically focused on") a second "dynode." Their impact on this dynode produces more secondary emissions; between four and five new electrons are produced for each electron impacting the dynode. These are drawn to a third dynode, and further amplification. The process continues for a total of nine stages, achieving a total amplification of more than 2,000,000 (Rajchman and Snyder 1940) (see fig. 4.4).

The operating characteristics of these tubes make them ideal for use in a direct-reading spectrometer. They are extremely sensitive—due, of course, to their high degree of amplification:

> A spectral line so weak as to require an exposure of several hours with a photographic plate will, when measured with a multiplier tube, give a current of the order of 0.01 microampere, sufficient to give a good sized deflection with a sensitive galvanometer. Thus, in the application of electron multipliers to spectrochemical analysis, the photocurrents are usually of such size as to require no further amplification. (Saunderson 1947, p. 25)

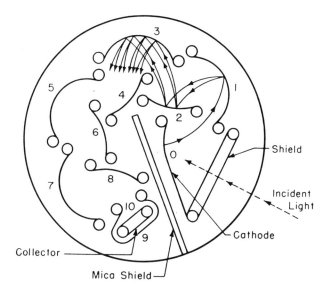

FIGURE 4.4 Schematic diagram of a photomultiplier tube (from Saunderson 1947). Reprinted by permission of the Materials Information Society.

Also, the tubes respond linearly to increases in light intensity (Rajchman and Snyder 1940, p. 22). Another nice feature of these tubes is that—if not mistreated—they can be used indefinitely (Saunderson 1947, p. 25).

In a direct-reading spectrometer, instead of recording light on photographic film, light is used to produce currents in photomultiplier tubes. In the Dow direct reader, "exit slits" were positioned on the Rowland circle to collect light of predetermined wavelengths—those useful for determining concentrations of preselected elements of interest. Thus, an exit slit was positioned to collect light at 3,934 Å—a "calcium line." Currents produced in the photomultiplier tubes behind these exit slits would charge condensers, one condenser for each tube. The amount of charge accumulated in a given condenser, then, would reflect the amount of light that reached that condenser's photomultiplier tube.

To determine concentrations by the internal standard method, electronics were used to determine the relative amounts of charge accumulated on the internal standard's condenser as compared to the unknown element's condenser (see fig. 4.5).

During the sparking, charge is accumulated on the condensers connected to each exit slit's photomultiplier tube. In figure 4.5, condenser C_2 accumulates charge produced by the magnesium—Mg—reference or "in-

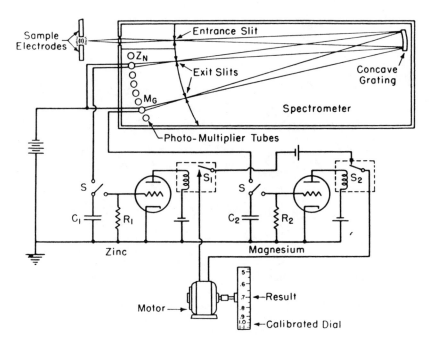

FIGURE 4.5 Schematic diagram of a direct-reading spectrometer (from Saunderson 1947). Reprinted by permission of the Materials Information Society.

ternal standard" photomultiplier tube, while C_1 accumulates charge for zinc—Zn—the unknown element's tube. The amount of time it takes the condensers to discharge, then, determines relatively how much charge each condenser has accumulated.

The theory of condenser discharge allows a fairly straightforward determination of the relationship between the ratios of the light intensities reaching their respective photomultiplier tubes (Saunderson et al. 1945, p. 682). One can show that the difference in the amount of time it takes the two condensers to discharge, Δt, is proportional to the ratio of the logarithms of the intensities of the light hitting the two relevant photomultiplier tubes.[4] What is needed to make a working instrument, then, is a way

---

4. Given a condenser of capacity C discharging through a resister of resistance R, the voltage E at any given time t on the condenser is a function of the initial voltage E_0:

$$E = E_0 e^{-t/RC}$$

Given that the two condensers, C_1 and C_2, for reference and unknown, have accumulated voltages of E_1 and E_2 respectively, the time each takes respectively—

to measure the relative time of discharge and to have this measurement connected to a scale that is calibrated for the relationship between light intensity and concentration.

5. DOW CHEMICAL AND DIRECT READING

In his informative history and assessment of the analytical instrument industry, Frederick White cites six factors that drove the development of instrumentation: the military, universities, electronics, government, nonphysical sciences, and patent and copyright law (White 1961, ch. 5). Although all of these contributed significantly, the importance of the role played by the military, particularly in the context of World War II, cannot be overestimated.

World War II interrupted the practice in the United States of importing materials and instruments from Europe, which had already begun to erode during World War I. The demands of the war for various materials, from aircraft-grade aluminum and magnesium alloy to rubber, resulted in a massive effort to find new sources of raw materials or the means to manufacture synthetic substitutes. In all such cases, instruments were needed to ascertain the properties of the new materials:

> The millions of crystals needed for special war communications provided a tremendous impact on x-ray diffraction; and the synthetic rubber program, as well as the need for penicillin, provided important stimuli in the development of infrared. Even the shortage of India mica had its effect in the development of superior electrical components. The search for substitute, synthetic, or new materials was one of the major factors which made scientists aware of their complete dependence on instrumentation. (White 1961, p. 41)

The result was a tremendous increase in demand for analytical instruments. Baird Associates, one relatively small instrument-making firm, saw

---

t_1 and t_2—to discharge to a given reference voltage, E_s, is

$$t_1 = R_1 C_1 \ln(E_1/E_s) \quad \text{and} \quad t_2 = R_2 C_2 \ln(E_2/E_s)$$

The resisters and condensers are calibrated so that $R_1 C_1 = R_2 C_2 = RC$, and these equations are subtracted to find the difference in discharge times, Δt:

$$\Delta t = RC \ln(E_2/E_1)$$

And since light intensities, I_1 and I_2, are linearly proportional to the amount of charge, E_1 and E_2, accumulated on the condensers, we have

$$\Delta t = RC \ln(I_2/I_1) + K$$

for some constant K.

its revenue jump from $27,486 in 1942 to $353,645 in 1946 (1953) (see chapter 10, table 10.1). World War II was good to the fledgling analytical instrumentation industry.

The exigencies of the war called for greater efficiency. Chemical analyses were needed more rapidly, at lower cost, and were conducted by less highly trained personnel. This accelerated the shift from wet chemical techniques toward instrumental techniques:

> It also saw a shift in scientific thinking, a greater emphasis being given to a physical rather than to a chemical approach. Metallurgy was transformed from a pathological to a clinical or predictive science, as it was necessary to ascertain in advance the operational behavior of crucial parts under various conditions of stress. This demanded a more intimate understanding of structural materials—by the use of new instrumental techniques. An immense saving in time and manpower was effected by spectrographic analyses, and spectroscopy was indispensable for supplying the aluminum needs of the wartime aircraft industry. (White 1961, p. 41)

It was in this context that Jason Saunderson went to work for the Dow Chemical Company in 1939. He had received his Ph.D. in physics from the University of Michigan at the age of twenty-six.[5] His dissertation, under the supervision of D. S. Duffendack, focused on the scattering of electrons by thin foils of metal. However, he had worked in Ralph Sawyer's spectroscopy lab (for $.50 an hour) to earn extra money. It was this experience that paved the way to his being hired to work in Dow's spectroscopy lab.

By 1943, Dow was producing large quantities of magnesium alloy for airplane construction. Calcium was a critical element in magnesium alloy. If made with too much calcium, the metal would not roll properly; if made with too little, the metal would burn when welded. The tolerance was very narrow. Without a means to determine the amount of calcium in the melt before the alloy was poured, a large quantity of metal had to be scrapped. Wet chemical methods were much too slow, as were photospectrographic methods. Saunderson conceived a way to use photomultiplier tubes to yield information on concentrations in the melt virtually immediately.

Work began in January 1944, and an operational instrument was up and running by September. In the meantime, Dow had gone ahead—on the

---

5. Except where otherwise noted, information about Jason Saunderson was obtained from a personal interview with him on March 8, 1997, and correspondence with him in 1998.

unverified promise of a successful instrument—and built a spectroscopy lab in the basement of the foundry. This required a considerable investment, for the lab had to be air-conditioned—to control both temperature (for optical stability) and humidity (for electronic reliability)—and connected to the foundry floor by pneumatic tubes. Interviewed in 1997, Saunderson guessed that Dow risked more than $50,000 on his "32-year-old's" idea.

6. DIFFICULTIES

As is always the case, and as figure 4.6 suggests, the path from idea to working instrument involved a variety of difficulties. Here I briefly consider four areas that posed problems—optical, electronic, mechanical, and material.

Figure 4.6 shows that a significant number of additional optical elements had to be added to fit the photomultiplier tubes physically with the exit slits. An aluminum line—3,944 Å—was only slightly more than a millimeter from a calcium line—3,934 Å—as the instrument dispersed light to 8 Å per millimeter (Saunderson et al. 1945, pp. 683–84). However, these difficulties, subtle as their optical solution had to be, were not new or unusual, although line choice and photomultiplier tube sensitivity were.

One might think that the easy solution to the aluminum/calcium crunch would be to choose different lines that are further apart. However, the lines used were dictated by the behavior of the photomultiplier tubes. In a "photo"-spectrographic instrument, weak lines—lines of low light intensity—were preferred to strong lines. Strong lines tended to be "hollow," appearing almost as two lines. The hollowness was the result of reabsorption of light in the spark. The most intense radiation came from the hottest—central—part of the spark. However, as this light passes through the cooler parts of the spark, some of its energy is reabsorbed there. A hollow line is not ideal for photographic intensity reading. In contrast, with a direct-reading instrument, strong lines were preferred because, while sensitive, the photomultiplier tubes worked more accurately with higher-intensity light.

The use of photomultiplier tubes posed a second problem. The cathodes that initially received the light in the photomultiplier tubes turned out to be finicky. Saunderson and his co-workers studied the relationship between where light hit the initial cathode and the output of the tube. The result is

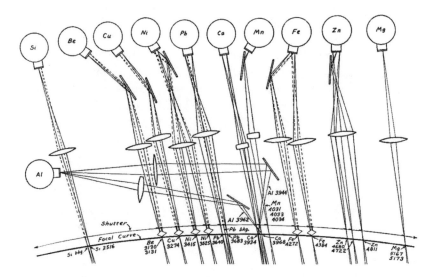

FIGURE 4.6 Direct-reading spectrometer optics diagram (from Saunderson et al. 1945). Reprinted by permission of the Optical Society of America.

shown in figure 4.7 (Saunderson et al. 1945, p. 685). Curves (a) and (b) in figure 4.7 show how slight variations where the tube's cathode received light resulted in large variations in the tube's output. Curve (c) in figure 4.7 was obtained when a ground quartz plate was used to "fuzz" the line over the cathode to produce stable average sensitivity.

Where Saunderson brought optical expertise to the direct reader project, V. J. Caldecourt brought electrical expertise. He developed a way to solve the problem of dark current. Photomultiplier tubes produce current when not illuminated, called "dark current." It was this property of the tubes that made them useful in the production of radar-jamming signals. However, in spectrochemical analysis, dark current is noise, a source of error. To control for this, Caldecourt devised a system for subtracting out the dark current contribution:

> During the sparking period, the reversing relays are operated periodically with a cam system. The relays are reversed once a second, and synchronized with this reversing is the motion of the shutter [allowing light to enter the spectrometer]. With the shutter in position to pass the spectral lines, the relays are in one position, and with the shutter in the background position, the relays are reversed. Thus the condensers are alternately charged with the photo-current from the intensity of the line + background and then discharged with the photo-current from the intensity of the background. . . . It will be noticed that this

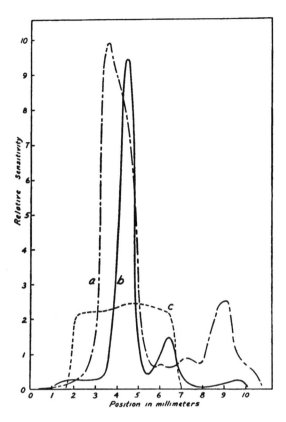

FIGURE 4.7 Photomultiplier tube sensitivity graph (from Saunderson et al. 1945). Reprinted by permission of the Optical Society of America.

method eliminates the effect of dark current upon the final charge on the condenser. (Saunderson et al. 1945, pp. 687–88)

The Saunderson direct-reading spectrometer measured the charge that had accumulated on the condensers by determining how long it took the condensers to discharge. Initially, a "quick and dirty" approach had this information recorded by a line drawn on electrical marking paper advancing at an even rate for the time of condenser discharge. Line lengths were read manually against calibrated scales. This proved cumbersome and time-consuming.

In short order, this approach was replaced by rotating drums: a drum with a calibrated scale on it would rotate for the time of discharge. The trick was to control drum rotation. An electric motor drove a shaft continuously. Shaft rotation was connected to recording drums by means of pulleys and "dental cloth" belts. While the drive shaft turned continuously, each drum was allowed to rotate only when "its" condenser was discharging. Drum rotation was stopped by snagging the dental cloth with a steel phonograph needle controlled by relays sensing the discharge of the condensers.

Finally, Saunderson had to obtain photomultiplier tubes. These tubes had high war priority because of their use in radar jamming and were thus difficult to obtain. However, as Saunderson relates the story, Dow persuaded the government that the control of magnesium alloy production was a high enough priority that a supply of tubes was also made available for this project.

7. A SUCCESS STORY

Saunderson's instrument was a great success. Within a month of its installation, it was routinely analyzing 4,000 samples a month. In 1952, Saunderson was awarded the Willard H. Dow Memorial Award for Research in Magnesium for his work developing the direct reader. The award citation reads: "This new tool has been a very significant contribution to the rapid advancement of magnesium technology and represented pioneering work in the whole field of analytical techniques" (Nelson 1952).

A company publication, the *Dow Diamond*, published an article about the direct reader in March 1946. The article tells a story from the foundry floor:

"Will you send this sample down?" the older man asked his companion, . . .

"Sure thing," the new employee answered, carefully breaking the glass from around the solid cylinder of grayish-white magnesium. He . . . placed the sample cylinder inside . . . a pneumatic tube carrier. . . .

. . . "Why do you take so many samples for analysis?"

"Well, the hard thing to understand is that in making magnesium alloys, you just don't add one part of aluminum, two parts of calcium, and three parts of something else. Those elements are put in there in very close amounts, accurately measured. . . . And while this molten mag is in the pots, it's changing those percentages, so on some alloys we run tests every 15 minutes. The alloys are changing because the flux and metal react all the while, so if tests aren't run often, we'll be pouring a batch of metal that wouldn't pass inspection. And you know what that means."

The new man looked a little puzzled, "Not exactly." . . .

"There was a time when you'd have learned in a day what rejected metal means. It had to be melted, alloyed again, analyzed further and finally cast again. We were running as high as 15 percent rejected metal for a while. Then we got even closer specifications on a special mag for aircraft parts, which would have made rejects even higher. But about that time we got this new analysis machine, and since then we get the tests made in a few minutes, where it used to take half an hour and even longer. That's what caused a lot of the rejects—that half hour when percentages were changing all the while. That's all different now—with this new machine . . ."

Before he could finish his sentence there came the clatter of the carrier as it fell out of the pneumatic tube into a waiting basket. (Dow Chemical Company 1946, p. 2)

The title of the *Dow Diamond* article is revealing too: "Mechanical Brain for Magnesium Analysis." Saunderson's instrument did not simply measure molten alloy for needed information. It took care of all the previously time-consuming cognitive chores of normalization, recording, and interpretation, and the results came in a format that was immediately useful. In the words of Ralph Müller that serve as an epigraph to this chapter, the Saunderson direct reader was a "true instrumental method of analysis": an instrument with "cognitive skills" that allowed it to provide the desired information in final form. It amounted to a mechanical brain.

In 1947, Saunderson's instrument was licensed to Baird Associates for commercial manufacture and sale. Baird further developed the instrument to make it useful in other metal industries. The first Baird/Dow direct reader was sold to the Timken Roller Bearing Company in 1947. E. R. Vance, the Timken chemist who made the decision to purchase a direct reader, was awarded a $1,000 prize by Timken for this decision (Vance 1947, 1949). In 1952, Saunderson came to work for Baird Associates, where he further developed his direct-reading spectrometer. (More details of this work are given in chapter 7.)

8. MATERIAL KNOWING IN THE MATERIAL WORLD

At the beginning of this chapter, I listed a number of skills, or their functional equivalents, that had to be encapsulated in the instrument for it to serve as a reliable, useful means for making elemental concentration measurements on molten alloy. These include knowledge of the spectral fingerprints of the elements of interest, the accurate normalizing of spectral lines as to both place and intensity, the determination of relative intensities of light energy reaching different exit slits, and the encoding and displaying of this information. My story here is of how all this was accomplished.

Knowledge of spectral fingerprints is built into the placement of the exit slits. Normalizing of line placement and intensity is accomplished by precision optical alignment on a mechanically stable frame (an issue I have not discussed), and condenser-discharge electronics was used to put Gerlach and Schweitzer's "internal standard method" in material form. Photomultiplier tubes and the associated electronics allowed the instrument to make relative intensity determinations. Encoding and displaying the signal, now given in the form of information, was accomplished with dental tape, phonograph needles, servomotors, and more electronics.

The knowledge encapsulated by the direct reader is of a variety of different "fields," optics, electronics, and spectrochemical analysis among them. The particular knowledge encapsulated in the direct reader synthesizes knowledge from these various fields in an integrated way. Two fundamentally different kinds of thing knowledge get integrated in materially encapsulated knowledge: working knowledge and model knowledge. Analytically, we can distinguish these in the direct reader.

The instrument includes a model of (some) spectrochemical knowledge. A strip of metal is bent into a Rowland circle, with a radius determined by the radius of the concave grating used in the instrument. Exit slits are cut into this strip of metal at points that correspond to specific wavelengths of light emitted by the elements of interest, a material representation of (some of) the spectrochemistry of these elements. By shaping the strip of metal in a certain way and then by cutting slits in it at specific points, we get a material presentation of a selection among a field of possibilities. Information is built into the instrument, and this then allows us to take information from the signal produced by the instrument.

This signal is also essential to the instrument. The instrument, in interaction with the sample or input, has to create a phenomenon. When accurately calibrated, the instrument produces reliable outputs for given inputs. By preparing samples with known concentrations of various elements of interest, instrument makers and users confirm the reliability and validity of the numerical regularities produced by the instrument. In this way, they confirm the phenomenon produced by the instrument interacting with the sample. In this sense, the instrument stands as working knowledge.

This is analysis. We can distinguish the model knowledge, built into the instrument as a strip of metal in the shape of the Rowland circle, from the working knowledge, constituted by the instrumental crafting of a reliable phenomenon. In the instrument, both epistemic modalities are synthesized to produce a reliable, informative, and useful instrument.

Another part of the direct reader nicely illustrates the synthesis of two epistemic modalities. The electronics that transforms the light energy captured by the photomultiplier tubes into concentration readouts shows how the two kinds of knowledge are integrated into encapsulated knowledge. On the one hand, there is the theory that relates the variables of time, voltage, and resistance for the phenomena of condenser discharge—pretty standard theoretical knowledge. On the other hand, it is the instantiated physical phenomena of condenser discharge, an instance of working knowledge, that allows the instrument maker to deploy a material encapsulation of this theoretical knowledge. This allows the instrument to convert relative amounts of collected light energy into relative times of condenser discharge—and thence into a concentration readout. The final circuit is the synthesis of both modalities. It synthesizes the theoretical knowledge of condenser discharge with the working knowledge constituted by the phenomenon of condenser discharge. The result presents a material functional equivalent of the skill of determining relative spectral line intensities, which previously required human work with spectrograms and densitometers.

The difficulties that Saunderson had to overcome were material. "In principle," the direct reader worked well in January 1944. "In material reality," nine months of hard work were necessary to make it do so. It is easy to conceive the "ideal" photomultiplier tube, where output does not depend on where on the cathode the light hits. The actual material object does not behave this way. In order to achieve an accurate enough direct reader, Saunderson et al. had to deal with this annoying behavior of the tubes. This was true of many of the specific detailed problems that had to be materially solved to make an accurate working instrument, which included line choice (and hence exit slit placement), dark current, and stopping and starting the drums. And these, of course, are merely a sampling of the difficulties that Saunderson and his colleagues had to surmount to get their instrument working. They also confronted a host of other problems. The two points that I wish to emphasize here, however, are, first, that it is a solution to such detailed problems, which litter the path from "clean" idea to working material instrument, that makes instrument development possible, and, second, that these problems more often than not are material.

The first point is widely known. Edison put it well: "It has been just so in all my inventions. The first step is an intuition, and comes with a burst, then difficulties arise—this thing gives out and then that—'Bugs'— as such little faults and difficulties are called—show themselves and months of intense watching, study and labor are requisite before commercial success—or failure—is certainly reached" (quoted in Friedel et al. 1987, pp. 28–29). The initial idea—although very important, indeed, necessary—is the easy step.

The second point is central to my epistemic thesis. A "skilled" instrument is not simply the material encapsulation of propositional knowledge, of ideas. It brings together ideas and material realities. If, contrary to fact, instruments were simply the instantiations of ideas, one could readily argue that knowledge is fundamentally a matter of ideas, which can be instantiated in instruments. This is not how it is. Materials and ideas are both necessary, and materials do not behave like ideas (on this point, see chapter 7). It was Saunderson's understanding and ability to manipulate both the ideas and the material realities involved in direct reading that made his instrument, his contribution to thing knowledge, possible.

This point about the material aspects of encapsulation can be more directly seen in terms of the high degree of thermal and mechanical isolation necessary for the instrument's accuracy. In order to work reliably, to produce the necessary phenomena for measurement, the instrument has to be built to withstand the thermal and mechanical conditions of its use. The instrument had to be designed and built to withstand these conditions. While these conditions could be altered—as Dow Chemical did in building an air-conditioned analytical laboratory in the basement of the foundry—an understanding, at the level of manufacturing practice, of how to control for mechanical and thermal variations had to be built into the instrument. This understanding is part of the working knowledge encapsulated in the instrument. Without it, the instrument would not produce a phenomenon, and measurement would not be possible. In contrast, for its commercial success—even simply its value to Dow as a "one-of" addition to their magnesium foundry—the direct reader had to provide the desired information in a timely and cost-efficient manner. Such economic knowledge, however, is not encapsulated in the instrument, for it is neither working nor model knowledge.

The net effect, when the instrument is well calibrated and operating correctly, is a useful tool for measuring elemental concentrations in metal alloy melts. It also is encapsulated thing knowledge synthesizing working knowledge, model knowledge, theoretical knowledge, and functional equivalents to skill knowledge.

5 The Instrumentation Revolution

A good machinist is worth 10 lousy PhDs.
MORRIS SLAVIN,
Atomic Absorption Spectroscopy

1. REVOLUTIONARY CHANGE IN ANALYTICAL CHEMISTRY

The direct-reading spectrometer developed at Dow Chemical during the 1940s (see chapter 4) was one piece of a major epistemological change in science. By the middle of the twentieth century, the epistemic centrality of instruments, the fact that they are bearers of scientific knowledge, had become a matter of scientific self-awareness. This is seen most easily in analytical chemistry, but these changes were widespread in the physical sciences. Ernest Lawrence's cyclotron, discussed in chapter 3, is a prime example from the heart of physics. This is the scientific instrumentation revolution.

The changes analytical chemistry experienced during the middle years of the twentieth century have been called "the second chemical revolution." Prior to 1920, analytical chemists determined the chemical constitution of some unknown by treating it with a series of known compounds and observing the kinds of reactions it underwent. After 1950, analytical chemists determined the chemical constitution of an unknown by using a variety of instruments that allow one to identify chemicals from their physical properties.

This transformation did not involve changes in theory. Rather, it involved changes in the practice of analytical chemistry. It involved changes in the limits of possible analyses—with respect to the amount of sample required for an analysis, the time necessary for an analysis, and the precision with which trace quantities could be analyzed. It involved the development of a new family of companies that made scientific instruments and a new level of capital expenditure necessary to do analytical chemistry. It involved the development of new means to disseminate information about scientific instruments. It promoted scientific instruments as bearers of scientific knowledge. With these changes in analytical chemistry, we have widespread recognition that building a new instrument can teach us about the world, just as devising a new theory can. "That the history of physical science is largely the history of instruments and their intelligent use is well known," Ralph Müller wrote unambiguously at the time these changes were under way (see the epigraph to this book, from Müller 1940, p. 571).

This revolution is not of the kind discussed by Thomas Kuhn ([1962] 1970; 3d ed., 1996) and his followers (see, e.g., Hacking 1981, pp. 1–5, 169–76). It is more akin to the "probabilistic revolution," where the possibility of probabilistic scientific knowledge emerged (Krüger et al. 1987). I argue in this chapter that it is best understood as an example of what Ian Hacking has called "big revolutions" (Hacking 1983b, 1987).

My claim that scientific instruments bear scientific knowledge, the thesis of thing knowledge, must be understood historically and normatively. Scientific knowledge is not an eternally unchanging category. Scientists and instrument makers from the eighteenth century hesitated to include their devices under this heading. James Ferguson and John Smeaton (see chapter 2) bear witness to this. Here I show that the concepts of knowledge and instrumentation shifted during the twentieth century. This change in how these categories were deployed "on the ground," so to speak, by scientists and engineers asks for a revision of our philosophical analysis of them. Here is the normative dimension to thing knowledge. To adequately understand current science and technology, philosophy *should* articulate an account of knowledge that qualifies instruments as knowledge bearers. This is the project of chapter 6. First, in this chapter, however, I present the evidence for instruments coming into their own epistemically during the twentieth century.

Virtually every history of analytical chemistry notes the revolutionary character of the changes in analytical chemistry between 1920 and 1960. Here, for example, is John K. Taylor:

> In 1985, it is hard for anyone to remember, and most analytical chemists have never known, an instrumentationless world. When one enters a modern analytical laboratory, one is surrounded by equipment so that the analyst may be dwarfed by the instruments at his or her command. Contrast this with the laboratory of the 1930s; the analyst was surrounded by chemical reagents and the most conspicuous installation was a fume hood. Several drawers contained the tools of the profession—beakers, filters, burets and pipets. (Taylor 1985, p. 1)

Section 6 of his article is titled "The Chemical Revolution." In it he writes:

> Chemical analysis is undergoing a change of operational mode similar to the industrial revolution of a century ago. . . . The trend is from

individual craftsmanship to mechanical outputs, using apparatus and equipment that is often poorly understood by the technical operator. (ibid., p. 8)

Many other examples can be found.[1] None of the authors who discuss this transformation of analytical chemistry assert a detailed sense of "revolution" with their use of the word. Their speaking of revolutionary change, however, does signal dramatic developments in the field. This was not a period of "work as usual."

2. TEXTBOOKS, THEN AND NOW

Textbooks provide nice summary pictures of analytical chemistry before and after these changes. Consider, for example, W. A. Noyes's elementary text *The Elements of Qualitative Analysis,* first published in 1887 and revised with George McPhail Smith in 1911. The book has three main parts. The first part (16 pages) provides the theory of qualitative analysis; precipitation is qualitatively explained by ionization theory. The second, and longest, part (82 pages) presents an empiricist's gold mine of descriptions of chemical reactions. Substances are classified according to their "deportment toward various reagents" (1911, p. 17). Reactions are discussed with the aim of separating and distinguishing the elements. The third part of the text (10 pages) presents an algorithm for determining the nature of an unknown, drawing on the reactions studied in the first two parts of the book. In short, qualitative analysis works by running an unknown through a series of reactions designed to separate the various components and allow their identification from the kinds of reactions they participate in.

Quantitative analysis, in contrast to qualitative analysis, is concerned with determining the relative amounts of the different elements present in an unknown. Prior to 1920, quantitative analysis used two methods, gravimetric analysis and volumetric analysis. A brief example from George McPhail Smith's 1921 text *Quantitative Chemical Analysis* explains both approaches:

[L]et us consider the determination of silver in a silver coin.
(a) Gravimetric Method. The weighed sample is dissolved in nitric acid, the solution diluted, and the silver separated from copper, by precipitation as insoluble silver chloride, with dilute hydrochloric acid.

---

1. See, e.g., Melville 1962; Kolthoff 1973; Ewing 1976; Laitinen and Ewing 1977; Ihde 1984.

The precipitate is filtered off, washed, dried, and weighed. From its weight, the weight of silver is calculated as follows:

Ag/AgCl × wt. of precipitate = wt. of silver. . . .

(b) Volumetric Method. The weighed sample is dissolved in nitric acid, diluted as before, and the silver converted into the insoluble chloride by the gradual addition, from a burette, of a solution of sodium chloride of known concentration. As soon as, after stirring each time and allowing the precipitate to settle, the first drop is added which fails to induce further precipitation, the reaction is known to be complete; and the number of cubic centimeters required, multiplied by the silver equivalent of the sodium chloride solution per cubic centimeter, gives directly the weight of silver in the sample. (Smith 1921, pp. 2–3)

Smith's work continues with detailed discussions of a large number of examples that illustrate both basic approaches.

A few other methods are mentioned in other, more advanced, texts. J. C. Olsen's 1916 text *Quantitative Chemical Analysis* is subtitled "by Gravimetric, Electrolytic, Volumetric and Gasometric Methods." Still, gravimetric and volumetric methods make up the greatest proportion of the 555-page text. The book includes a thirty-page chapter on electrolytic methods. Here, by dissolving materials and passing a current through the solution, different substances are deposited on the different electrodes. It is clear from the discussion that these methods suffered from a lack of a dependable source of electricity. Twenty-three pages are devoted to gas analysis. Here the main difficulty lies in finding appropriate substances with which to absorb different gases. Once they have been absorbed, a more standard gravimetric approach can be pursued.

John Muter's 1906 *Short Manual of Analytical Chemistry* also is primarily devoted to gravimetric and volumetric methods. Muter includes an eight-page chapter on "alternative methods." Here he discusses analysis by circular polarization with the saccharometer (two pages), spectrum analysis with a Bunsen burner and a prism spectroscope (one page), and gas analysis with Hempel's "gas-measuring apparatus which is reasonable in price, and yet is capable of measuring gas volumes with very fair accuracy" (four pages) (Muter 1906, p. 232). It is clear, however, given their short treatment, that these methods were not central to the practice of analytical chemistry.

Finally, it is worth mentioning William Lacey's 1924 *Course of Instruction in Instrumental Methods of Chemical Analysis*. This is the earliest textbook with an explicit instrumental focus. The instruments, however, are fairly simple devices developed for special analytical needs. The polarimeter, which measures the angle through which polarized light rotates when passing through a substance, is particularly useful for determining the percentage of sugar in a sample, a commercially important piece of information. The book pays scant attention to the two areas that have become most important to instrumental analysis. Spectrographic analysis is covered in two pages. Electrochemical analysis is covered in one chapter, where we find:

> Apparatus: Aside from the cell and burettes, the apparatus consists of some means of measuring the electromotive force produced. If a potentiometer with standard cell for comparison is used, the actual electromotive force may be determined. . . . [I]n most cases, the method [is] used merely for the location of endpoints of titrations; and for this purpose it is only necessary to be able to follow relative changes in voltage without reference to the actual magnitudes. (Lacey 1924, p. 83)

The book continues with a circuit diagram for constructing a simple means of measuring these relative changes. For all its shortcomings, the book does suggest the importance of using instruments to make various determinations of physical properties. During the following decades, this became the source of the radical transformation in analytical chemistry.

By way of contrast, consider a more recent text, *Quantitative Analytical Chemistry* by George H. Schenk, Richard B. Hahn, and Arleigh V. Hartkopf (1977; 2d ed., 1981). The first part of the book, "Fundamentals," provides a general introduction to chemical analysis, covering important theoretical bases of chemistry such as solution equilibria, acid-base reactions, and oxidation-reduction reactions. The student is taught some of the important procedures of chemical analysis (data handling, sampling the material for which an analysis is sought, preparation of the sample). This is also where the classical—gravimetric and volumetric—methods of analysis are dealt with.

The second part of the text covers a variety of instrumental methods of analysis. Four chapters are devoted to optical methods of analysis. Here the student is taught about spectroscopy, use of the fluorescence of molecules and ions—where atoms absorb radiation at one wavelength and emit it at another wavelength—and the refractive properties of some materials—where radiation is "bent" when passing through these materials. Two chapters are devoted to electrochemical methods of analysis. Here analyses are accomplished by making measurements of various electrical properties. pH is routinely determined by measuring the electric potential across a special electrode. Electrogravimetry uses an electric current to cause deposits—

which can be weighed—of ions on the electrodes in a solution. Coulometric analysis is accomplished by measuring the amount of current necessary to reduce or oxidize ions in solution. Polarography depends on the fact that different ions require different potentials to participate in a current; from a plot of applied voltage versus current—a "polarograph"—an analyst can determine the concentrations of the different ions involved. All of these approaches rely on special optical and electrical instrumentation.

Schenk, Hahn, and Hartkopf's text is aimed at students who do not intend to become analytical chemists but may use analytical methods in their work. Douglas Skoog and Donald West have written a pair of texts, more thorough in treatment, aimed at students pursuing a career in chemistry (1971, 1976 [1st ed. 1963]). Their first text, *Fundamentals of Analytical Chemistry*, does all that the Schenk text does, but in greater theoretical detail. Ten chapters (225 pages out of 765) are devoted to volumetric methods. Nine chapters (207 pages) are devoted to instrumental methods—electrochemical (five chapters) and spectrochemical (four chapters). Gravimetric methods receive a treatment similar to Muter's 1906 treatment of "alternative" methods—one (thirty-page) chapter with the following apology:

> Some chemists are inclined to discount the present day value of gravimetric methods on the grounds that they are inefficient and obsolete. We, on the other hand, believe that the gravimetric approach to an analytical problem—like all others—has strengths and weaknesses, and that ample situations exist where it represents the best possible choice for the resolution of an analytical problem. (Skoog and West 1976, p. 135)

Skoog and West's second text, *Principles of Instrumental Analysis*, focuses exclusively on instrumental methods. They begin the preface noting, "Instrumental methods of analysis have become the backbone of experimental chemistry" (Skoog and West 1971, p. v). The book has detailed treatments of spectrochemical analysis (ten chapters), other electromagnetic-radiation-based methods (three chapters), mass spectroscopy (one chapter), radiochemical methods (one chapter), electrochemical analysis (six chapters), and chromatographic methods of separation and analysis (two chapters).

3. ANALYTICAL CHEMISTRY

We can also get a sense of the changes in analytical chemistry by looking at the changes in the central American journal of research in analytical chemistry, *Analytical Chemistry*. It was born in 1929 as an offshoot of *Industrial and Engineering Chemistry*. From 1929 to 1948, it was published as *Industrial and Engineering Chemistry, Analytical Edition*. After 1948, adopting its current name, *Analytical Chemistry*, it became autonomous, with its own subscription list and editorial policies. Volume numeration was kept continuous. The journal has experienced dramatic growth. The first, 1929, volume, contains 238 pages. The 1948 volume contains 1,250 pages. The 1989 volume contains 2,850 pages. The 1996 volume contains 5,384 pages.

In February 1943, editorial responsibilities passed from Harrison Howe to Walter Murphy, who took an active role in promoting the changes taking place in analytical chemistry. Several regular columns were introduced, the first on instrumentation. The scope of papers appropriate for publication in the *Analytical Edition* was broadened to included more theoretically oriented papers and papers focused on instrumentation. The editors were particularly insistent that one must take the "chemistry" in analytical chemistry very liberally: "The tools used may be chemical or physical. . . . The physical chemistry, in many cases may approach pure physics" (Murphy et al. 1946).

Analytical Chemistry published three surveys of trends in the field. The first, in 1947, responded to the perception that the field was being taken over by instruments.

> Columns and editorials in *Analytical Chemistry* and the correspondence they quote show that many chemists are asking, "Where is analytical chemistry heading, technically and professionally?" . . .
>
> Though many teachers of quantitative analysis are adding as much material on the newer instrumental methods of analysis as time and equipment permit, there are many shades of opinion on what is significant enough to include and whether the new methods are important enough to be given at the expense of material on the classical methods. (Strong 1947, p. 968)

Of the papers on analytical chemistry published in 1946, 56 percent were on instrumental methods (Strong 1947, p. 969).

Similar studies were done in 1955 and again in 1965 (Fischer 1956; Fischer 1965). By 1965, 40.5 percent of all papers concerned optical methods alone. Only 3.6 percent of papers concerned gravimetric methods, down from 10.7 percent in 1946 (Fischer 1956, p. 968). Perhaps the most important point is that the 1965 analysis is not concerned with the percentage of instrumental as opposed to noninstrumental methods. That issue has been settled. Analytical chemistry has been won by the instrumental approach, although the early courses still present much basic chemistry.

4. SEPARATION AND MANUFACTURE VERSUS IDENTIFICATION AND CONTROL

Currently, analytical methods are distinguished as either "classical" or "instrumental." Typically, contemporary textbook authors play down differences between classical and instrumental methods. Everyone agrees that one mandate of the analytical chemist is to determine the constitution of the sample. On a cursory analysis, instrumental methods simply augment the arsenal of methods available to an analytical chemist. But there are subtle differences between analytical chemistry then and now that are important to notice.

In his 1969 *Instrumental Methods of Chemical Analysis*, Galen Ewing writes:

> Historically, the development of analytical methods has followed closely the introduction of new measuring instruments. The first quantitative analyses were gravimetric, made possible by the invention of a precise balance. It was soon found that carefully calibrated glassware made possible considerable saving of time through the volumetric measurement of gravimetrically standardized solutions.
>
> In the closing decades of the nineteenth century, the invention of the spectroscope brought with it an analytical approach which proved to be extremely fruitful. (Ewing 1969, p. 1)

Contrast this with the remarks of H. Laitinen and W. Harris, in their "noninstrumental" text, *Chemical Analysis: An Advanced Text and Reference:*

> Classical methods of final measurement will long continue to be important. In the first place, they are inherently simple. For an occasional determination or standardization the use of a titration [volumetric] or gravimetric determination often will require the least time and effort and will involve no investment in expensive equipment. Second, classical methods are accurate. Many instrumental methods are designed for speed or sensitivity rather than accuracy, and often must be calibrated by classical methods. . . .
>
> In summary, the thesis of this book is that knowledge of chemical reactions is important, first because it is needed for direct application to classical methods, and second because it is essential in instrumental methods where chemical reactions are involved in operations preceding

the use of an instrument in the final measurement. (Laitinen and Harris 1975, pp. 2–4)

There is no contradiction between Ewing's and Laitinen and Harris's remarks, but there is a difference in emphasis. For Ewing, new and better instruments are the bellwether of progress in analytical chemistry. One could imagine a Ewing-style analytical "chemistry" that had little to do with chemistry per se and a lot to do with physics. Laitinen and Harris are not banking on such a course of events.

Instrumental methods do not work the same way as classical methods. Contrast gravimetric methods with spectrographic methods. Put simply, atomic-emission spectroscopy works because the wavelengths of light that an atom emits are characteristic of that kind of atom. When an analyst measures these wavelengths, the analyst is directly "fingerprinting" the atom. In contrast, how much some precipitate weighs is not, in any general sense, characteristic of the composition of the precipitate. This measurement allows identification only within the context of the chemical reactions involved in the initial chemical separations.

This difference has ramifications for how analytical chemistry is conceived. The most careful theoretical development of analytical chemistry prior to 1920 is Wilhelm Ostwald's *Scientific Foundations of Analytical Chemistry* (1895). Ostwald starts at a high level of abstraction. Substances are distinguished by differences in their properties. Two substances are identical when they agree on all their properties. Here Ostwald is only concerned with *distinguishing* elements from one another. The hard part of analytical chemistry, however, comes in *separating* a complex mixture into its elements: "From what has been said in the foregoing chapter it is apparent that the task of recognizing any given substance . . . is always more or less easy of accomplishment. . . . But the problem becomes far more complicated when we have to deal . . . with a mixture; separation must here precede recognition, and the first-named operation is naturally much the more difficult of the two" (Ostwald 1895, p. 9). It was in separating substances that the subtlety and craft of the analytical chemist was displayed.

Ostwald spends the remaining theoretical portion of the book discussing the various means available to separate different substances from one another. He discusses various *physical* means of separation—for example, using filters to separate liquids from solids—but by far the bulk of his text concerns *chemical* methods of separation. He focuses on the way in which ions behave in solution. The material is developed in considerably greater theoretical detail than in Noyes or the other early texts mentioned above.

But from a practical point of view, precipitation is the primary means of accomplishing chemical separation. Ostwald does, however, consider two other means of separation: the liberation of a gas from a solution and the electrolytic method.

Ostwald spends one chapter on quantitative analysis. As with the more elementary texts, he focuses on the two basic means of obtaining quantitative data: gravimetric and volumetric. He distinguishes two kinds of quantitative problems: when the elemental components of a substance have already been separated out into their pure forms, and when the elemental forms are still combined. In the first case, one merely (!) needs to measure the quantity of the different pure forms involved. Unfortunately, substances are frequently not suitable for weighing in their natural state— they may too easily absorb water from the air, for instance. For this reason, substances are frequently weighed while in combination with some other elemental substance. Atomic weights and the law of constant mass proportions can then be used to determine the quantity required.

When pure substances have not been obtained, analytic chemists can resort to other tricks to find the amounts of the components without separating them. For instance, in the case of two mixed liquids, one can determine the proportions of each in the mixture by comparing the specific gravity of the mixture with the known specific gravities of each substance in their pure states. Any such property in which the two substances differ and that can be measured in the mixture can be used in this way.

The second half of Ostwald's book concerns "applications." Here he briefly discusses the characteristic ways to identify and separate the various elements from one another. There is no attempt to present a systematic algorithm for doing so. Rather, he discusses each element in turn, mentioning the more important means available for separating and distinguishing it from other elements.

Prior to the instrumental revolution in analytical chemistry, chemical separation, and not physical identification, was the central feature of this science. Noyes, in his elementary text, follows Ostwald: "Qualitative analysis, with which we are here concerned, deals with the qualitative composition of bodies; i.e., with the separation (either free or in the form of characteristic compounds) and identification of the various elements present in them" (Noyes 1911, p. 1). Indeed, as late as 1929, the analytical chemist was defined as "a chemist who can quantitatively manufacture pure chemicals" (Williams 1948, p. 2). Such manufacture is the result of separations performed by appropriate chemical reactions. With the introduction of instrumental methods of analysis, analytical chemists came to focus on the physics of elemental properties as a means of identification, rather than on the chemistry of reactions as a means of separation.

5. A CRISIS OF IDENTITY

In March 1947, Walter Murphy published an editorial describing how the profession of analytical chemistry had changed. Previously, analytical chemists had been hired to do work that was "largely repetitive, usually long drawn out, tedious, dull, uninteresting and therefore uninspiring to the truly professional" (Murphy 1947a, p. 145). By 1947, however, because of advances in analytical instrumentation, things were quite different:

> The widespread introduction of instrumentation has caused a sharp division in the analytical laboratory between those of professional and subprofessional training, experience and ability. Today thousands of analytical procedures are carried on readily by laboratory technicians. The true professional is expected to direct, to administer, and to pioneer research in analytical chemistry. He is therefore required to be an organic chemist, and may, at times, be expected to be a biochemist, a metallurgist, a specialist, if you will, in a dozen or more highly specialized fields. He most certainly must be somewhat of an expert in electronics—he must be almost as much a physicist as physicists themselves. In addition, he is usually expected to be specially skilled in some field within the profession of analytical chemistry. (ibid.)

Unfortunately, Murphy noted, outside the field of analytical chemistry, the impression remained that the analytical chemist was only suitable for routine chemical determinations.

Murphy made some specific proposals for changing the perception of his field. These included insisting on a sharp line of separation between analytical chemists and technicians, updating curricula to come to terms with advances in analytical instrumentation, the establishment of an award for outstanding work in analytical chemistry, and the "[c]onsideration of ways and means of educating industry and particularly top-flight management on the true importance of analytical chemistry" (ibid., p. 145).

Murphy was remarkably successful in implementing his program. Distinctions between technicians and analytical chemists did develop. Curricula were revamped (Lingane 1948). Awards were established to promote advanced research in analytical chemistry (Murphy 1947e, 1948b). Even before the end of the year, Murphy commented on an article in *Fortune* discussing new methods of spectroscopic analysis: "Modern chemical analysis has arrived! . . . Top management and executives are beginning to have their attention directed to the wonders of modern chemical analysis" (Murphy 1947d).

Perhaps the most important consequence of Murphy's editorial were the responses it provoked concerning the nature of the profession. In May 1947, Murphy reprinted at length the response of William Seaman of the Analytical Research Laboratory at American Cyanamid. Seaman expanded on the difference between the professional analyst and a technician; the analyst is not so much "a pharmacist filling a prescription" as "a doctor planning a course of treatment" (Murphy 1947b, p. 289). The June editorial consisted of three pages of letters responding to Murphy's editorial (Murphy 1947c, pp. 361–63). In August, a guest editorial by D. B. Keyes on the importance of analytical chemistry to industry was published (Keyes 1947). Finally the November and December 1947 and January 1948 editorial pages consisted of invited responses to the question "What is analysis?"

The responses point up the several ways in which analytical chemistry was in a state of confusion. B. L. Clarke of Merck & Co. starts with the old-fashioned notion that analytical chemistry is the science of separating substances from one another, but he goes on to recognize the analyst's goal of determining the constitution of substances and the importance of instrumental methods of analysis:

> Thus, the analytical chemist is one who breaks substances down in order to find out of what they are made.
>
> Two points deserve emphasis. Because the analytical chemist is really a manufacturing chemist who works on a reduced scale, his basic training in the understanding of chemical reactions cannot be very different from that of the factory chemist. . . . Thus the analytical chemist is first and foremost a chemist. . . .
>
> The other point is that modern analysis frequently avoids the actual physical destruction of the sample, by the use of instruments, like the spectrophotometer, that in effect extend the senses and allow the analyst to observe molecular structure without the crudity of picking the molecule apart. Not only are these instrumental methods more elegant; they are potentially more efficient, and are more and more used in industry where efficiency counts.
>
> Obviously, then, the curricula for the training of analytical chemists must give great emphasis to analytical instruments and to the physical basis underlying their operation. (Clarke 1947, p. 822)

Clarke vacillates precisely on the question that the development of the new instrumental methods raised: Is analysis primarily a chemical process of separation and identification, or a physical process of direct identification?

Everyone recognized the importance of these instrumental methods, yet few were able to embrace them wholeheartedly.

W. C. McCrone of the Armour Research Foundation took a more "liberal" stand:

> The analytical chemist has been replaced not by a man having a different training but by a group of specialists in the determination of physical properties. In general, these specialists resent being referred to as analysts. They are instead physicists or chemists trained in the study of electron microscopy, tracer techniques, infrared spectrophotometry, x-ray diffraction, mass spectrometry, chemical microscopy, polarography, etc. A group of people qualified in each of these phases of analytical work make up the modern analytical laboratory. (McCrone 1948, pp. 2–3)

This crisis of identity also produced problems in the administration of analytical laboratories. McCrone continues:

> The most appropriate name for such a group has not yet been found; the Armour Research Foundation has used Analytical Section, some groups prefer Chemical Physics, other possibilities are Instrumental Analysis, Analytical Physics, and Physical Analysis. It is desirable to have a new name, more dignified than "analytical" alone, yet it is essential to retain the word, or at least the connotation, "analytical." Instrumental Analysis Laboratory is perhaps the best compromise. (ibid., p. 4)

The confusion expressed itself in arguments about appropriate curricula for training in analytical chemistry. Most respondents urged that instrumental methods have a greater portion of available course time. J. J. Lingane—noted for his work on electrochemical methods—disagreed:

> I venture the opinion that it is neither desirable nor feasible to attempt much serious instruction in "instrumental analysis" in the undergraduate course in quantitative analysis. True, one can place potentiometers, spectrophotometers, pH meters, polarographs, and the like in the laboratory and have the student "make determinations" with them, carefully selecting the "unknowns," of course, so no "difficulties" are encountered. But since the undergraduate quantitative course is peopled chiefly by sophomores and juniors, who have not begun the study of physical chemistry, and whose background in physics and mathematics is meager, the educational value of such a scheme is questionable. Too much superficial "modernization" of this kind tends to dilute the instruction in more fundamental aspects of analytical chemistry, which many will agree are still as essential to the education of an analytical chemist as they ever were.

> In our justifiable enthusiasm for the truly great accomplishments
> of "instrumental analysis" it is easy to lose our sense of proportion
> and forget that the most important factor in a chemical analysis is the
> chemical experience of the analytical chemist rather than the final de-
> terminative techniques at his disposal. (Lingane 1948, p. 2)

For Lingane, *chemical* experience was still central to analytical chemistry.

Lingane was not opposed to instrumental analysis. Nor did he doubt the
need for instruction in these areas, saying: "No one will deny the increasing importance of physicochemical determinations in modern analytical
practice, and the concomitant need for more systematic and more extensive
education in these methods" (ibid., pp. 1–2). He preferred, however, to
postpone such instruction to graduate-level courses. Lingane was inclined
to agree with Ralph Müller's idea for special departments of instrumentation (about which, more later in this chapter). This would promote research
in instrumentation and allow analytical chemistry to remain chemistry:

> But the science of instrumentation itself presents a larger problem.
> Month by month in this journal for two years our colleague Ralph
> Müller has been presenting convincing evidence that instrumentation
> in the broad sense has grown to such proportions that it merits recog-
> nition as a new branch of knowledge. Many others share the belief that
> haphazard instruction in this subject is no longer adequate if we wish
> to realize its potentialities fully. Perhaps graduate courses in instru-
> mentation will suffice, although there are some who believe that special
> curricula will be required. (ibid., p. 2)

These editorial remarks expose a crisis of identity for analytical chemists. Instrumental methods need not be chemical in nature. The theoretical
underpinnings could come from physics, electrical engineering and instrumental design. The outcome made it unclear in what sense analytical chemistry was chemistry. New chemical principles were not the only or primary
goal for analytical research. A good portion of analytical chemical research
focused on the development of new instruments.

By the 1960s, the crisis had resolved. "Like it or not, the chemistry is
going out of analytical chemistry," H. A. Liebhafsky argued in his 1962
Fisher Award Address (1962, p. 23A). Instead, Liebhafsky saw "modern analytical chemistry as the characterization and control of materials" (ibid.).
Characterization involves ascertaining a material's composition, properties, and qualities. Control involves using various kinds of sensors and
feedback mechanisms to control the production and use of materials. Control is one new feature of postrevolutionary analytical chemistry made
possible by the introduction of instrumentation. Even characterization,

which bears the greatest similarity with prerevolutionary analytical chemistry, is different. Liebhafsky says:

> Mellon (1952) described the older analytical chemistry as consisting of separation preceding determination: separation usually involving chemistry, determination being based on physics. If we adopt characterization as the essence of modern analytical chemistry, then separation needs replacing by the broader preparation, a change made necessary by the decreasing emphasis on ascertaining composition.
>
> Two trends are noticeable: toward less chemistry in the preparation, and toward less preparation prior to the determination. (ibid., p. 24A)

Liebhafsky further notes that with the de-skilling brought about by the introduction of instrumental methods, analytical chemists are increasingly required to act as personnel managers directing the technicians running the instruments.

6. RALPH MÜLLER'S SCIENCE OF INSTRUMENTATION

Not satisfied simply with soliciting papers on the application and development of new instruments, the editors of the *Analytical Edition* took an active role in providing information on instrumental methods of analysis. The entire October issues for 1939, 1940, and 1941 were devoted to instrumentation (*Industrial and Engineering Chemistry* 1939; Müller 1940, 1941). Ralph H. Müller wrote the entire October issues in 1940 and 1941.

After World War II, the editors decided on a more regular means of providing information on instrumentation in analysis. The first monthly column Murphy introduced into the *Analytical Edition* was Müller's "Instrumentation in Analysis." Müller's first contribution appeared in January 1946, and he continued to write this column until the end of 1968, after which the column was written by invited authors, with comments by Müller.

Müller did a variety of things in his column. He frequently discussed new instruments that would be of interest to analytical chemists. Initially, Müller discussed instruments in the research literature. In his first column, he described a paper by Lingane on measuring the amount of material deposited on an electrode by measuring the amount of current used (Müller 1946a). In his second column, he described the paper by Jason L. Saunderson, V. J. Caldecourt, and E. W. Peterson announcing the development of their direct-reading spectrometer (Saunderson et al. 1945; see chapter 4) (Müller 1946b). Eventually, many of the instruments Müller described were production models from commercial instrument makers. In April 1946, Müller described a new kind of vacuum gauge sold by the National Research Corporation (Müller 1946d). In July 1947, he described the Baird Associates–Dow Chemical direct-reading spectrometer, a commercially made instrument based on Saunderson et al.'s spectrometer (Müller 1947c) (see chapters 4 and 7).

Müller also used his column to discuss the basic principles of the emerging "science of instrumentation." His third column discussed the "three Rs of instrumentation, reading, 'riting, and 'rithmetic," which is to say "indication, recording and computing" (Müller 1946c). Müller noted that the recording of data had become particularly important because of the complexity of the indications that newly developed instruments provided. Infrared-absorption spectrometers—which note relatively how much infrared radiation a substance absorbs as a function of wavelength—would not be a useful analytical tool without recording absorption values as a function of wavelength; too many data are provided in too short a time. Müller's discussion of computations presaged the dramatic developments in computing that have marked the past thirty years.

When the three Rs are appropriately built into an instrument, we have a device that directly provides the desired information. Müller defined an "instrumental" method of analysis, as opposed to "mere" instruments, in terms of the ability of instrumentation to take care of all the intermediate steps. With instrumentation, an analyst merely had to insert an "unknown" into the instrument, push a button, and get the desired information about the unknown. (See the epigraph to chapter 4 by Müller, and the discussion of "push-button objectivity" in chapter 9.) One can also see here why John Taylor likens the instrumental revolution in chemistry to the industrial revolution. Both produced the same de-skilling of routine analytical work. Müller's dream was that once relieved of routine analytical determinations, analysts would be able to investigate other phenomena.

Müller advocated a science of instrumentation with its own departments in universities. "The annual instruments issue of *Science* (1949) contains a number of articles which we believe, will interest the analyst," he wrote in November 1949. "In the first of these, E. U. Condon, director of the National Bureau of Standards, raises a question to which we supplied an affirmative answer ten years ago: 'Is there a science of instrumentation?'" (Müller 1949, p. 23A). Indeed, in 1946, Müller had written:

> September 16 to 20 [1946] represents an important landmark in American instrumentation. The first National Instrument Conference and

Exhibit was held in Pittsburgh with the theme "Instrumentation for Tomorrow," . . .

. . . This meeting has demonstrated that all the factors essential for a true profession [of instrumentation] are in evidence: a common interest, a well defined set of principles and practices, a wide assortment of special skills, and a well educated and trained body of experts completely dedicated to this field. (Müller 1946f, p. 25A)

The main issues for Müller were where the instrument scientists would be trained and where the research into instrumentation would take place. He continued his comment on Condon's question about a science of instrumentation, expressing the following concerns: "We are in complete and enthusiastic agreement with, but wish to repeat that a profession cannot exist without adequate professional training. Consequently, we have been asking, by what type of academic osmosis are the prerequisites for this profession to be absorbed from our present curricula?" (Müller 1949, p. 23A).

In numerous columns, Müller called for more instrumentation research in universities. Unfortunately, to his way of thinking, industry had taken the lead in training and developing instrumentation research:

One of our academic friends expressed surprise and some resentment at the preponderance of industrial and instrument company representatives at this conference [the AAAS Chemical Research Conference, Colby College, August 18–22, 1947]. By actual count we found that the universities were represented to the extent of about 15%. . . . This situation emphasizes the fact that the initiative and intelligent prosecution of instrumental research have long since passed to industrial research laboratories and a few instrument companies. (Müller 1947a, p. 26A)

The consequence was that general principles of and approaches to instrumentation would not be developed. Instead, specific, commercially viable, instruments would be developed:

We have long insisted that research in analytical instrumentation of the "useless" variety is urgently needed and that its proper place is the university. Not that this will be conceded in academic surroundings, because there one hears the constant complaint that there are already so many instruments that it is not possible to tell the students about them. This attitude cannot halt the march of progress, but it helps immeasurably. (Müller 1948, p. 21A)

Müller had in mind research into instrumentation on the model of pure theoretical research.

While the universities may have missed Müller's boat, industry did not. The development of instrumental methods of analysis went hand in hand with the development of a new class of instrument makers. All of the instruments for instrumental analysis had to be developed, produced, and marketed by instrument-making companies. These companies had to hire personnel with an understanding of the physical principles underlying the operation of the instruments, of appropriate design for rugged, reliable instrumentation, and of the manner in which these instruments would perform useful analytical tasks. New companies, such as Perkin-Elmer, Beckman, ARL, and Baird Associates, sprang up to fill this need (D. Baird 1991). These new companies pursued research into instrumentation, although with an eye toward commercial markets for their instruments (although see the discussion of gift economies in chapter 10).

7. SCIENTIFIC REVOLUTIONS

There is little doubt that analytical chemistry has undergone a radical change. The practice of the analyst, who now deals with large, expensive equipment, is different than it was in 1930. Modern instrumental methods are by and large more sensitive and accurate, have lower limits of detection, and require smaller samples; different kinds of analyses can be performed. Analytical chemistry is much less a science of chemical separations and much more a science of determining and deploying the physical properties of substances. This is not to say that separations have disappeared from analytical chemistry; rather, they are no longer the centerpiece of the analyst's craft. Analytical chemistry is now a central part of much industrial research and control, and analytical chemistry is integrated into the business of making instruments both commercially and in the academy.

Given the extent of these changes, it is significant that none of the standard models for revolutionary scientific change fit this case. The revolutionary phase of Thomas S. Kuhn's *Structure of Scientific Revolutions* starts with a crisis, a problem that the established methods of normal science cannot solve (Kuhn [1962] 1970; 1996, ch. 5). There was no such crisis in analytical chemistry. While one might imagine that analytical chemistry underwent a change of paradigm, there was no crisis that provoked this change. Pre-1930 analytical chemists did not bemoan the inability of their chemistry to solve certain problems. Instead, new methods were developed that could solve established—solved—problems, but solve them better: more efficiently, with smaller samples, greater sensitivity, and lower limits of detection. These changes in analytical chemistry do not suffer from any kind of incommensurability: today, one can easily enough understand what analytical chemists were doing in 1900—although the idea that the analytical chemist is one who can quantitatively manufacture pure chemicals is startling on first encounter.

I. B. Cohen provides a broader, more historical framework for the discussion of scientific revolutions, with criteria for judging whether or not a given event in the history of science should be judged a revolution. A genuine revolution must:

1. Be identified as such in the testimony of scientists and/or non-scientists active at the time.

2. Have an impact on the treatises and textbooks written.

3. Be judged a revolution by competent historians of science.

4. Be judged a revolution according to the current opinion of scientists. (Cohen 1985, ch. 3)

The transformation in analytical chemistry passes all of Cohen's tests. The scientists active at the time were well aware of the radical—revolutionary—changes that were taking place in their field. The changes in analytical chemistry had a substantial impact on journal articles and textbooks. There has not been any discussion by professional historians of these changes in analytical chemistry.[2] But there have been several historical studies by chemists, all of which note the dramatic changes in analytical chemistry.

Cohen also provides a general schema for the stages of a revolution in science. According to Cohen, a scientific revolution starts with a creative act that "is apt to be a private or individual experience" (ibid., p. 29). Here, a scientist conceives of a radical means to solve some pressing problem. Already there is trouble fitting Cohen's model to the changes in analytical chemistry. There was no single "purely intellectual exercise" that was the fountainhead for the succeeding changes in analytical chemistry.

One might look to Bunsen's 1860 invention of spectrochemical identification. But the revolution in analytical chemistry was the result, not simply of the development of spectrochemical methods, but of the confluence of many events, all of which showed how the introduction and development of physically based instrumental methods would improve the abilities of analytical chemists. One might say there were many small "Cohen

2. See, however, Morris 2001; Shinn and Joerges 2001.

revolutions," one in emission spectroscopy, one in pH meters, and so on. But this would miss the central feature of this revolution: it was the introduction of the instrumental outlook that transformed analytical chemistry, not the introduction of one or other particular instrumental method.

There is another model of scientific revolution that is more promising. This is the sense of revolution upon which talk of *the* scientific revolution calls. *The* scientific revolution was a large-scale transformation in the nature of scientific knowledge itself. Kuhn has described the rise in importance of measurement in early nineteenth-century physics as "the second scientific revolution" (Kuhn 1977, p. 220). Given how common Kuhn thought the kind of scientific revolution described in his *Structure of Scientific Revolutions* ([1962] 1970, 1996) was, his speaking of a "second revolution" must refer to a different kind of revolution.

Ian Hacking has developed this idea further in his discussion of "the probabilistic revolution" (1983b; 1987). Hacking uses the phrase "big revolutions" to distinguish such historical mutations from small revolutions of the sort Kuhn writes of in *Structure*. Big revolutions have many characteristics, of which Hacking singles out four. First, they are interdisciplinary or, better, predisciplinary. Second, new social institutions appear with these revolutions. Third, dramatic social changes are part and parcel of these revolutions; societies in general organize themselves in different ways. Finally, these revolutions involve substantial changes in our attitudes to the world; Hacking uses Herbert Butterfield's language: big revolutions are "accompanied by a change in our sense of the 'texture' of the world, in a different 'feel for the world'" (Hacking 1987, p. 51).

8. THE FOURTH BIG REVOLUTION

Hacking's first rule is: "Don't look for a big revolution until you find new kinds of institution that epitomize the new directions created by the revolution" (Hacking 1987, p. 49). The revolution in analytical chemistry involves instrumentation research, development, marketing, and use. When scientific experiments were done with one-of-a-kind instruments, a single person or research lab would both perform all the research and development and, of course, use the instrument. Marketing was not necessary. Now that many instruments are bought off the shelf, however, the research, development, marketing, and use of instruments have become separate functions. This gives rise to a need for ways for the people involved in these separate functions to get together to coordinate their activities. New institutions have developed to fill this need.

Spectroscopy was one of the first instrumental methods to have a big impact on analytical chemistry. But the scientists involved were scattered in many different academic disciplines and industrial and government laboratories. These scientists needed a means of getting together to discuss their common interests. MIT's summer conferences on spectroscopy filled this need. Starting in July 1932, one was held each summer until World War II intervened. The conferences brought together people with various professional affiliations. Eighty-eight papers were published in the proceedings for the 1937, 1938, and 1939 conferences. Of these, forty-one (46 percent) were authored by university employees, twenty-five (28 percent) by employees of industry, and seventeen (19 percent) by government employees (Harrison 1938b, 1939b, 1940).

Papers were presented by invitation, and George Harrison, who organized the conferences, clearly had it in mind to bring together the diversity of interests in spectroscopy. Some papers focused on new developments in spectrographic technique; R. A. Sawyer (at the lab Jason Saunderson worked in for $.50 an hour) and H. B. Vincent of the University of Michigan reported on "Characteristics of Spectroscopic Light Sources" at the 1938 conference (Sawyer and Vincent 1939). Some papers focused on new instruments; at the 1937 conference, M. F. Hasler of Applied Research Laboratories described ARL's commercial grating spectrograph (Hasler 1938). Some focused on applications; Joseph Walker of the Massachusetts State Police reported on using the spectrograph to assist criminal investigations at the 1938 conference (Walker 1939). Some compared different kinds of instruments; G. R. Harrison and Morris Slavin argued separately for grating as opposed to prism instruments (Harrison 1938a; Slavin 1940).

After the war, a variety of forums cropped up to provide a means for instrument researchers, makers, and users to get together. The Instrument Society of America put on the first National Instrument Conference and Exhibit, September 16–20, 1946. The conference also had exhibits of instruments by commercial instrument makers (Müller 1946f). In 1947, 7,000 persons attended this meeting, and it offered 139 instrument exhibits (Hallett 1947). This conference and exhibit became an annual September event. In addition, there were other, one-shot conferences and exhibits devoted to providing information about new instruments. Lawrence Hallett hailed the freer exchange of information between makers and users, noting that it "marks real progress and will result in faster development of this very important and fascinating part of applied science" (Hallett 1948).

The most successful forum for the exchange of ideas between makers and users of instruments is the Pittsburgh Conference, created from the marriage of the Society for Analytical Chemistry of Pittsburgh and the Spectroscopy Society of Pittsburgh. The Society for Analytical Chemistry formed in 1942 and began holding conferences in 1946. In 1949, eleven commercial instrument companies exhibited at the meeting. The Spectroscopy Society had held annual meetings since 1940. In 1949, in light of their common interests in analytical/optical instrumentation, the two societies decided to merge their meetings. Analytical chemists were very interested in learning about the possibilities of spectrochemical analysis, and the spectroscopists were interested in closer contact with those who applied their techniques. The result was a great captive audience for the makers of spectrographic equipment. At the first joint meeting of the two societies in March 1949, there were fifty-six papers and fourteen exhibits by commercial instrument makers. The conference has been held every March since. In 1964, the "Pittsburgh Conference" was incorporated, and since 1968, because of its size, it has been held in various cities other than Pittsburgh (Pittsburgh Conference 1971, p. 123, "Historical Notes"; Wright 1999).

The Pittsburgh Conference—"Pittcon"—has grown to enormous proportions. The 1998 conference was held at the Morial Convention Center in New Orleans. There were 28,118 registered attendees, the technical program included 1,931 papers, and over 3,100 instrument exhibits represented more than 1,200 different commercial instrument makers. This meeting is one key place where people in industry, government, and the academy can meet, find out what one another are doing, share the results of their research, and negotiate plans for pursuing cooperative research (Wright 1999, p. 179). The book of abstracts for the fiftieth Pittcon, held at the Orange County Convention Center in Orlando, Florida, in March 1999, is over 800 pages long, with 2,329 abstracts (Pittsburgh Conference 1999).

Besides new institutions, Hacking identifies three other central aspects of big revolutions. They are interdisciplinary, they are associated with dramatic social changes, and they are associated with changes in the "texture of the world."

The interdisciplinary nature of the instrumentation revolution is an obvious characteristic, notwithstanding that this chapter has focused on one particular discipline, analytical chemistry. A flock of new journals devoted to instrumentation were founded during this period. The *Review of Scientific Instruments* first appeared in 1929, and its British counterpart, the *Journal of Scientific Instruments*, first appeared in 1930. *Instruments: Industrial and Scientific* first appeared in 1928. *Instrument Abstracts* first appeared in 1945. These journals are not devoted to a single science but cover the spectrum. Cyclotron researchers read and contributed to them. Instrumentation is interdisciplinary, and if Ralph Müller's dreams of a science of instrumentology are fully realized, these developments in instrumentation are appropriately predisciplinary.

Hacking finds dramatic social changes associated with big revolutions. Here I must be more circumspect. I would point to the rise of big government and the "military-industrial complex." Spurred by the demands of World War II, the federal government took the lead in paying for and promoting the dramatic buildup of the analytical-instrumentation industry. Many of the companies originally founded to develop and supply analytical instruments would not have survived had it not been for governmental contracts during the war (D. Baird 1991). The social implications of these developments are too vast to bear analysis here.

Hacking's notion that big revolutions provide a different "feel for the world" deserves more extensive discussion. In chapter 9, I discuss how changes in the concept of objectivity and associated changes in a wide variety of practices from childbirth to teaching to steel manufacture have provided a different texture to our world, a texture tied to the rise of "objective instrumentation."

This "big instrumentation revolution" has not been discussed by other scholars. Several scholars, however, have described changes that coincide with this revolution (Cohen 1985, ch. 6; Brush 1988). I. B. Cohen, for example, identifies four big revolutions and characterizes them in terms of institutional and conceptual changes: *the* scientific revolution is institutionally characterized by the first organizations, such as the Royal Society, devoted to science. Cohen's second big revolution—identical to Kuhn's "second scientific revolution"—is associated with the rise in the importance of measurement during the first half of the 1800s. Cohen's third big revolution occurred around the end of the 1800s, when scientific research centers and schools for the graduate training of scientists first appeared. Finally, there is Cohen's fourth big revolution, "one that has occurred during the decades since World War II" (Cohen 1985, p. 93). Given the time frame, this big revolution is of particular interest. Cohen identifies this revolution with the expenditure of large sums of money on science and the necessary institutions to make this possible: "In the United States these have included not only the specially created National Science Foundation (NSF) and the National Institutes of Health (NIH) but granting divisions in the armed forces, the National Aeronautics and Space Administration (NASA), and the Atomic Energy Commission" (ibid., p. 94). Of the conceptual changes associated with this fourth big revolution, Cohen writes:

> It is difficult to think of any . . . single intellectual feature that marks the fourth Scientific Revolution. But of major significance is the fact that a considerable part (though by no means the whole) of the biological sciences can be construed as almost a branch of applied physics and chemistry. At the same time, in the world of physics, the most revolutionary general intellectual feature would be the abandonment of the vision of a world of simple elementary particles with only electrical interacting forces between them. (ibid., p. 96)

The major conceptual change associated with Cohen's fourth big revolution is the rise in the epistemic importance of scientific instrumentation. Among other things, this explains why science has become so expensive. Instruments cost money; theories are cheap. High-energy physics is big science, not because of the abstract theories it involves, but because of the mammoth instruments that it develops and works with. Cohen notes that biology could almost be a "branch of applied physics and chemistry." He could have said the same for analytical chemistry. One way in which the importance of physics has developed in these sciences is through the incorporation of physical approaches to measurement into instruments serving chemical or biological ends. Cohen's fourth big revolution is the instrumentation revolution, in which analytical chemistry has played such a significant part.

6   Thing Knowledge

What I cannot create I do not understand.
RICHARD FEYNMAN

1. DOES IT MATTER?

Does it matter that we call the various devices discussed in chapters 1–4 "knowledge"? Is the scientific instrumentation revolution of chapter 5 a revolution in name only? Why not content ourselves with the observation that much analytical skill can be encapsulated in a direct-reading spectrometer, as described in chapter 4? Why not be content to say that Faraday made a new instrument that provoked the development of our theoretical *knowledge* of electromagnetism and the development of *useful* machines? Why not be content to admire the skills of eighteenth-century orrery makers for their beautiful devices that so closely mimicked the motions of the heavenly bodies? What is gained in collecting spectrometers, electromagnetic motors, orreries, and a vast array of material products of cunning, skill, insight, understanding and luck under the heading of knowledge, along with theories, great and small, that warrant being called contributions to our technological and scientific knowledge of the world?

Skeptical questions such as these may be variously interpreted. They may express hostility to all knowledge talk. Some may argue that knowledge talk at best covers over the detailed, contingent, social and political negotiations that lie behind establishing one set of propositions and practices instead of other sets of propositions and practices. These questions may also express a neutral attitude to knowledge talk. Talk of knowledge if you like, but there is no value added in doing so. Nothing changes if we call Einstein's general theory of relativity or Jason Saunderson's direct reader contributions to knowledge. No work is done beyond noting the various particular—historically contingent—reasons why Einstein's theory and Saunderson's instrument were enfolded into the ongoing theoretical and instrumental practices of the cultures that embraced them. Finally, these questions may express skepticism about extending knowledge talk from

theories—where historical and philosophical precedents have long established such talk—to parts of the material world. Knowledge concerns a
special kind of human belief, belief that can be justified in some special—
perhaps even historically evolving—manner. Material instruments certainly cannot be beliefs, and hence it makes no sense to speak of them as
knowledge.

A general hostility to knowledge talk has been one of the salutary contributions of certain strains of the "strong programme in the sociology of
scientific knowledge" (Pickering 1995). I say "salutary," not because I agree,
but because these arguments force us constructively to reexamine issues
that lie at the foundations of the epistemology of science and technology.

It is possible for a focus on epistemology to distort one's understanding
of the history of science. Such a focus easily slips into a view of rational—
epistemological—forces behind the progress of science in battle with ir-
rational—social, political, financial, and so on—forces holding back the
progress of science. But it is not necessary to make this move. An epistemologist can acknowledge the importance and positive value of nonepistemological forces in the development of science but still want to mark a distinction. World War II certainly was the key reason for the development of
Saunderson's direct-reading spectrometer (see chapter 4), along with many
other analytical instruments. The war may even have been responsible for
a shift in the very category of what it is to know—as I argue in chapter 5.
But the development of the photomultiplier tube also played a key, indeed
necessary, role in the development of the direct-reading spectrometer. The
war and the photomultiplier tube made different kinds of contributions to
the development of technology and science. Marking the distinction between these two different kinds of contribution need not imply anything
about the relative importance or value of either.

Epistemology can grant the importance of social, political, and financial
contributions to establishing theories, practices, and instruments. Epistemology can grant the historicity of the categories of knowledge and the
justifications for its acceptance. Such concessions, if, indeed, it makes sense
to call them concessions, do not necessarily impugn the project of epistemology. In writing "What I cannot create I do not understand" on his
chalkboard, Richard Feynman was posing a challenge to epistemologists to
articulate what their understanding amounts to.[1] If Feynman's understanding was a product of his times—and it would not have been Newton's

1. This was written on Feynman's office chalkboard at the time of his death
(Gleick 1993).

understanding—it is an epistemological challenge to articulate the history of this transformation. The fact that nonepistemological forces may play important or even determinative roles in how science and technology develop implies neither that epistemological forces play no role (surely a historically contingent question) nor that it is impossible to draw a distinction between the epistemological and the nonepistemological, to analyze the difference between them.

How we mark the distinction between the epistemological and the non-epistemological makes a difference. Practices are affected by the way the distinction is made. A century ago, it was widely held on theoretical and empirical grounds that the only "natural" kind of variation was variation that formed a Normal (Gaussian, or "bell-shaped") distribution. Karl Pearson, because of his commitment to a now discredited positivism, argued for and established the point that natural variation can be other than Normal. Pearson's epistemology—even though it would be unlikely to persuade many people today—mattered to the future of statistical science (see D. Baird 1983). Pearson presents one example, but many others could be found. How a particular scientific community conceptualizes knowledge affects how knowledge develops in that community. This surely is one of the central lessons in Peter Galison's *Image and Logic* (1997).

The material epistemology I articulate here has important implications. The boundary between science and technology, and perhaps even the contemporary validity of that boundary, is affected by a shift to include the material as epistemological. Faraday's material manipulations, and not simply their bearing on theory, become part of the history of scientific *knowledge*. So does Thomas Davenport's work constructing an electromagnetic motor (see chapter 1). Thing knowledge has implications for how we regard the work of engineers—for the category of "applied science." It could have implications for the kind of work that is rewarded in institutional settings: publish or perish, or demo or die? When we create scholastic aptitude tests, we create a powerful force for change in school curricula (see chapter 9). Does scholastic aptitude include the ability to make something? If not included in scholastic aptitude tests, the teaching of such abilities will be marginalized or lost.

Putting aside these deeper skeptical questions about the very project of epistemology, however, there remains the question of extending the concept of knowledge to include the material products that I focus on in chapters 1–5. In the first place, I have argued that instruments have played roles epistemologically analogous to theories. They have provided a medium in which to express, explore, and develop our understanding. They have provided a medium for explanation and prediction. In the second place, while instruments and theory typically work together, I have presented cases where they have not, where instruments have developed autonomously or in spite of bad theory. Such cases show that it is not possible to reduce the epistemological value of instruments to the epistemological value of theory. Together, these two points argue for finding a way to think of instruments epistemologically on a par with theory. Finally, there is Feynman's remark; creation is essential to understanding. Making is essential for Feynman's brand of subjective knowing. This remark is not an idiosyncratic fluke of Feynman's. It speaks to the epistemological transition of his time, the scientific instrumentation revolution. The situation calls for an epistemological analysis capable of including instruments.

2. DONE AND YET TO DO

So I take it that it does matter how we conceptualize knowledge, and I take it that the examples and arguments of chapters 1–5 call for a conceptualization that includes the material products of science and technology. More than this, the work done in the first five chapters goes some distance toward articulating new material epistemologies. Material models are a material form of representational knowledge. Devices that produce phenomena are instances of working knowledge, a kind of pragmatic knowledge that is constituted by effective action, but effective action with a twist, for the locus of the action is the device itself, not a human being. Measuring instruments present a third kind of material epistemology. They encapsulate in their material form not only both model knowledge and working knowledge but also, in many cases, theoretical knowledge and functional substitutes for human skill. In their material form, measuring instruments integrate all these different kinds of knowledge into a device that is at once both an instance of materially encapsulated knowledge and a source of information about the world.

The epistemological importance of instruments is not ahistorical. To paraphrase H. A. Liebhafsky (see chapter 5 above, end of § 5), science and technology became disciplines devoted to characterization and control during the twentieth century. Characterization is one kind of representation, and control is a matter of effective action. John Taylor (ibid., § 1) has compared what he calls "the second chemical revolution"—which I call "the instrumentation revolution"—with the industrial revolution, in which mass production displaced human craftsmanship. Instruments that encapsulate knowledge take this a step further with the appropriation of human skill and subjective knowledge. The three kinds of thing knowledge presented in chapters 2–4 are the essential components of the instrumentation revolution, in which characterization and control, encapsulating subjective human knowledge and skill in material—instrument—form, is a fundamental component of contemporary scientific-technological knowledge. This is what I call thing knowledge, and the five preceding chapters take the first steps in saying what it is and how it is central to current science and technology.

But much remains to be done. In the first place, I have to address head on the conceptual puzzle that thing knowledge poses to philosophy. It is the thesis of this book that we need to stretch the concept of knowledge to include the things of science and technology. But this stretching requires attention to the broader conceptual landscape. Knowledge has a long history of connection with concepts such as truth justification and belief. What can we say about these concepts in light of a stretched concept of knowledge? The next five sections of this chapter, where I articulate the concept of an instrumental function as a kind of material surrogate for truth, address this concern.

The final six sections of this chapter present and argue for a more general epistemological picture with which to embrace the various material epistemologies I have been concerned with—as well as more traditional proposition-based epistemologies. This picture draws on Karl Popper's "objective knowledge," but with a decidedly non-Popperian materialist basis. I find this neo-Popperian picture both compelling and useful. I know, however, that many find Popper's epistemology implausible at best, and I respond to some of the more fundamental criticisms of Popper in sections 9–12.

More work remains to be done. The new material epistemologies that I advocate have a variety of consequences that take us well beyond epistemology per se. The last four chapters of this book examine four of the most significant consequences to thing knowledge. To come to terms with knowledge borne by things, and not simply ideas or propositions, we have to recognize the difference between things—as a medium—and ideas. There are fundamental differences, and setting them out is the project of chapter 7, "The Thing-y-ness of Things." Thing knowledge has consequences for how we lay down boundaries between science and technology, for how we tell the history of science and technology. Chapter 8, "Between Technology and Science," presents a history of an instrument, the steam engine indicator, that crossed old boundaries between science and technology. Seen in the context of thing knowledge, the history of the indicator makes more sense than a history based in traditional idea epistemology. Objectivity is another concept that is transformed by thing knowledge. Chapter 9, "Instrumental Objectivity," examines this transformation, with respect to both its promise and its problems. When objectivity resides in instruments, what is the role of human judgment? Finally, an epistemology that includes things changes the economics of epistemic exchange. Chapter 10, "The Gift," examines the nature and ramifications of this change.

3. CONCEPTUAL PROBLEMS WITH MATERIAL KNOWLEDGE

I claim that material products such as Davenport's motor bear knowledge, and that the kind of knowledge they bear is typically different from the kind of knowledge borne by theories. But the concept of knowledge is tied to other concepts. A well-worn road in epistemology speaks of justified true belief. My project is one of expanding the domain of knowledge, and doing this requires rethinking the concepts with which we analyze knowledge.

Belief is a big problem. Whatever Davenport's motor may be, it is not a belief. It is not that I deny the sense or value of speaking of a person's subjective knowledge, and of doing so in terms of a person's beliefs. Rather, I assert that in addition to subjective belief, we need an analysis of objective knowledge, of knowledge that can be distinguished from its subjective origins. Both subjective and objective points of view are important to epistemology. I take up this relationship in more detail in section 9.

I have never been wedded to a literal use of "truth" in the analysis of knowledge. Here my roots in Popper's and Lakatos's philosophy show (Lakatos and Musgrave 1970; Hacking 1981). "Every theory is born refuted" (Lakatos 1978, p. 5). But there is something about "truth" that is important. Popper writes of truth as a "regulative ideal . . . that is, of a description which fits the facts" (Popper 1972, p. 120). We should seek true theories, and Popper offers an elaborate theory of verisimilitude as a central component of his method of "systematic rational criticism" (ibid., ch. 2, §§ 8–10). But Popper's theory of verisimilitude has been beset by empirical and conceptual problems, and it has not been persuasive. Still, accuracy remains a regulative ideal of science. We want good representations, true to what we know of the objects they claim to describe.

The fundamentally new contribution, necessary for understanding material knowledge, is that of an instrumental function. Material models, since they operate representationally, can call on the extensive literature on representation, some of which I employ at the close of chapter 2. Working knowledge is not being representational, and it needs something else. Instrumental function is this something else. To motivate and justify this conclusion, I first ask the more fundamental question, "What does knowledge do for us?" In answering this question without presupposing a propositional—ideational or belief-centered—concept of knowledge, we shall be in a position to understand how instrumental function serves to give material devices the values of knowledge.

4. WHAT DOES KNOWLEDGE DO FOR US?

If I want some information about plutonium, I can easily look it up:

> Plutonium. Actinide radioactive metal, group 3 of the periodic table. Atomic number 94. Symbol Pu. This element does not occur in nature except in minute quantities as a result of the thermal neutron capture and subsequent beta decay of ^{238}U; all isotopes are radioactive; atomic weight tables list the atomic weight as [242]; the mass number of the second most stable isotope ($t_{1/2} = 3.8 \times 10^5$ years). The most stable isotope is ^{244}Pu ($t_{1/2} = 7.6 \times 10^7$ years). (*Van Nostrand's Scientific Encyclopedia* 1983, p. 2262)

I do not have to read about Glenn Seaborg's discovery of the element in 1940 through the deuteron bombardment of uranium accomplished with UC Berkeley's 60-inch cyclotron. Nor do I have to read about all of the various ways in which the above information has been ascertained and justified. This information has been detached from the context of its discovery and can be used elsewhere without reference to its discovery (which, I note, is lacking in this encyclopedia entry).

This is a feature of scientific knowledge that is of signal importance. Knowledge can detach from its context of discovery to be used elsewhere. It comes with a kind of guarantee that when used appropriately, it can be depended upon. Knowledge is efficacious in this respect. Finally, knowledge comes with a guarantee of a kind of longevity. Knowledge is more than mere opinion, more than a fashionable whim.

To these three ideals—detachment, efficacy, and longevity—I add two others. The first is obvious, but important in ways that emerge in subsequent discussion. Knowledge establishes a relationship between humans and the world. We may assert a fact or develop a detailed picture of "how we think things are." Knowledge serves to connect our thinking with the world—either the world is, is not, or is in certain important respects as we represent it to be. And note that I do not thereby claim there is a single correct representation. There may be more than one adequate representation, more than one expression of our knowledge of some topic.

The last ideal I am concerned with is objectivity. Knowledge stands in a special relationship between an individual and the world, where the world's voice has a kind of priority. I may have wished that Al Gore had won the popular vote in the state of Florida in the 2000 presidential election. But my wishing it were so won't make it so. The votes make it so. "The votes" stand as impartial arbiters between camps with conflicting wishes. They provide an objective standard independent of subjective wishes.

I use the Florida election pointedly, for it was a flawed election that revealed the difficulty with the idea of the world's voice having priority. How is the world's voice "heard"? In Florida, there were moves and countermoves. The wishes of the various camps directed the reading of the chads on the ballots. Some are tempted to conclude that that world has no voice. There are only the voices of the warring camps, each enlisting features of a mute world to support projection of its voice. If one accepts this, one cannot be dismayed by the manner in which the election was brought to closure through legal action and the more easily counted votes of nine Supreme Court justices. We should prefer to accept as an ideal a different view of the matter: as a matter of objective fact, either Al Gore or George Bush did receive more votes in Florida and should have won the election on that basis. Unfortunately, our methods of ascertaining this objective fact were not up to the task. Objectivity, like the other features I have identified, is an ideal.

We have, then, five ideals that encompass core values to knowledge:

1. Detachment: technological and scientific knowledge can detach from its context of discovery

2. Efficacy: technological and scientific knowledge can be depended upon to accomplish appropriate ends

3. Longevity: technological and scientific knowledge can be depended upon into the indefinite future

4. Connection: technological and scientific knowledge establishes a relationship between the world and us

5. Objectivity: "the world's voice" has a kind of priority in the relationship between the world and us

These are ideals. As such, we don't expect any specific claim to knowledge to live up to them without controversy and struggle. But also as ideals, they tell us why knowledge is important, and why, in the domain of material knowledge, instrumental functions are important.

5. INSTRUMENTAL FUNCTION, MATERIAL TRUTH

Each of the five ideals of knowledge describes important central features of the instrumental functions we develop and deploy in our artifacts. Efficacy falls out almost by definition. When we build an artifact to accomplish some goal, we depend on the efficacy of our material contrivance to accomplish the goal. If it fails to accomplish the goal—if it fails to function—we have to keep at it or abandon the project and/or goal. The point of a material function is to accomplish something, to be efficacious.

Detachment, not quite as obvious as efficacy, is an equally central feature of the functions of our artifacts. Photomultiplier tubes were developed in the late 1930s as part of a research program at RCA. Spectrometry was not RCA's target application. When these tubes were used in a direct-reading spectrometer, their function of sensing light was detached from their original context of development. This "material detachment" is not simple. The quality control on RCA's manufacture of the tubes was relatively loose, and individual tubes had to be individually checked for adequate performance in a spectrometer. Tubes that checked out were expected to perform their function into the foreseeable future.

"Into the foreseeable future" speaks of longevity. Material artifacts are perhaps more prone to wear and tear than theoretical knowledge. They cannot be depended on to work forever. But if we couldn't depend on them to work for a reasonable—sometimes carefully quantified—amount of time, they wouldn't be of much use. Whatever else they are, functions must have material forms that behave as do the phenomena Peirce speaks of in *Pragmatism and Pragmaticism* as "a permanent fixture of the living future."

Functions must have a kind of objectivity too. I may wish that the Ethernet circuitry card in my computer were not broken. I may even behave as if it were not broken, reloading software and replacing other components. But, at the end of the day, if it is broken and I want to connect to an ether network with my computer, I am going to have to find a replacement or substitute for my Ethernet card. Now reliability is not a black-and-white concept. Perhaps my Ethernet circuit has a "flaky" component that only works some of the time. Here we can develop the statistical theory and practice of reliability.

I have saved connection, which seems the simplest feature of knowledge, for last. Both scientific knowledge and engineered function connect us with the world. Theoretical knowledge connects how the world is with how we represent it to be. Functions connect how an artifact behaves with how we want it to behave. Here is an obvious and fundamental feature of functions, but while it may seem to be the simplest function of functions, it is indeed deeply complex and problematic and requires, finally, a closer examination, which I shall put off until section 10.

Roughly speaking, then, I claim that an artifact bears knowledge when it successfully accomplishes a function. This claim requires elaboration, most particularly with respect to the concept of function itself. The concept I employ is relatively thin, stripped of any heavy load of intentional baggage and focused on the reliable, regular predictable performance of the artifact. It might best be characterized in terms of mathematical functions rather than biological or more broadly teleological functions. A function, for me, is a crafted and controlled phenomenon.

There is linguistic evidence to support my association of function with knowledge and truth. Philosophers are accustomed to think of truth in terms of propositions or sentences, and so ignore turns of phrase such as "a true wheel." A golfer has spoken to me of a "true drive down the fairway." Among the more philosophically common senses of "true," we also find "9. Accurately shaped or fitted: *a true wheel*. 10. Accurately placed, delivered, or thrown" (*American Heritage College Dictionary*, 3d ed., s.v.). But a "true wheel" is not true simply because it properly conforms to a particular form; a true wheel spins properly, dependably, regularly. A wheel that is out of true wobbles and is not dependable. Ultimately, it will fail. This sense of "truth" picks out those contrived constellations of materials that we can depend on. A public, regular, reliable phenomenon over which we have material mastery bears a kind of "working knowledge" of the world and "runs true" in this material sense of truth.

The need for the wheel to spin properly to be true immediately intertwines this material sense of truth with the notion of function. Barring aberrant contexts, the basic function of a wheel is to spin smoothly, regularly, and reliably. Of course, we may deploy such a function as a component serving the broader purpose of some device. Bicycle wheels spin to move the bicycle, gyroscope wheels spin to provide a sense of balance. But it is because a bicycle maker can depend on the spinning function of the wheel that the maker can deploy this function to serve the broader goal of locomotion; the same may be said for a gyroscope maker.

Knowledge, expressed in propositions, provides fodder for further theoretical reflection. These resources—sentences with content—are manipulated linguistically, logically, and mathematically. Theoreticians are "concept smiths," if you will, connecting, juxtaposing, generalizing, and deriving new propositional material from given propositional material. In the material world, functions are manipulated. In a spectrograph, photographic film is used to record spectral lines. In a direct-reading spectrometer, photomultiplier tubes replace photographic film. This is a functional substitution. One material truth is substituted for another that serves the same function. Photomultiplier tubes perform the function of intensity recording instead of photographic film. "Instrumenticians" are "function smiths," developing, replacing, expanding, and connecting new instrumental functions from given functions.

6. THICK AND THIN FUNCTIONS

In my analysis, a function couples purpose with the crafting of a phenomenon. A function is a purposeful phenomenon. But adding purposes adds problems. There are problems ascertaining purposes or intentions. Without access to a designer's mind or a design team's interactions, determining the intention behind some part of an instrument can be a difficult matter of reconstruction and interpretation. Reverse engineering is not an automatic process. There are problems with unintended uses. The designers of photomultiplier tubes did not intend their tubes to be used for radar jamming, but they were so used because of the "black current" they produced (see chapter 4). They also were used to check for defective fuses in grenades (White 1961, p. 143). There are problems with intended consequences based on mistaken understandings. M. S. Livingston focused his cyclotron's beam by shimming the magnet, incorrectly thinking that he was fixing irregularities in what he imagined should be a homogeneous magnetic field (see chapter 3). There are problems of unintended consequences. In the early days of word processing, the idea was to decrease, not increase, paper consumption. Football helmets were meant to decrease serious injury. Unfortunately, despite the best intentions, things frequently "bite back" (Tenner 1996).

Function also has a normative dimension, which adds another set of difficulties. In certain respects, the direct-reading spectrometer was better at determining elemental concentrations in samples of metal. It was quicker than photographic spectroscopy or wet chemical methods—enough to make a major difference in the manufacture of metal. Less human labor and judgment were necessary. However, although it was more accurate for many important chemical elements, this was not the case with all of them, and it could be used to analyze only certain preselected elements. It was much more expensive. The direct-reading spectrometer changed forever the role of the chemical analyst in metal manufacture. There never is a simple "worse/better" with the kind of normative judgments involved with functions. Trade-offs are an inescapable part of work in the material world. Consequently, it is difficult to determine how normative judgments were applied in making certain choices in the development of an artifact, and it is more difficult, if, indeed, it is possible at all, to determine what normative judgments *should* be applied.

A full analysis of the role of function in design requires attention to all of these problems. Functional design, like theoretical representation, is a deeply intentional arena.[2] When we speak of the knowledge an engineer has of the artifact he or she is working with or on, we must include the engineer's understanding of the purposes of the various components to the artifact and the overall purpose of the artifact itself. Knowledge of purpose is an essential part of the subjective knowledge engineers must have to make and work with artifacts.

My aim here, however, is not an analysis of the subjective knowledge of engineers. I am concerned with the objective knowledge borne in the artifacts engineers develop and deploy. For these purposes, a "thinner" notion of function suffices. I acknowledge that functions are connected with intentions in some way. But I sidestep a detailed analysis and focus on phenomena. The epistemological work I extract from instrumental function can be accomplished by our crafting a phenomenon. Here we get the ideals of knowledge—detachment, efficacy, longevity, objectivity, and connection.

While we may draw on the concept of a function as used in biology—the function of the heart, for example, is to pump blood—for an analysis of the thicker conception of function, the thinner concept I am interested in draws on a different discipline. A mathematical function, as opposed to a biological function, is an association of values, or, to put it another way,

---

2. Research on functions and their dual aspects both as purveyors of phenomena and as material constructions of human purposes is being vigorously pursued by the "Dual Nature of Functions" program based at the University of Delft in the Netherlands.

a set of ordered pairs of values. We can talk of how "the function *produces* an output value for a given input value." We can think of a mathematical function in quasi-teleological terms: the x^2 function has the purpose of giving as output the square of a number given as input. But from a definitional, set-theoretic point of view, a function simply is a set of ordered pairs: (1, 1), (2, 4), (3, 9). . . . This is how to think about crafted material functions. What we want is a device—an artifact—that reliably associates inputs and outputs, a device that is, in a possible-world kind of way, a set of ordered pairs of inputs and outputs.

Consider the work that went into crafting photomultiplier tubes for use in a spectrometer. As it happens, the tubes were sensitive to exactly where the light struck the initial cathode. They did not instantiate a univocal set of ordered pairs, for a given input of light intensity could be associated with a spread of possible output values (see chapter 4, § 5). Jason Saunderson did not know the reason for this undesirable spread. What to do? By inserting a quartz plate between the light source and the tube's cathode, he "fuzzed" the light over the cathode. This produced a material kind of averaging, with the result that the outputs were more closely univocally tied to the inputs.

As with the other ideals I discuss earlier, material functions do not live up to their ideal mathematical counterparts. We do not have an absolutely straight horizontal line for Saunderson's fixed photomultiplier tubes (curve *c* in fig. 4.7). But this is clearly what he was aiming for: One output associated with one input.

7. JUSTIFICATION

The eliciting, stabilizing, routinizing, even black-boxing, of functions—in my mathematical sense—is hard work. Galison has documented this work of justifying material knowledge in great and fascinating detail (1987, 1997), and Hacking, Buchwald, Gooding, Latour, Pickering, and others have addressed similar points.[3]

Justification of material truths—model knowledge, working knowledge, and encapsulated knowledge—is a matter of developing and presenting material, theoretical, and experimental evidence that connects the behavior of a new material claim to knowledge with other material and linguistic claims to knowledge. In some cases, a phenomenon is sufficiently compelling on its own. Such was the case with Faraday's motor. Typically, how-

3. Hacking 1983a; Latour 1987; Gooding 1990; Buchwald 1994; Pickering 1995.

TABLE 6.1 Spectrometer/Spectrograph Calibration

Element	Chemical Analysis	Extremes, Spectrometer	Spectrograph % Standard Deviation	Spectrometer % Standard Deviation
Manganese	0.55	0.54–0.56	1.82	1.35
Silicon	0.28	0.27–0.29	1.97	2.46
Chrome	0.45	0.44–0.47	1.92	2.06
Nickel	1.69	1.68–1.71	1.85	0.79
Molybdenum	0.215	0.21–0.22	2.66	1.68

SOURCE: Vance 1949, p. 30. Reprinted by permission of the *Journal of Metals*.

ever, it is important to connect the phenomena an instrument deploys with other instrumental, experimental, and/or theoretical knowledge. This situates new working knowledge in the field of material and theoretical knowledge. Such connecting work provides depth and justification to new knowledge. Thus, in a report on the first commercial use of a direct-reading spectrometer for steel analysis, a table is included (see table 6.1).

The table shows, first, that for the five elements measured, the range of concentration readings provided by the spectrometer centers on the concentrations found by wet chemical analysis. Secondly, the table shows that for manganese, nickel, and molybdenum, the precision of the spectrometer is better than the spectrograph in terms of percentage of standard deviation. With silicon and chrome, it is the reverse. The table thus connects the behavior of the new instrument with other techniques (wet chemistry) and instruments (a spectrograph).

Work such as that reported in table 6.1 justifies the subsequent use of the new instrument. Analysts can use it with the degree of confidence justified by the data in the table. Another way of thinking about this is that such work justifies the transition to a new material form of knowledge. It ensures the appropriate kind of stability through change. The instrument is *calibrated*, relative to other material and conceptual knowledge, for its range of appropriate—trustworthy—uses.

This is the work of creating instrumental functions, material knowledge. An instrument maker has to produce, refine, and stabilize a phenomenon—working knowledge—that serves some instrumental purpose. These instrumental functions, then, can be manipulated, conjoined, combined, adapted, and modified for the overall purpose of the instrument in question. The behavior of the resulting material device, then, is connected to established apparatus, theories, and experiments. The result is growth in material knowledge.

The fact that it is hard to establish an instrumental function materially has a corollary. Where truth serves as one regulative ideal for theory construction, the regularity and dependability of a phenomenon serve for instrument construction. This is where the material sense of "true"—as opposed to out of true, as in the case of a wobbly wheel—points us in the right direction. "Material truth"—working knowledge—serves as a regulative ideal for material knowledge, just as "theoretical truth" serves as a regulative ideal for theoretical knowledge.

8. POPPER'S OBJECTIVE KNOWLEDGE

Thus far I have argued that we need to understand instruments themselves as knowledge bearers, on a par with theory. I have articulated three different kinds of knowledge borne by instruments, and I have offered several thing-centered substitute concepts for the key epistemological concepts of truth and justification. I close this chapter with a more general epistemological picture that speaks of objective knowledge, borne by, among other things, things—scientific instruments. My picture draws on Karl Popper's account of "objective knowledge" or "epistemology without a knowing subject" (Popper 1972, ch. 3). But where Popper restricts his epistemology to the "world of language, of conjectures, theories, and arguments" (ibid., p. 118), I include things.

Popper's ontology includes three distinct, largely autonomous, but interacting "worlds" (ibid., p. vii and ch. 3). The first is the material world of stones and stars—"the first world," or "world 1." Next is the world of human (or possibly animal) consciousness, of beliefs and desires—"the second world," or "world 2." Finally, Popper proposes a "third world," or "world 3," of objective knowledge. Popper's third world consists of the content of the propositions that make up the flow of scientific discourse. Each world emerges from, and is largely autonomous from, its predecessor world. Conscious states may require material instantiation, but they are not explicable in purely material terms. Objective knowledge may depend on human consciousness, for conscious humans (typically) produce knowledge, but objective knowledge is not explicable purely in mental terms.

Popper's third world may sound dubiously metaphysical, but the kinds of objects he populates it with bring it down to earth. These include "theories published in journals and books and stored in libraries; discussions of such theories; difficulties or problems pointed out in connection with such theories; and so on" (ibid., p. 73). It is not the physical marks on journal paper that Popper points to but the assertions these physical marks express.

There is an ontological issue that differentiates my epistemological picture from Popper's. It makes some sense to think of language in immaterial terms. "The proposition expressed by the sentence, 'There is no highest prime number'" surely is a candidate for an immaterial object. It is quite natural to think of propositions, ontologically, as something akin to Plato's forms. The material products of science and technology with which I am concerned most certainly are material, and the "idea of a thing" cannot be identified with the thing itself. In Popper's terms, the material creations would seem to occupy world 1. I claim they are in world 3. I conclude this chapter—in section 13—considering this ontological problem.

9. SUBJECTIVE AND OBJECTIVE REVISITED

Popper strongly criticizes those whom he calls "belief philosophers," who "studied knowledge . . . in a subjective sense—in the sense of the ordinary usage of the words 'I know'" (1972, p. 108). Such a focus, says Popper, leads to irrelevancies. Our focus should rather be on *"knowledge or thought in an objective sense,* consisting of problems, theories, and arguments as such. Knowledge in this objective sense is totally independent of anybody's claim to know; it is also independent of anybody's belief, or disposition to assent; or to assert, or to act" (ibid., pp. 108–9; emphasis in original). Imre Lakatos's rational reconstructions of scientific research programs radically extend Popper's proposal for objective epistemology (Lakatos 1970; see also Hacking 1983a, ch. 8).

I prefer a less extreme version of objective epistemology. Popper focuses on problems, theories, and arguments, the stuff that might be found preserved in libraries. In most cases, the sentences that make up these problems, theories, and arguments are connected with beliefs held at some time singly or jointly by the author(s) of the sentences. People, with their subjective beliefs, are almost always involved in one way or another with objective knowledge. Popper's example of tables of logarithms produced by machine and never used by humans (see § 10 below) is exceptional and probably related to beliefs in a second-order analysis. In many cases, the sentences preserved in libraries are one way to understand the beliefs of the actors involved. Thus, my brief reconstruction of Livingston's beliefs about the operation of his cyclotron in chapter 3 is based on the written historical record. But it goes beyond the specific sentences in the record, and Livingston's beliefs are a useful historical category on which to pin the reconstruction.

There is a similar relationship between the things we make and a complex of human capacities that include skills, know-how, the ability to visualize, and, indeed, beliefs, the nexus often referred to as "tacit knowledge." David Gooding's discussion of the work Faraday did that led up to the making of his electromagnetic motor provides insight into exactly this relationship (1990). Gooding's reconstruction of Faraday's work, using the written record to direct reenacting this work, provides valuable insight into the motor Faraday ultimately made and its relationship to Faraday's skills, know-how, and so on. Both the more objective epistemological object—Faraday's motor—and the more subjective epistemological object—Faraday's skills, know-how, and so on—provide insight into Faraday's knowledge and the knowledge borne by his work. Understanding either the subjective or objective objects helps one to understand the other.

With these concessions to critics of Popper in mind, I nonetheless agree with the thrust of Popper's push for a focus on objective epistemological objects. There are several reasons for this.

Objective epistemological objects, sentences, and things are public. In principle, they are open to examination by anyone. For this reason, they can provide insight into the more private domains of beliefs and skills. This surely is one of the reasons why work in artificial intelligence promises insight into natural intelligence. Artificial intelligence is public, open to scrutiny and manipulation in a way that natural intelligence is not. Harry Collins and Martin Kusch's theory of action presents a theory of public behaviors as a way to understand skill and know-how and our relationships with machines (Collins and Kusch 1998).

In a similar vein, historical reconstruction must depend on evidence that can be examined. For the most part, this consists of texts, although artifacts have increasingly become important. Klaus Staubermann's work presents an interesting dialectic between objective and subjective (1998). Staubermann recreated Karl Friedrich Zöllner's nineteenth-century astrophotometer, starting with the public record—both written and artifact. He made a public object and used it to rework Zöllner's experiments. The result is insight into Zöllner's skills, both in making and in using the instrument. But Staubermann's insight into this subjective epistemological object—Zöllner's skills and beliefs—was then reflected back and provided a deeper understanding of the public materials, written and artifact, that were the basis of early astrophysics.[4]

With both historical reconstruction and the contemporary construction of theory, objective epistemological objects play an essential role. While we do not have to join Popper in abandoning subjective epistemological objects, the fact that objective objects can be shared is of fundamental importance.

Objective epistemological objects are also important because they are what can qualify as scientific knowledge. Individual beliefs might at best be called "candidate claims" to scientific knowledge.[5] Individual skills might lead to reliable instruments, but in themselves, they do not qualify as scientific knowledge. It is the community that determines what scientific knowledge is, and communities have to act on public—objective—objects.

Related to this point is the fact that scientific knowledge transcends the subjective beliefs and skills of any individual. This is true in the simple sense that there is more "known" than any single person could subjectively know. But it is also true in the more complicated sense that the tools we have for making beliefs public—speaking, writing, engaging in dialogue— allow us to articulate beliefs in a way that is not possible purely subjectively. My beliefs about Livingston's cyclotron, for instance, develop and crystallize as I write about Livingston's cyclotron. Writing enables us to build more content into our beliefs, creating objective epistemological objects in the process.

A similar point can be made about the tools we have developed to work materials, which dramatically exceed the level of our skills and know-how. As I write, Bostonians are remaking their city, and cranes tower over the Boston skyline. They call it "the big dig." It is a vast project to build a tunnel under the city to remove traffic from city streets; elevated expressways will be a thing of the past.[6] Huge projects such as this, of course, involve a tremendous amount of politics. They involve selling visions of a future Boston to skeptics and those with large purses. They also involve machinery that vastly extends our skills in making things. If we want to understand the growth of our abilities to make things, we have to understand the development of our tools for doing so. The big dig is a visually and financially remarkable project. Our abilities to make tools capable of working

4. Otto Sibum's work presents a similar dialectic (Sibum 1994, 1995).
5. On this point, see Gooding 1990 and Pitt 1999.
6. On the big dig, see T. P. Hughes 1998.

at finer and finer degrees of precision, reliably mounting untold thousands of transistors into smaller and smaller integrated circuits, for example, and now engineering at the "nano-scale," is having and will have a much broader impact. Thing knowledge stands on the shoulders of giants, giant machines. Only at its peril can a materialist epistemology ignore these objective epistemological objects.

10. IS THERE AN "EMPIRICAL BASIS"?

Both theories and instruments express knowledge of aspects of the universe. Knowledge can be expressed in many different ways. Theories express knowledge through the descriptive and argumentative functions of language. Instruments express knowledge both through the representational possibilities that materials offer and through the instrumental functions they deploy. Both should be understood to populate a neo-Popperian world 3.

In some of his more striking passages Popper writes as if objective knowledge, world 3, could exist without human help. He considers the possibility of books of logarithms, produced by computer, distributed to libraries, yet never read. "Yet each of these figures [of logarithms] contains what I call 'objective knowledge'" (Popper 1972, p. 115). In my discussion of functions (§§ 5–6 above), I noted that they connect humans with the world, but I was intentionally vague about the nature and depth of this connection. I focused on a function's making up a phenomenon. Popper's possibility of knowledge entirely disconnected from a knowing subject reappears. Must an artifact be crafted by a human being to count as knowledge? And how clearly must those doing the crafting understand conceptually what they are doing? Jason Saunderson did not know why photomultiplier tube output was sensitive to precisely where light struck the tube's cathode. But he could deal with this mystery without knowing its source. Livingston clearly misunderstood what he was doing in getting his early cyclotron to work. And several of the early uses of photomultiplier tubes relied on a different conceptualization of their function from that of their designers. The "dark current" the tubes produced was, in their designers' view, noise. For others, it was useful in the generation of radar-jamming signals. What about the creations of biological evolution? Do spiderwebs bear knowledge of insect catching? Do naturally occurring phenomena bear knowledge? Does our solar system bear knowledge of gravity?

My distinction between thin and thick notions of function is connected to the distinction between objective and subjective concepts of knowledge. Subjective knowledge is closely tied to subjects and draws on a thick, intention-laden notion of knowledge. As such, it is saddled with the host of problems of intention that I have spelled out at the beginning of section 6. Objective knowledge divorces itself from subjects and requires only a thin notion of function. Popper's minimal criterion is that "in order to belong to the third world of objective knowledge, a book should—in principle, or virtually—be capable of being grasped (or deciphered, or understood, or 'known') by somebody" (Popper 1972, p. 116). Extend such a view to material artifacts and we are led down the path that leads to spiderwebs and solar systems bearing knowledge—knowledge that has never subjectively been embraced by anyone. With the development of black-boxed instrumentation and, more recently, of "expert systems," Popper's logarithmic fantasy becomes more pressing. Recently, a medical expert system was used to gauge the performance of doctors at Massachusetts General Hospital. In 3 percent of cases, doctors' orders were assessed by the expert system to be of no help; in 0.3 percent of cases, they were judged harmful.

Susan Haack, in a series of publications (1979, 1991, 1993), has taken strong issue with Popper's elimination of the knowing subject:

> I agree, of course, that our theories may have unforeseen consequences, that scientific knowledge far exceeds what is known or believed by any individual, that journals, computers, and libraries are vital for the transmission of scientific knowledge, and that the contents of journals, etc., may, for some purposes, be fruitfully studied in their own right. But, unlike Popper, I don't allow scientific knowledge to include "knowledge" *no one* ever has, had, or will have, and I won't allow epistemology to renounce its interest in the cognitive agents who devise, study, learn, transmit, test, and reject scientific theories. (Haack 1979, p. 326; emphasis in original)

Haack presents a series of carefully articulated arguments to show that humans are essential to knowledge, that Popper's talk of the autonomy of world 3 is wrong, confused, or metaphorical at best.

Of her arguments against epistemology without a knowing subject, Haack's most fundamental arguments focus on the empirical basis for putative Popperian world 3 knowledge. At some point, whatever is known must have some kind of empirical justification. Good guesses don't count as knowledge. For Popper, justification lies in critical testing. A theory in world 3 must be capable of being tested against "basic statements" that are taken as stating basic empirical truths. If accepted basic statements contradict predictions (deductions) from a theory, the theory should be abandoned (Popper 1959, [1962] 1969). Where do "basic statements" come from? According to Popper, they are adopted as a result of a kind of decision on the part of the scientific community; they are accepted as a matter of convention. Experience itself does not justify basic statements: "Experiences can motivate a decision, and hence an acceptance or rejection of a statement, but a basic statement cannot be justified by them—no more than by thumping the table" (Popper 1959, p. 105; quoted in Haack 1991, p. 371). Haack finds Popper's turn to something like "empirical truth by community decision" both surprising, given Popper's strongly held rationalism, and deeply troubling.

She argues that Popper is forced into this unsatisfactory position regarding the empirical basis for scientific knowledge by his view that nothing beyond strictly deductive arguments serves to underwrite the rationality of science. This fuels both an "anti-inductivist" argument and an "anti-psychologistic" argument against the possibility of justifying basic statements directly by experience. The anti-inductivist argument notes that a basic statement cannot simply report experience. The very terms in which a basic statement is couched already commit it to content well beyond a local empirical report. Noting, for example, that magnesium has a spectral line at 5,167 Å presupposes a load of knowledge about the decomposition of substances into elements, the stability of elemental spectra, and so on. Since such basic statements cannot be justified inductively by experience for Popper, they must instead be accepted "by convention" as according with both accepted theory and experience. The anti-psychologistic argument notes that it would be a category mistake to say that an experience can stand in any kind of logical relationship, let alone a deductive relationship, to a statement. At best, an experience can be psychologically causally related to statements. But for Popper, psychological causes are not rational justifications (Haack 1991, pp. 370–74; 1993, pp. 98–102).

Popper then opts for an epistemology rooted in a world largely divorced from human consciousness. It is a world of propositions that stand in various deductive relations to one another. Humans interact with this world, examining and articulating these propositions and their relations. But, ultimately, the empirical justification for any of the basic propositions in this world of objective knowledge is a matter of conventional choice on the part of the scientific community.

Haack is not the first to take issue with Popper on this point. She herself considers some early versions of this criticism leveled against Popper by Anthony Quinton and A. J. Ayer (Quinton 1966; Ayer 1974). She does not, however, take note of a large literature that, among other things, has concerned itself with Popper's turn to conventionalism. Imre Lakatos's essay "Falsification and the Methodology of Scientific Research Programmes" is the first important contribution to this literature (Lakatos 1970). Lakatos abandons truth in favor of the growth of scientific knowledge, what Hacking has called "a surrogate for truth" (Lakatos 1970; Hacking 1983a, ch. 8). But Lakatos characterizes knowledge in purely theoretical terms, leaving little room for advances in experimental or instrumental aspects of science. Work on the philosophy of experiment, starting with Hacking's 1983 *Representing and Intervening,* has provided a much-needed articulation of the variety of components in the creation of the empirical end of science.

Hacking's 1992 essay "The Self-Vindication of the Laboratory Sciences" reaches a conclusion that is a wonderfully developed version of Popper's "conventionalism." Hacking distinguishes fifteen basic elements in laboratory science. He groups these under three basic headings, ideas, things, and marks. Ideas include questions, background knowledge, systematic theory, topical hypotheses, and models of the apparatus. Things include the target, the source of its modification, detectors, tools, and data generators, and marks include data, data assessment, data reduction, data analysis, and interpretation (Hacking 1992, pp. 44–50). Hacking proposes that laboratory science consists of bringing these fifteen elements into "some kind of consilience" (ibid., p. 58). This is the self-vindication of laboratory science:

> We create apparatus that generates data that confirm theories; we judge apparatus by its ability to produce data that fit. There is little new in this seeming circularity except taking the material world into account. The most succinct statement of the idea, for purely intellectual operations, is Nelson Goodman's summary (1983 p. 64) of how we "justify" both deduction and induction: "A rule is amended if it yields an inference we are unwilling to accept; an inference is rejected if it violates a rule that we are unwilling to amend." . . . The truth is that there is a play between theory and observation, but that is a miserly quarter-truth. There is a play between many things: data, theory, experiment, phenomenology, equipment, data processing. (ibid., pp. 54–55)

Popper brought "basic statements" taken to describe the empirical world into agreement with theoretical statements. Hacking proposes a similar kind of epistemology with many more elements.

Andrew Pickering extends the number of elements that must be brought into mutual agreement further (1995). For Pickering, all of the elements of the "cultural front" of science and technology can be "plastic resources" in establishing consilience. These include theoretical, material, natural, social, and intentional dimensions of science and technology. If one is having difficulty doing something, for example, making an instrument work in a certain context, one can change intention and stop trying to get it to work in that context (Pickering 1995, ch. 2).

Our ability to articulate exactly how the scientific community "reaches decisions" concerning what "basic statements" are taken to describe experience has come a long way from Popper's largely a priori arguments. Indeed, we would not now speak of "basic statements," but rather of "how experiments end" (Galison 1987). Haack would be right, however, to express concern over the result. We still describe the empirical basis of scientific knowledge as one plastic resource to be molded with other plastic resources to yield a coherent result: "A coherence theory of truth? No, a coherence theory of thought, action, materials and marks," Hacking says (1992, p. 58).

While I am quite comfortable thinking that much of the roughly propositional content of science and technology (what Hacking calls ideas and marks) is a plastic resource, I am less comfortable with the purported plasticity of (at least some of) the material content of science and technology. Faraday's electromagnetic motor (see chapter 1) was not a plastic resource, but an empirical anchor in a sea of theoretical confusion. Exactly how we talk about this working knowledge, from the most basic "phenomenological descriptions" to the deepest theoretical explanations, is an arena with considerable room for maneuver. But the phenomenon itself will not go away. It may turn out to be uninteresting and/or unimportant, perhaps, like the pulse glass (see chapter 3). But even that unimportant phenomenon would not go away.

Is this an empirical basis for science? No, but it is a mistake to think of science as a theoretical construction "resting on" an empirical basis. These technological creations, model knowledge, working knowledge, and encapsulated knowledge, are all equally part of scientific and technological knowledge. They interact with theoretical knowledge in numerous ways. They can stand in need of theoretical description and explanation. Usually together with theory, but sometimes alone, they can provide us with an understanding of the world. They can encapsulate theory into their functions. And, appropriately set up, they can render information about the world that speaks to other technological or theoretical creations.

I find Haack's concern about the empirical basis for epistemology without a knowing subject appropriate but incorrectly described. A fully plastic theory of consilience in science will not serve. There are differences between the theoretical resources and the material resources that need recognition. But there is no "basis" for science and technology. There are different modes of engaging the world and of understanding the world. Some of these are theoretical and some material. They interact.

Haack might be concerned with our recognition of thing knowledge. She might ask, "What justifies the conclusion that Faraday's motor is a genuine phenomenon and not a fluke?" While this is a legitimate question, its form suggests semantic ascent, "the conclusion *that*. . . ." When we treat this contrived part of the material world as a phenomenon, manipulating its parts in various functional ways—perhaps to create Barlow's star or Davenport's motor—we have already incorporated it into our toolbox of working knowledge. We are fallible, however. It could have turned out to be a fluke, not suitable for any further material manipulation, let alone replication. Polywater and N-rays come to mind (Franks 1983; Ashmore 1993). One way of thinking of our material manipulation of some bit of working knowledge is as a test of its stability and reliability. Herein lies empirical justification, but it must not be understood foundationally. All this work is part of making our thought, action, materials, and marks cohere.

11. WORDS, THINGS, AND HISTORY

There is an asymmetry in the "plasticity" of Hacking's things and ideas or marks. Things are less plastic than ideas and marks. Two examples, one from the eighteenth century, another from the twentieth, clarify the point.

James Watt is remembered for his improvements to the steam engine. He also engaged in a bitter priority dispute with Henry Cavendish over who discovered that water is not a simple substance, or element. Watt was up on the chemistry of his day, but much of what he says he is doing makes little sense by today's standards. He believed in a modified phlogiston theory. Despite this outdated way of *talking* about various substances, however, Watt was fully able to do things with these substances. His work on the steam engine harnessed the power of water, which he deployed and developed despite his erroneous theoretical views (see chapter 8 for more detail on this point).

Watt first communicated his discovery that water is not a simple substance in a letter to Joseph Priestley. "Water is composed of dephlogisticated air and phlogiston deprived of part of their latent or elementary heat," Watt writes (quoted in Muirhead 1859, p. 321). Later, in 1783, he wrote to Joseph Banks, the secretary of the Royal Society, with a recipe for making water:

> To make Water:
>   R. Of pure air and of phlogiston Q. S., or if you wish to be very exact, of pure air one part, of phlogiston, in a fluid form, two parts, by measure. Put them into a strong glass vessel, which admits of being shut quite close; mix them, fire them with the electric spark; they will explode, and throw out their elementary heat. Give that time to escape, and you will find the water, (equal in weight to the air), adhering to the sides of the vessel. Keep it in a phial close corked for use. (quoted in ibid., p. 322)

Watt described what he was doing incorrectly, but we know what reaction he was experimenting with. The "pure air" he writes of is what we now call oxygen. Phlogiston is what we now call hydrogen. Before 1778, phlogiston was supposed to be a substance that, when combined with metallic ore, produced a metal; it was also a substance that humans threw off in respiring. This stuff does not exist. But what we now call hydrogen combines with what we now call oxygen to produce water and has many of the other properties phlogiston was supposed to have had. This was the phlogiston of the "modified phlogiston theory" current in 1785 (Conant and Nash 1957, p. 110). Watt was quite able to manipulate this stuff reliably to make water. However we bring our ideas and marks into consilience with it—in terms of phlogiston and pure air or of hydrogen and oxygen—the phenomenon was reliable. Was then, still is.

Consider a more recent example from the history of artificial intelligence. In his seminal paper "Computing Machinery and Intelligence," Alan Turing seems to say that "computer thought" is the same as human thought if a computer's typewritten linguistic behavior cannot be distinguished from a human's typewritten linguistic behavior: the "Turing test." Questions about the similarity of the internal mental states of humans and the (possible) internal states of computers would thus be answerable on the basis of the external behavior of both kinds of entity. We know that humans have internal mental states, and Turing seems to say that computers have internal mental states too if their external behavior is sufficiently similar to external human behavior. Turing apparently gives us a criterion both for the reality of internal mental states of computers and for the similarity of those states to human mental states.

On the contrary, however, Turing actually rejects the question about the reality of computer thought: "The original question, 'Can machines think?' I believe to be too meaningless to deserve discussion," he says ([1950] 1981, p. 57). However, he further believed that in the near future (for Turing, within fifty years of 1950), it would be possible to construct machines that could *imitate* typewritten human language interaction to such a degree that "an average interrogator will not have more than 70 percent chance" (ibid.) of correctly distinguishing language generated by a computer from that generated by a human being. As a consequence, "the use of words and general educated opinion will have altered so much that one will be able to speak of machines thinking without expecting to be contradicted" (ibid.).

Turing sees the relationship between our talk about computer thought and our interventions with computers historically. With the emergence of a new technology (new ways of doing) comes new ways of speaking; in particular, Turing says, we shall find that it is natural to speak of computer thought. The (predicted) reliable public behavior of computers will result in an alteration in the language with which we talk about computers.

Both of these examples show our ideas being brought into consilience with our interventions in the world. But in both cases, it is our ideas that must accommodate established phenomena (Watt) or hypothesized future phenomena (Turing). Watt was able to produce a reliable phenomenon despite having a theory for the substances and interactions involved that was controversial in his day and that we now regard as wrong. As the ideas attached to these substances and their interactions changed, Watt's phenomenon remained a reliable stable phenomenon, just described differently. It would be astounding if it hadn't stayed stable, for the natural world neither understands nor responds to our descriptions of it. This is a respect in which the natural world is markedly different from the social world.

12. POPPER ON LIBRARIES AND THINGS

Early on in his essay "Epistemology without a Knowing Subject," Popper presents an argument that could seem to shed doubt on the epistemological place of thing knowledge. He has us consider two thought experiments:

> Experiment (1). All our machines and tools are destroyed, and all our subjective learning, including our subjective knowledge of machines and tools, and how to use them. But *libraries and our capacity to learn from them* survive. Clearly, after much suffering, our world may get going again.

Experiment (2). As before, . . . But this time, all libraries are destroyed also, so that our capacity to learn from books becomes useless.
If you think about these two experiments, the reality, significance,
and degree of autonomy of the third world (as well as its effects on the
second and first worlds) may perhaps become a little clearer to you.
For in the second case there will be no re-emergence of civilization for
many millennia. (Popper 1972, pp. 107–8; emphasis in original)

Popper's argument here is aimed, not at demoting the importance of
"machines and tools," but rather at urging the autonomy of his linguistically based world 3. But the fact that he mentions "machines and
tools," and that their existence, absent libraries, does not support the "re-
emergence of civilization," may seem to put their epistemological importance into question.

I have two responses to this argument of Popper's. First, as with any
thought experiment, the conclusion Popper draws from the experiment ex-
poses his conceptual commitments, not "the truth of the matter." Second,
Popper's experiments are not set up to test for the relative importance of
machines and propositions. To do this, we would need to consider an alternative pair of thought experiments, one where the machines and tools are
destroyed but the libraries remain intact, and another where the libraries
are destroyed but the machines and tools remain intact. I urge a different
conclusion—exposing my different conceptual commitments—to this alternative thought experiment.

Popper is optimistic about a civilization that has had its "material infra-
structure" destroyed, but that retains libraries and the "capacity to learn
from them." This reveals his commitment to the importance of the written
word. Nothing I have to say would question the importance of the written
word. Popper certainly is right that the preservation of libraries and our capacity to learn from them is epistemologically very important. But Popper
does not consider the importance of tools and machinery and *our capacity
to use and learn from them.* Much recent historical work has demonstrated
that the written record is not sufficient to allow us to reproduce instruments and machinery. We need to learn from the machinery and from our
collective experiences with the machinery. No matter how much we might
learn from a library, we would not be able to make a shelter unless we were
able to convert natural resources, such as trees, into appropriate components (such as boards) and join those together with appropriate tools (such
as a hammer and nails). Furthermore, our ability to make new, *better* machinery and tools depends on previously not-quite-as-good machinery and

tools. It is worth considering that in most stories of life after an apocalyptic collapse of civilization, people who can tinker with things are key to progress. If our machinery and tools and our knowledge of how to use them were destroyed, it would indeed be a long time before civilization reemerged.

Popper's two thought experiments are aimed at showing the autonomy of his world 3. Were he to consider thought experiments aimed at demonstrating the relative epistemological merits of book knowledge as opposed to material knowledge, he would have come up with two thought experiments such as these:

> Experiment 1: All our machines, tools and all our abilities to make things in the material world are destroyed. All our subjective knowledge of machines and tools (and everything else) is lost. But libraries and our capacity to learn from them survive.
> Experiment 2: All our libraries and our capacity to learn from the written word are destroyed. But our tools and machines remain, as do our abilities to use and manipulate them.

These thought experiments are much more difficult to read morals from. Indeed, it is difficult to imagine the two scenarios, given the degree to which literary and material modes of knowing interpenetrate each other; in this sense, both may be inconsistent. Both represent drastic losses.

But were I to choose, I would guess that civilization of a sort would emerge more quickly in the second case. Experiment 1 is something akin to the state of most nonhuman animals, with the added ability to read (and write, I suppose). Most nonhuman animals live in a world that is not, as the human world is, overwhelmingly populated by things of their making, a "technosphere." Yes, there is some primitive tool use, yes, birds make nests and beavers make dams. But for most nonhuman animals, most of their world is not a world of their conscious design and making. Were humans to lose our technosphere and our abilities to make things, we would be put in the position of these animals, with the added ability to read books in libraries. Could these books teach us how to make things? That depends on the degree to which this ability has been lost. If we lost our "hand-eye" coordination, I think it would be a very long time before we created anything remotely like our current civilization.

Experiment 2 is something akin to the state of many people today, according to studies of world literacy, and if one goes back in time a few hundred years, it is akin to the state of most people in "advanced societies." Widespread literacy is a relatively modern development. Again, depending on the degree to which our abilities to read and write were destroyed, it would be a long time before civilization was restored. All of our political, legal, and commercial structures would have to be recreated. If we did not have the ability to read and write because of some kind of universal brain damage, this would take a very long time. If we had these abilities, but had lost our libraries, then much would depend on human memory and determination to reestablish these structures. My guess, however, is that it would come faster than in experiment 1.

13. THE METAPHYSICS OF THING KNOWLEDGE

I close with the ontological problem thing knowledge poses. Popper's world 3 is not a domain of things. For Popper, our material creations are world 1 applications of world 3 theories: "It cannot seriously be denied that the third world of mathematical and scientific theories exerts an immense influence upon the first world. It does so, for instance, through the intervention of technologists who effect changes in the first world by applying certain consequences of these theories" (Popper 1972, p. 155).

Viewing the fruits of technology as applications or instantiations of theoretical knowledge will not stand historical scrutiny. Faraday's motor was not an instantiation of his theory of electromagnetism. But the alternative is perplexing. It would seem that including such world 1 objects in Popper's world 3 produces ontological confusion. One would like to know what difference there is, if any, between my world 1 / world 3 objects and regular world 1 objects.

The first thing to realize is that theories themselves require material expression. Popper himself speaks at length of libraries being the repositories of world 3. Anyone who has moved even a small collection of books knows that they are distressingly material! Popper also writes of "paper and pencil operations" in the solution of problems (e.g., the product of 777 and 111) (1972, p. 168). Paper and pencil operations are operations in the material world. Of course, Popper might say that these operations are linguistic items with world 3 meaning, what he calls "third-world structural units." They are "capable of being grasped (or deciphered, or understood, or 'known')" (ibid., p. 116). With instruments, tools and other material products of human ingenuity, it is not quite the same. They don't have meaning in the same sense that propositions do. Yet it is possible to grasp "a meaning" of a material object. Davenport did so with Henry's electromagnet; Maurice Wilkins and Rosalind Franklin did so when they saw Watson and Crick's model of DNA.

So the question remains. What distinguishes a part of world 1 that is also a part of world 3 from that which is not? What are the differences between a riverbed, a spiderweb, and the things I call thing knowledge?

First of all, I insist on these differences. Whatever the analysis of them, we can distinguish objects of human manufacture—both linguistic and material—from other natural products of life. Both can be distinguished from the products of purely physical forces. A moonscape differs from a landscape, which in turn differs from a painting of a landscape. What an art historian writes about a landscape is different yet again.[7]

Second, I recall one of Hacking's observations about phenomena: naturally occurring phenomena are rare. Before one protests that phenomena are ubiquitous—"phenomenon. 1. An occurrence, a circumstance, or a fact that is perceptible by the senses" (*American Heritage College Dictionary*, 3d ed., s.v.)—let me clarify. Hacking follows an established usage in the sciences: "A phenomenon is noteworthy. A phenomenon is discernible. A phenomenon is commonly an event or process of a certain type that occurs regularly under definite circumstances. . . . A phenomenon, for me, is something public, regular, possibly law-like, but perhaps exceptional" (Hacking 1983a, pp. 221–22). He is at pains to dissociate his use of the word from other usages where "phenomena" denotes the nearly constant ebb and flow of sensual appearances: "My use of the word 'phenomenon' is like that of the physicists. It must be kept as separate as possible from the philosophers' phenomenalism, phenomenology and private, fleeting, sense-data" (ibid., p. 222). Hacking's use of "phenomenon" allows him to draw a distinction between what William James called the "blooming, buzzing confusion" (James [1890] 1955, 1: 488) that presents itself to our senses and the ordered regularities that are the bread and butter of the natural sciences. Following James here, Hacking writes: "In nature there is just complexity, which we are remarkably able to analyze. We do so by distinguishing, in the mind, numerous different laws. We also do so, by presenting, in the laboratory, pure, isolated phenomena" (ibid., p. 226). Beyond these manufactured—pure, isolated phenomena—naturally occurring phenomena are rare: "Outside of the planets and stars and tides there

---

7. There are mixed cases, such as, for example, a managed forest reserve. But it seems to me that we shall be better equipped to deal with such cases once we have considered the less difficult cases.

are few enough phenomena in nature, waiting to be observed. . . . Every time I say that there are only so many phenomena out there in nature to be observed—60 say—someone wisely reminds me that there are some more. But even those who construct the longest lists will agree that most of the phenomena of modern physics are manufactured. . . . [T]he Faraday effect, the Hall effect, the Josephson effect—are the keys that unlock the universe. People made the keys—and perhaps the locks in which they turn" (ibid., pp. 227–28). The "expressivity" of instruments—how they are part of both world 3 and world 1—is a consequence of their making up such Hackingesque phenomena, what I call "working knowledge."

It is significant that both Hacking and Popper waffle on biological phenomena. Popper sees many biological products as akin to theories: "The tentative solutions which animals and plants incorporate into their anatomy and their behavior are biological analogs of theories" (Popper 1972, p. 145). Yet he does not include them in his world 3. Hacking writes, "Each species of plant and animal has its habits; I suppose each of those is a phenomenon. Perhaps natural history is as full of phenomena as the skies of night" (Hacking 1983a, p. 227). Yet earlier, he writes:

> It will be protested that the world is full of manifest phenomena. All sorts of pastoral remarks will be recalled. Yet these are chiefly mentioned by city-dwelling philosophers who have never reaped corn nor milked a goat in their lives. (Many of my reflections on the world's lack of phenomena derive from the early morning milkstand conversations with our goat, Medea. Years of daily study have failed to reveal any true generalization about Medea, except maybe, "She's ornery often.") (ibid., p. 227)

Hacking's and Popper's ambivalence about the putative phenomena of natural history suggests a further distinction. Thing knowledge, existing in a more refined, constructed space, exhibits greater simplicity—although perhaps less robustness—than do the adaptive living creations of natural history. Perhaps more important, our material creations, through our various acts of calibration, connecting them with one another and with what we say, have a greater depth of justification than do animal phenomena. Spiderwebs are well adapted to catch flies. But there is no connection established between this approach to catching spider food and other possible and actual approaches. We can and do connect direct-reading spectrometers with other spectrographs and with wet chemical techniques.

In the end, then, we have a material realm of thing knowledge, fallible and dynamic like Popper's world 3. A realm with objects we can think about and intervene in to change our physical surroundings—a realm that interacts with worlds 2 and 1. This is a realm where we encapsulate different kinds of knowledge—theoretical, skillful, tacit, and material—into statements, performances, and material bearers of knowledge. It is a material realm that is simultaneously an epistemological realm.

7   The Thing-y-ness of Things

> No mechanism operates perfectly—its design must make
> up for imperfections.
>
> HENRY ROWLAND

1. IDEAS AND THINGS

With Richard Ray, a civil engineer at the University of South Carolina, I
co-teach a course in the philosophy of technology. Our first assignment is
to build a bridge from Popsicle sticks and glue. It must span thirty inches,
provide for a five-inch roadbed, and support at least one pound in the center. Such an assignment, while not uncommon in engineering, is almost
unheard of in philosophy.

For most of our students who are not engineering majors—and even
for those who are—the time spent on design and analysis is much less
than that spent on construction. The major problems that students con-
front building these bridges are material: How can one glue the Popsicle
sticks together in a straight line? How can the sticks be held together while
the glue dries? How can one cope with the individual differences and irregularities in the Popsicle sticks? How should one cope with unexpected
difficulties—for example, when the sticks are not absolutely straight, or
when two (or more) structural members are trying to occupy the same
space? Building takes creativity, time, patience, and some faith that one's
design will work, even when one has less than ideal reason to think it will.
Hands get sticky. The assignment reminds students that making things is
different from thinking thoughts.

To appreciate the demands of the materialist epistemology I advocate,
one needs to appreciate the "thing-y-ness" of these knowing things. One
has to recognize the fact that things occupy space, have mass, are made of
impure materials, and are subject to dust, vibration, and heating and cooling. Things are built in "real time" and must produce their work in real
time. They must be used—safely—by humans.

In this chapter, I discuss the specifically material aspects of the development of spectrographic instrumentation in the mid twentieth century. I

start with Henry Rowland's production of diffraction gratings, and I conclude with Spectromet, a "laboratory in a box" that brought spectrographic analysis to the foundry floor in the mid 1950s. This "laboratory in a box" is an example of what is called a black box. When it is operating in place, its innards are opaque to its users, who may have little or no understanding of spectrographic analysis. Black-boxed instruments detach from their context of discovery in the manner discussed in chapter 6. Black-boxed instruments also hide their thing-y-ness. This is one of the ironies that confronts thing knowledge. Instruments, when they are working, connect seamlessly with theory; they provide information, data that can be enfolded into the propositional life of theory. This is why epistemology has been able to carry on under the illusion of knowledge solely as a play of ideas. The materiality of instruments only surfaces in their making and breaking. One needs to appreciate this essentially Heideggerian point (1977) to recognize that and to see how material knowledge complements knowledge borne by ideas.

2. JOY IN MAKING STUFF

There is another common result from the bridge assignment. Generally speaking, the students who are not engineering majors enjoy it. They may complain during the two weeks or so of gluing and waiting. But in the end they enjoy it. One student confessed that the sole reason he signed up for the course was that he had heard about the bridge assignment.

In his book *What Painting Is*, the artist and art historian James Elkins writes:

> But I know how strong the attraction of paint can be, and how wrong
> people are who assume painters merely put up with paint as a way
> to make pictures. I was a painter before I trained to be an art historian,
> and I know from experience how utterly hypnotic the act of painting
> can be, and how completely it can overwhelm the mind with its smells
> and colors and by the rhythmic motions of the brush. Having felt that,
> I knew something was wrong with the delicate dry erudition of art history, but for several years I wasn't sure how to fit words to those memories. (Elkins 1999, p. 6)

Elkins reminds us that there is a genuine human joy in making stuff. But little is written on this. Elkins notes that of the more than 8,900 books cataloged in the Library of Congress on the history, criticism, and techniques of painting, fewer than six "address paint itself, and try to explain why it has such a powerful attraction *before* it is trained to mimic some object, *before* the painting is framed, hung, sold, exhibited and interpreted" (ibid.; emphasis in original).

My father, Walter Baird, co-founded Baird Associates in 1936. The company's first important product was a grating spectrograph suitable for quantitative chemical analysis. More detail on the founding and early history of Baird Associates is given in chapter 10 (and see also D. Baird 1991). Here, I would note something my father told the *Johns Hopkins Magazine*. He said that one of the most important things he had learned as a graduate student at Hopkins was "how to work with his hands—running a lathe, learning how to build something from scratch" (R. L. 1958, p. 11). While traveling on business, he wrote John Sterner, co-founder of Baird Associates, "I want to get back. I have not loafed but I want to get my hands on things again" (W. S. Baird 1936a).

3. THE DESIGN PARADIGM

Since many engineers spend their lives engaged with the material world, one might expect the epistemology of technology and engineering to be more receptive to the importance of materials. Alas, even here epistemology focuses on ideas, not things. Walter Vincenti's terrific book *What Engineers Know and How They Know It* provides a telling case in point: "I concentrated on *ideas rather than artifacts* and sought to trace the flow of information," Vincenti says (1990, p. 10; emphasis added). There is irony here, for Vincenti documents the intimately interwoven nature of ideas and materials in terms of building and gaining experience with material models and prototypes.

Carl Mitcham, in his *Thinking Through Technology* (1994), puts the point directly: "According to a widely accepted analytic definition (which can be traced back to Plato), knowledge is justified true belief. True beliefs concerning the making and using of artifacts can be justified by appeal to skills, maxims, laws, rules, or theories, thus yielding different kinds of technology as knowledge" (Mitcham 1994, p. 194).

Mitcham has "skills, maxims, laws, rules, or theories" justifying "beliefs concerning the making and using of artifacts." This is contrary to usual usage, where evidence—experiential, observational, or experimental—justifies knowledge—maxims, laws, rules, or theories. Mitcham has gerrymandered the category of knowledge claims into the category of evidence. The only reason to do this is to avoid the material in favor of beliefs about the material. Semantic ascent is hard to resist.

But beliefs about artifacts are not artifacts themselves. I have many beliefs about artifacts. If I want to understand or, more important, if I want to use or modify the knowledge an artifact bears, I am better off attending to the material thing itself. Engineers work with thing knowledge in conjunction with propositional knowledge—frequently through the intermediaries of visualized drawings and materialized models—to accomplish their ends. Both the material and the propositional play a role, and neither is reduced to the other.

An effort must be made to avoid semantic ascent. Thus, while I wholeheartedly approve of Peter Kroes's articulation of "design" as the central element in technological knowledge, I object to his writing, "Physical constraints are factual statements about nature" (Kroes 1996, p. 63). As far as I am concerned, physical constraints should be physical. But for Kroes, "physical constraints" are a class of ideas we have about the behavior of objects: "many of them [physical constraints] find their origin in physically necessary (lawlike) relations. They are 'brute facts' about nature that are not negotiable at all; they transcend human power" (ibid., p. 63). Seeing physical constraints in semantic, potentially lawlike, terms draws our attention from the contingencies that much design is concerned with. How can more photomultiplier tubes be crammed into the small space available in a spectrometer? No doubt geometric laws are involved here. But it is the specific contingencies of what the instrument maker was trying to accomplish that play the predominant role. When we move the level of analysis to lawlike relations, we no longer see such issues, issues that in fact take up much design time. Semantic ascent distorts our understanding of design. This is one of the important lessons of the Popsicle-stick bridge assignment.

Expression in things themselves, not simply in words, must be recognized as part of design. Consider the following from Anthony F. C. Wallace's discussion of the way nineteenth-century mechanics thought:

> The kind of thinking involved in designing machine systems was unlike that of linguistic or mathematical thinking. . . . To the mechanical thinker, the grammar of the machine or mechanical system is the successive transformations of power—in quantity, kind, and direction—as it is transmitted from the power source . . . through the revolutions of the wheel, along shafts, through gears and belts, into the intricate little moving parts, the rollers and spindles and whirling threads of the machine itself. The shapes and movements of all these hundreds of parts, sequentially understood, are a long yet elegantly simple moving image

in three-dimensional space. In this mode of cognition, language is auxiliary — often so lagging an auxiliary that the parts and positions of a machine have no specific name, only a generic one, and if referred to in words, have to be described by such circumlocutions as "the 137th spindle from the left," "the lowest step of the cam," or "the upper right hand bolt on the governor housing." (Wallace 1978, p. 238)

The term "design" covers the mutual employment of the material and the propositional, as well as hybrid forms such as drawings, computer simulations, and material models. However, design must be understood to embrace material knowledge as well as ideational knowledge. The "design paradigm" is the most promising recent development in the epistemology of technology, but it must not lose track of this central insight about design.[1] Thought and design are not restricted to processes conducted in language. And working with models and prototypes is not more primitive (see Wallace as quoted in the Preface) than working with words and equations. This is a central tenet of thing knowledge, and it is the purpose of this chapter to articulate how working with things differs from working with words.

4. HENRY ROWLAND'S SCREWS

When my father realized — to his distress — that I was pursuing a doctorate in philosophy of science — and not physics — he gave me a book, *Selected Papers of Great American Physicists* (Weart 1976), which he inscribed: "To Davis, Read all — but be sure to read Henry Rowland." The book contains two articles by Rowland, his 1899 American Physical Society Presidential Address, "The Highest Aim of the Physicist," and his article "Screw" for the ninth edition of the *Encyclopædia Britannica.* I dismissed Rowland. What could screws have to do with the epistemology of science? Rowland had been R. W. Wood's predecessor in the Johns Hopkins Physics Department, and Wood had been one of my father's teachers at Hopkins. I thought my father's interest in Rowland was simply "familial."

Only several years later, alas, after my father died, did I give up my youthful, perhaps Freudian, rejection of Rowland's screws. These two articles present a powerful epistemological lesson. In "The Highest Aim," Rowland argues that "the aims of the physicist, . . . are in part purely intellectual" (Weart 1976, p. 102). In "Screw," we have an example of one

---

1. See Vincenti 1990; Bucciarelli 1994; Dym 1994; Mitcham 1994; Kroes 1998; Pitt 1999; Kroes 2000.

FIGURE 7.1 Henry Rowland and his ruling engine (from Rowland 1902)

such intellectual aim. Rowland and my father were urging me to notice something in science beyond ideas—its things.

Rowland was an expert on screws: how to make them, how to test them for various imperfections, and how to use them despite their imperfections. Rowland's expertise allowed him to rule diffraction gratings that were more than an order of magnitude larger and more accurate than any previously made. Rowland's gratings made possible the spectrochemical transformation I have written about in several chapters in this book. Spencer Weart notes that of Rowland's various scientific contributions—to electromagnetic theory, for the authoritative determination of the value of the ohm, for the variation of the specific heat of water with temperature, and for supervising work leading to the discovery of the Hall effect—his "greatest contribution to science was the construction of diffraction gratings" (1976, p. 84). Rowland's greatest contribution was thus a material achievement made possible by his expertise with screws (fig. 7.1), without which spectrographs of the requisite quantitative accuracy would not have been possible.

Rowland had a dictum, the epigraph to this chapter: "No mechanism operates perfectly—its design must make up for imperfections."[2] John

2. Strong 1984, p. 137. This is known as "Rowland's dictum."

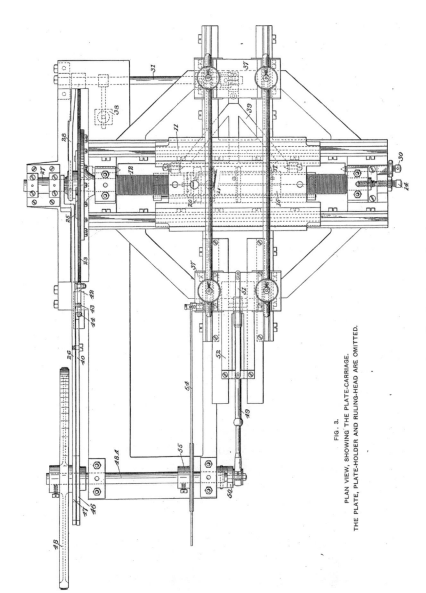

FIG. 3.
PLAN VIEW, SHOWING THE PLATE-CARRIAGE.
THE PLATE, PLATE-HOLDER AND RULING-HEAD ARE OMITTED.

FIGURE 7.2 Rowland's ruling engine blueprint (from Rowland 1902, fig. 3)

Strong, who worked with R. W. Wood, relates an example of Rowland's dictum in operation. Describing Rowland's "ruling engine" (fig. 7.2), he says:

> The grating grooves are ruled on the grating blank by repeated, straight-line strokes of a diamond point—a point guided by a carriage that spanned the blank. It is carried on a divided cross-ways; guided by one sliding shoe on the right side of a rectangular-bar . . . together with a second shoe . . . bearing on the left side of another rectangular bar, aligned and parallel.

It was suggested that the shoes might slide more easily if they were on the same side, both right or both left:

> In Rowland's arrangement, using opposite sides, the motion of the diamond midway between the two shoes becomes immune to lateral shifts due to the lubricating oil thickness, as long as variations of the oil film during the ruling stroke are equal. And the arrangement also makes the motion immune to wear. (Strong 1984, p. 137)

Rowland knew that minute variations in the thickness of lubricating oil could produce lateral shifts in the stroke of the diamond cutting head. The result would be a groove that was not straight. Since lubricating oil was necessary (a point easily missed when not thinking in terms of real materials), Rowland designed his ruling engine to compensate for this source of error.

Rowland understood that no screw is perfect, and that both in order to make a better screw (from a master screw) and to use a screw, one has to work with a screw's imperfections. Rowland's ruling engine for making diffraction gratings was an exemplar of construction compensating for error. Rowland's dictum is my first of six lessons that follow on the thing-y-ness of things. We can imagine a perfect screw, but we cannot make a perfect screw. And if we don't recognize that all material reality departs from the ideal of perfection—and design and build to compensate for this—we won't get very far. Ideas may be perfect, but reality is more interesting.

5. MOVING THE INSTRUMENT

In the 1930s, when my father first got into the spectrograph business, grating spectrographs suitable for quantitative analysis of metals required an entire light-tight room. A track, supported on massive concrete piers to eliminate vibration, followed the "Rowland circle" (see chapter 4) around

FIGURE 7.3 Spectrometry room, c. 1940 (from Harrison et al. 1948). Reprinted by permission of Pearson Education.

the room (see fig. 7.3) (Harrison et al. 1948, p. 30). In order to photograph different parts of the spectrum, the spectroscopist had to sneak around the room with a dim red light moving plates along the track. According to its co-founder, John Sterner, when I interviewed him in 1990, Baird Associates had in mind a self-contained unit that could easily be operated by people who lacked expertise in spectroscopy.

I shall skip the details that went into the design and construction of Baird Associates' first 1937 three-meter spectrograph here (see chapter 10 and D. Baird 1991). Their original instrument, minus spark gap and supports, could be fitted into a 2 ft. × 2 ft. × 12 ft. box. It could relatively eas-

FIGURE 7.4 Delivery of early Baird Associates spectrograph, c. 1940. Reprinted by permission of Thermo-ARL Inc.

ily be moved and installed in an appropriately prepared laboratory. The instrument was much easier to transport than an entire light-tight room (see fig. 7.4).

Only people with expertise in spectroscopy could use the 1937 Baird Associates spectrograph. People lacking this expertise could use the Baird/ Dow direct-reading spectrometer, first sold in 1947 (chapter 4). Although it was larger than the spectrograph, the direct-reading spectrometer was transportable and eliminated the need for developing and interpreting photographic film—spectrograms. A dark room was thus no longer necessary. Still, a special analytical laboratory was necessary to house the instrument.

Spectromet eliminated the need for a special room. Its 12 ft. × 4 ft. × 6 ft. cabinet contained all the necessary optics and electronics for a direct determination of the concentrations of elements of interest. The instrument was built to withstand and/or compensate for the conditions found on the foundry floor; temperature and humidity control was not necessary.

While there are obvious issues concerning size reflected in this series of improvements, I want to draw attention to transportation here. (I return to size below.) My second lesson on the thing-y-ness of things is that transportation is a serious obstacle to dispersion and progress. The instrumentation revolution required the development of instruments that could be built and easily transported to the site where they would be used. Smaller is better, because smaller can be moved. This is not simply an "external" issue about technology transfer. It is about expanding the reach of what Bruno Latour calls "technoscience," writing of expanding networks of technoscientific data production, consumption, and distribution (1987, p. 250). While I don't go along with Latour's notion that these networks are made of paper, I am persuaded by his concept of the expanding domains of technology and science. Transportation is central to this expansion, and it is central to the encapsulation, detachment, and use of material knowledge.

6. MATERIALS

Improvements in materials and their manipulation have been key to the progress of spectrochemical instrumentation. These improvements have neither been directed by theory nor directly promoted theoretical work. They lead to improvements in instruments, which in some cases have been essential for an instrument's success. Indirectly, an instrument's success will bear on various theoretical concerns. Direct engagement with materials, however, is one component of progress in our knowledge of the world—whether borne by things, ideas, or both.

R. W. Wood experimented with controlling the shape of the groove cut in a grating. By suitably modifying the "attack" of the diamond cutting head in the ruling engine, he was able to rule gratings with a different cross-section for the shape of the groove. Recall from chapter 4 that, as a result of the interference pattern produced by a diffraction grating, various "order images" (1st, 2d, 3d, etc.) of the entrance slit are focused on the Rowland circle (see fig. 4.1). The higher-order images are further from the central image of the slit. Depending on a variety of factors—the size of the spectrometer and the consequent range of the spectrum that can be brought into focus at one time, overlapping slit images of different elements, etc.—some order images can be more useful than others. Wood's innovation allowed him to rule gratings that would "throw" most of the light into a particular order image.[3] Thus, if one wanted to use the first-order images for analytical work, one could use a grating that threw as much as 80 percent of the light into the first-order image. This made identification of important spectral lines easier, both because different-order

---

3. See Wood 1911, 1912, 1935, 1944.

images are harder to confuse and because light intensity is channeled into working portions of the spectra.

In 1935, John Strong, also at Hopkins, showed how to make gratings on "blanks" of a thin layer of aluminum evaporated onto a glass surface (Strong 1936a, 1936b; see also Wood 1935). This greatly increased the reflectivity of the surface. Prior to this time, most gratings had been ruled on speculum metal, an alloy that can be brilliantly polished but that does not reflect light well in the far ultraviolet region of the spectrum (2,000–3,000 Å). A grating ruled on speculum metal reflected less than 10 percent of the light in the far ultraviolet—a region that was important for metal analysis. Strong's new surfaces, in contrast, reflected more than 80 percent of the light in the far ultraviolet (Harrison 1938a, p. 34).

In chapter 4, I describe several difficulties Saunderson and his team had to cope with to make a direct-reading spectrometer. Two further difficulties specifically with materials—condensers and wire—are worth mentioning here.

The direct-reading spectrometer needed good condensers to accumulate the charge received by the photomultiplier tubes. The best commercially available condensers were not good enough; they retained 0.4 percent of their charge between runs (Saunderson et al. 1945, p. 690). Saunderson's team therefore developed a new condenser with a dielectric of polystyrene, a material invented in 1930 by I. G. Farben in Germany and produced in the United States by Dow Chemical. Polystyrene turned out to be ideal for their purposes. Condensers made with a polystyrene dielectric were an order of magnitude better, retaining only 0.02 percent of their charge between runs (ibid., p. 690). Polystyrene condensers also leaked less charge than other commercially available condensers. In one test, a condenser with a 0.001-inch-thick polystyrene dielectric was charged to 135 volts; over a period of seventy-five days, it lost only 0.45 volts (Matheson and Saunderson 1952, p. 547).[4]

Eugene Peterson, one of the trio, with Victor Caldecourt and Jason Saunderson, who built the spectrometer, remembered one lesson they had learned the hard way. In a 1997 letter to me, he wrote:

> We made some mistakes in using what was at hand. We used some experimental insulated wire which had been made to check out a Dow plastic for such use. It was excellent wire but the copper was solid, not

---

4. Polystyrene turned out to be a very important material for electronics; Matheson and Saunderson 1952 provides a nice discussion of the extent and importance of its uses.

stranded. In those locations where parts received even slight mechanical stress, the solder joints eventually cracked. Little by little we replaced the solid wire with stranded.

One is inclined to think that, considered from the level of ideas, wire is wire—that line on the circuit diagram that connects one component with another. But because real wire is used in real situations where there are real mechanical stresses (however slight), the actual material performing the function matters a great deal. Stranded wire works reliably; solid does not.

My third lesson on the thing-y-ness of things is that the specific behavior of the materials used in instrument construction is essential to instrumental success. This behavior cannot (usually) be predicted on the basis of theory. This is why the instrument cookbooks I describe in chapter 3 are valuable. One must engage with materials to make thing knowledge. Learning to control groove shape and how to evaporate aluminum onto glass blanks, among many material innovations, was central to the development of spectrochemistry. Saunderson et al. needed a condenser that did not retain charge when discharged. From the standpoint of ideas, when a condenser is discharged, its charge is removed. From the standpoint of materials, its charge is *largely* removed. The difference between success and failure of the direct-reading spectrometer was determined by the ability of its inventors to find a material for the condenser dielectric that reduced this distance between reality and ideality. The difference between solid and stranded wire makes the same point, perhaps in more prosaic terms.

7. SPACE AND TIME

In 1947, Baird Associates negotiated a license with Dow to manufacture and market a modified version of the Saunderson direct reader. As Baird Associates worked to modify the Dow direct reader into a commercially viable instrument, a problem of space developed. One photomultiplier tube is needed for each element to be analyzed. How could so many tubes be fitted into the space available? (To get a feel for this problem see fig. 4.6.) Much later, my father described the situation:

> The problem was to record more elements from a single exposure. We had accomplished five, six, seven. Now, how to do more?
>
> The original photomultiplier tubes were about the size of a jar of jam. On the way back [from Dow Chemical in Midland, Michigan, to Baird Associates in Cambridge, Massachusetts] we took a plane, private, to get on a train for Boston. We had Drawing Room A. My friend, H. M. O'Bryan, thought I had the money. I thought he had. No money!!

FIGURE 7.5 Baird-Atomic photomultiplier tube rack, c. 1960. Reprinted by permission of Thermo-ARL Inc.

> We ended selling the side bench (Drawing Room A) to a chap who needed sleep for the price of the whole room.
> But the moral of the story. We invented the way to turn photomultipliers upside down, doubling the number of receivers. Our record, under considerable duress, some years later, was sixty plus—about the limit. (W. S. Baird 1979, p. 14)

Unable to sleep on the train, Henry O'Bryan and my father solved a space problem (see fig. 7.5).

The trajectory of spectrochemical instrumentation has been a steady decrease in size, from entire light-tight rooms to self-contained laboratories. It also has been a steady decrease in the time necessary for analysis. Wet chemistry took too long for useful prophylactic quality control. Spectrographs cut the necessary time to under an hour, tantalizingly close to something useful in controlling the melt, but even half an hour was still too long, both because keeping a pot of molten metal sitting around waiting for the lab report was expensive and because the constituents in the melt were still changing during the waiting period. Direct reading held the promise of useful quality control.

By bringing the time for analysis down to the order of minutes, Saunderson et al. pushed the time bottleneck outside the instrument. Now the problem was getting the sample from the melt to the instrument and getting the information from the instrument back to the foundry floor. Consequently, even before Saunderson and his team had successfully demonstrated their direct reader, Dow went ahead and built an air-conditioned analytical laboratory to house the instrument in the basement under the foundry. The lab was connected with the foundry floor by pneumatic tubes. Here was the solution to the time problem. With the development of Spectromet, the instrument could be brought right to the foundry floor, saving yet more time.

My fourth lesson on the thing-y-ness of things recalls modern philosophy's distinction between mind and matter. Matter is extended, and the manner in which material objects are extended in space—their "figure"—can pose significant constraints on design. Jam-jar geometry matters. Time also matters. Ideas may or may not be timeless. Metal alloy, in its molten state, certainly is not. Time very much matters in its production. Time and space are important in work with things in a way significantly different than in work with ideas.

8. SAFETY AND ERGONOMICS

The original spectrograph built by Baird Associates was dangerous. The electrode, where samples were sparked—brought to luminescence by a high voltage differential—was dangerous. In the first place, workers could slip and get parts of their bodies sparked. In the second place, these sparks produced stray ultraviolet light, which can burn an operator's eyes. Note the sunburn on the back of the cartoon character in figure 7.6, an early Baird Associates drawing of their wooden spectrograph. In his 1997 letter to me, Eugene Peterson recalled suffering from such eye burn after photographing the spectra of many samples of magnesium while developing the direct reader at Dow: "The effect appeared after I had gone to sleep that night, and I woke to pain in my eyes, like they were full of sand, and unable to see due to the copious tears. I was pretty scared, I can tell you, but by morning I could see again and went to work—'there was a war on.'"

Things, in their thing-y-ness, can be dangerous. They must be designed to be used safely by humans. E. Bright Wilson, in his marvelous but dated *Introduction to Scientific Research* (1952), makes a strong case for placing controls and meters—the "human interface" of the machine—in easily accessible locations. Experimenters should be able to operate the instrument easily, not simply to save time and irritation, but to allow for a clearer focus on the experiment the instrument is being used to investigate—as opposed to the instrument itself. Wilson also urges researchers to keep the parts of their instruments accessible, so that trial-and-error tuning and adjustment will not pose tremendous problems (Wilson 1952, p. 74). This is my fifth lesson on the thing-y-ness of things. When working in the me-

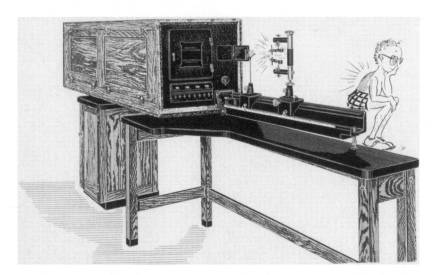

FIGURE 7.6 Drawing of Baird Associates three-meter spectrograph. Reprinted by permission of Thermo-ARL Inc.

dium of things, we have to attend to these important features at the human interface with the instrument. Safety and ergonomics are very important.

9. SPECTROMET

By 1952, Baird Associates had sold 37 BA/Dow direct readers. Unfortunately, many of them were not operating reliably, and payments were being withheld. In part to remedy this situation and in part to further develop this line of their business, Baird Associates induced Jason Saunderson to leave Dow Chemical and come and work for Baird Associates. Saunderson spent much of his first year on the road, visiting each malfunctioning direct reader and putting it right, "making it true."

One of the problems that he found repeatedly was misaligned optics. Part of the reason for this situation was organizational. When Saunderson arrived at Baird Associates, the Engineering Department was distinct from the Service Department. This administrative separation had an important consequence. Each instrument Baird Associates sold had to be customized; each customer had different analytical needs, and consequently each customer's instrument had to be set up to read just those spectrum lines useful for its particular analytical needs. The Engineering Department would ship an unfinished instrument to be installed and customized by the Ser-

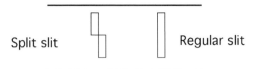

FIGURE 7.7 Diagram of a split slit

vice Department. This was unsatisfactory for several reasons. In the first place, it is much harder to accomplish optical alignment in the field. In the second place, Service personnel did not have adequate training for the job. Saunderson merged Engineering and Service, with himself as head. As he wrote in a letter to me in 1998 (also the source of the subsequent quotations in this section): "I set up the optical alignment facility in a special room, trained a man to do nothing but see to it that this all-important task was done perfectly. I issued an order that no one was to make any changes in optical alignment in the field, without my knowledge, under penalty of being fired. Unfortunately this order was carried out once."

Once the installed instruments were working again, Saunderson, prompted by a request from the Ford Motor Company, began thinking about how optical alignment could be performed automatically. Ford wanted direct readers that could sit right on the foundry floor, rather than having to be in an air-conditioned laboratory. Designing such a self-contained direct-reading spectrometer posed several problems, the major one being optical alignment. Temperature changes, which are to be expected on a foundry floor, have significant effects on optics.

Saunderson's solution to the problem of optical alignment was an automatic monitor: "Optical alignment was maintained by balancing two halves of a mercury line during the time that the instrument was idle. That is, the time just before starting to run a sample. This was done by having a servomotor rotate a 2mm thick quartz plate placed directly behind the entrance slit. This rotation produced small lateral displacements of all the spectral lines simultaneously." (See also Saunderson and DuBois 1958.) A mercury lamp, built into the instrument, would provide light for a "mercury line." This line would be focused on a special mercury exit slit and photomultiplier tube. By a clever split slit, the instrument could sense whether the optics were moving out of alignment; the servomotor would then rotate the quartz plate to compensate for any misalignment.

Saunderson's ingenious split slit works as follows. The mercury exit slit is split vertically (see fig. 7.7). The mercury lamp is also split vertically into two half-circle diodes, of which one lights on one half cycle of the 115-volt, 60-cycle supply, and the other lights on the other half cycle. The current from the photomultiplier tube behind the mercury split slit goes to a phase-sensitive amplifier that drives the servomotor controlling the rotation of the quartz plate. When aligned, both the top and bottom halves of the split slit receive the same amount of mercury light; the phases are balanced. When misaligned, however, either the top half or the bottom half (depending of the direction of misalignment) receives more light. The servosystem will detect an imbalance, and "will drive to correct the unbalance. And it will drive in one direction or the other depending upon which phase is the greater."

Saunderson well remembered the first demonstration of the automatic monitor:

> My chief assistant, Eliot DuBois, and an engineer we borrowed from Research, Bob Burleigh, did the actual work leading up to a demonstration we put on for the whole staff one afternoon. We had an optical alignment room which I had had set up in which we did all the optical alignment on massive steel "A" frames for the DRs. This involved focusing the grating and aligning all the exit slits on the proper spectral lines. So I had the staff gathered around the "A" frames in the darkened room, and I asked someone standing along side to lightly press down on the frame with their little finger. Of course this small pressure on the six inch I-beam frame displaced the spectrum lines, and the servomotor could be heard busily working to compensate. The demonstration was impressive.

The innovation, which subsequently was added to all Baird Associates direct-reading spectrometers, solved the problem of optical alignment, even under the harsh conditions of the foundry floor. The resulting instrument, dubbed "Spectromet," was a great success.

10. DETACHED BLACK BOXES

Spectromet is an example of "black-boxed" technology. I use the term "black box" not quite in the sense common in business history, where the internal workings of a business concern may be treated as a "black box" and ignored (Rosenberg 1982). Rather, I use the term with Bruno Latour's sense. In *Pandora's Hope*, Latour defines black-boxing as

> An expression from the sociology of science that refers to the way scientific and technical work is made invisible by its own success. When a machine runs efficiently, when a matter of fact is settled, one need focus only on its inputs and outputs and not on its internal complexity.

Thus, paradoxically, the more science and technology succeed, the more opaque and obscure they become. (Latour 1999, p. 304)

In one sense, this is exactly right; the internal complexity of Spectromet is invisible. Indeed, most of its users could not understand it if it were "cut open and made visible." Once built and installed, Spectromet could provide useful information for people with no understanding of its operation. Baird Associates advertising literature notes that one "regularly trained person, probably of shop origin, may operate Spectromet" (Baird Associates 1956). In the language of technology studies, the instrument de-skilled the analyst's job by encapsulating all the knowledge and skill required for spectrochemical analysis in its one-button automatic operation.

But I understand this feature of science differently than Latour. Spectromet encapsulates knowledge that can be taken to a new setting—a new foundry—and used. The knowledge used in this context is tacit in the sense that those using the instrument (typically) could not articulate the understanding of spectrochemistry they deploy in doing so. Nonetheless, they can use it. This spectrochemical knowledge has become detached. It has gone inside—inside the instrument—and can now tacitly serve other technical and scientific purposes.

Such encapsulation of knowledge into black boxes is one of the central features of the scientific instrumentation revolution. These black boxes, with their encapsulated knowledge, can detach from their context of creation to serve other technical and scientific needs. While Ralph Müller's story is perhaps overly utopian, he nonetheless was on the mark when he wrote:

Lord Kelvin once said that, "the human mind is never performing its highest function when it is doing the work of a calculating machine." The same may be said of the analyst and his chores. At present, under the compulsion of industry's pace, we are in a stage of extensive mechanization. That process cannot be stayed, however much the classical analyst bemoans the intrusion of the physicist and engineer upon our sacred domain. It is to be hoped, rather, that it will afford the analyst more time and better tools to investigate those obscure and neglected phenomena which, when developed, will be the analytical chemistry of tomorrow. (Müller 1946c, p. 30A)

The mechanization of science into detached black boxes has allowed science and technology to investigate other areas. The widely and portentously reported mapping of the human genome would not be possible without automatic methods of analysis, without knowledge encapsulated in detached black boxes. Medical technology has reached the point where few doctors understand the biophysics that produces the images with which they diagnose disease. While this situation does create the possibility (and, indeed, actuality) of misdiagnoses because of a failure to understand just how the pictures get made, there can be no question that our diagnostic capabilities are vastly improved with these new black boxes (Cohen and Baird 1999) (see chapter 10).

There is a tendency to associate the concept of black-boxing with infallibility, or perhaps inevitability. Much recent work in the sociology of science can be understood as opening up science's black boxes to show contents that are neither infallible nor inevitable. Things—quite literally "things," in the cases I focus on—could have been different. Mistakes are made. Illadvised trade-offs are accepted. Certain options may have been taken for whatever reason. Thus, it must be emphasized that my talk of "objective knowledge" and "black-boxing" does not imply that science is infallible, not subject to (material or conceptual) revision. It does not imply that things could not have been different. This is part of what it means to interact with world 3. An instrumental black box can be found wanting. Its results may not square with accepted theory; it may be less reliable than desired. It may produce data that are less precise than desired. It may cost too much. In chapter 10, I present several cases where magnetic resonance imaging equipment (MRI) has been found wanting and had to be refitted or changed.

There is one last feature of detachment that emerges from the story about the development of Spectromet. Knowledge, either in material or conceptual form, does not simply detach and "float free," going just anywhere. The original direct-reading spectrometers sold by BA encapsulated spectrochemical knowledge. In the right circumstances, they would have operated perfectly well. But they needed the right circumstances—operators who knew how to align the optics and an environment that wouldn't disturb the aligned optics. With pinched accounts receivable, BA found that these were not the circumstances in which their detached instruments found themselves. They were not working, and payments were being held back. BA therefore developed a hardier instrument capable of operating under these circumstances. But Spectromet, too, cannot be expected to work under just any conditions. Concentrations of only preselected elements can be determined. Operators have to prepare samples for the instrument. The electronics have to be checked periodically. And so forth. The reliability of detached black boxes is an open-ended process of adjusting or refining the instrument and its context of use, its niche. Adjustment happens at both ends. The instrument and its context of use are brought into mutual consilience. Bruno Latour tells just such a story as the "extension of Pasteur's laboratory to the farm" (1987, p. 249). It is also a matter of moving beyond the laboratory, an open-ended and fallible process of co-adaptation.

11. BLACK-BOXING THE MATERIAL WORLD

There is another feature of black-boxed instruments that is important for understanding the thing-y-ness of things. Latour's discussion, again, is a good place to begin. "When many elements are made to act as one, this is what I will now call a black box," he writes (1987, p. 131). All of the various elements that go into spectrochemical analysis—spectrum line choice, calibration, interpretation of output, and so on—are automated and built into Spectromet, so that the instrument can operate "as one." Of "modern machines," Latour later writes that "in the very process of their construction they disappear from sight because each part hides the other as they become darker and darker black boxes" (ibid., p. 253). Spectromet hides itself and the materiality of the world about which it provides information. The "ergonomic user interface" E. Bright Wilson advocated is yet another step on the road toward completely hiding the instrument. An instrument should be an invisible interface between its user and information about the object under study.

Another way to think about black-boxing is that the black-boxed instrument provides the interface between the material world and the world of propositions. With Spectromet, an analyst or a regularly trained "person of shop origin" directly obtains propositional knowledge of a piece of the world of interest and importance, namely, the melt: "The melt contains XYZ percent cadmium; ZXW percent calcium; etc." In order to accomplish this, all of the material aspects of the material world have to be transparently dealt with by the instrument.

Black-boxing renders the material transparent. This is my sixth and final, perhaps ironic, lesson on the thing-y-ness of things. When we black-box, we render the thing-y-ness of things invisible. In order to do this, the designers of the instrument—the black-boxers—have to recognize and work with the thing-y-ness of things. All of the previous five lessons on the thing-y-ness of things are dealt with in Spectromet's design and construction. Technical problems of size are hidden inside the cabinet. It operates in place, providing the desired information in such a manner as to be directly useful to the manufacture of metal. The distance between the perfection of ideas and the reality of materials is accommodated through careful choices of materials and compensating mechanisms such as the automatic monitor, Rowland's dictum in action. Foundry personnel could use the instrument easily and safely. "Pretty successful, I would say," Saunderson said of the instrument in his 1998 letter to me. "The performance was excellent, and the installations could be made quite rapidly." Transportation was straight-forward.

Spectromet hides the materiality of steel and the necessary material interactions to determine its qualities. The need for direct readers at Dow Chemical during World War II arose from demands on the quality of magnesium alloy used in aircraft construction. Specifically, aircraft manufacturers needed to be able to "roll out" and weld the metal easily. This material problem was solved by controlling for the percentage con-centration of calcium in the alloy. One forgets that it is actual magnesium alloy and focuses instead on a proposition about percentages. The "infor-mational shadow" of the molten alloy—"XYZ percent calcium"—substi-tutes for material reality. And Spectromet provides just such an informa-tional shadow. When the instrument directly controls these material parameters, directly intervening in the melt, we are at a further remove from the thing-y-ness of things.

We live in the "information age." Black boxes such as Spectromet sup-port this proposition, taking a sample of molten steel alloy as input and feeding us information. Forget the steel; what we want is its informational shadow. Analytical instruments have generally been widely viewed this way. The very first sentence of Bruce Pollard, Richard Papp, and Larry Tay-lor's 1994 *Instrumental Methods for Determining Elements* is: "A request for qualitative or quantitative *information* about the elemental composi-tion of a sample is common for the analytical laboratory" (p. 1; emphasis added). Similarly, the first sentence of the third edition of Howard Strobel and William Heineman's *Chemical Instrumentation: A Systematic Ap-proach* (1989) is: "A chemical measurement begins when *information* is sought about a system" (p. 1; emphasis added). So it is no surprise that two philosophers of science describe instruments in the following terms:

> Scientists naturally understand modern instruments as *information processors*. From this perspective many instruments function as com-plex systems of detecting, transforming, and processing *information* from an input event, typically an instrument/specimen interface, to some output event, typically a readout of *information*. (Rothbart and Slayden 1994, p. 29; emphasis added)

I myself, in an earlier paper, wrote of a class of instruments as "informa-tion transforming instruments" (D. Baird 1987).

In chapter 4, I discuss several reasons why we should think of instru-ments, acting in concert with the sample under study, as signal generators,

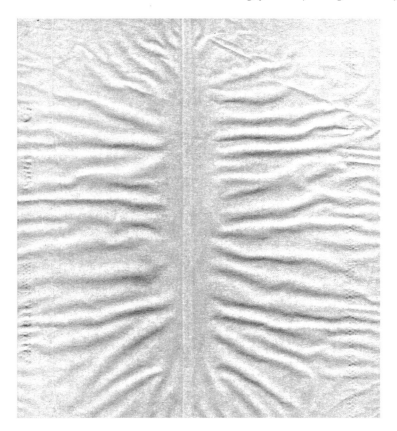

FIGURE 7.8 Scan of a Kleenex

not information processors. A century ago, James Clerk Maxwell described instruments in terms of energy, not information (Maxwell 1876). Maxwell wrote at the height of the "machine age," when the steam engine and the dynamo liberated us from natural sites for harnessing energy. The control of energy was the cutting edge of progress. Now the control of information is the cutting edge of progress. This and our black-boxed instruments make it easy to overlook the material basis that this information concerns.

As a counterpoint to this notion of the world, consider the following image from a dream I had some time ago. At various times in my life, I have been susceptible to violent allergic sneezing fits. In my dream I was faced with the problem of being in the middle of a sneezing fit, but only having a single Kleenex. What to do? In my dream, I solved the problem with a Xerox machine; I would make multiple Xeroxes of my one Kleenex (fig. 7.8).

On awakening—in a sneezing fit—I realized that when a Kleenex is needed, information is not enough. The thing-y-ness of things matters.

12. FILE TO FIT

In a 1997 letter to me, Eugene Peterson described some of the work done to develop the direct reader at Dow as follows: "The details were conceived in conversation, sketched out, and hardware generated from sketches. Sometimes we had parts fabricated by the main machine shop, but most were fabricated in the spectroscopy laboratory shop by Caldecourt and Peterson—'File to fit.'"

Working with the materials was an integral part of the creation of the instrument; design on paper was not the whole story. This is important, because things are not ideas. We shall misunderstand thing knowledge if we do not keep the thing-y-ness of things squarely in mind. Design, conceived as a play of ideas, neglects the essential role of experience—working materials—in solving the unique material contingencies that arise. Indeed, we entirely miss one draw of technology; getting one's hands on things can be a powerful incentive.

When Saunderson, Peterson, and Caldecourt were developing the direct reader, their abilities to work with materials—"file to fit"—was essential to their success. This kind of know-how is often called tacit knowledge (Polanyi 1966), but in this case it had a material outcome, the direct-reading spectrometer. This instrument is a public product; it can be shared and used by those without Saunderson et al.'s tacit know-how. It can be detached from its makers and assume a life of its own, helping in the production of magnesium alloy and the further development of spectrochemical analysis.

The significant point I wish to emphasize here is that it is as a material piece of the world that it has these epistemic functions. And, indeed, it is only through direct engagement with materials that there is any sense to Saunderson et al.'s know-how; "file to fit" requires real files and real things to fit together. Thus, understood both objectively—as a public, detached instrument—and subjectively—in terms of the interaction of hands and eyes, materials, and ideas—spectrochemical thing knowledge can be understood only with a thing-y dimension.

Finished installed instruments have a kind of concreteness that can be misleading. I emphasize their thing-y-ness as an antidote to the notion that knowledge is merely a production of mind, a play of ideas not borne in material form. But one can come away from my emphasis on the thing-y-ness of things with the idea that there is a single specific given thing—for example, *the* direct-reading spectrometer. Louis Bucciarelli rightly has emphasized the sense in which there can be no univocal *characterization* of "the thing" a group of designers are developing (1994, 2000). The mechanical engineer, focusing on mechanical concerns, sees "it" one way; the thermal engineer, focusing on thermal concerns, sees "it" a different way, and so on. There is no single "it."

Saunderson, coming to the direct reader with a background in optics, was primarily concerned with the optical aspects of the direct reader. Caldecourt was primarily concerned with the electronics. People in the magnesium foundry were concerned with how the machine might help them avoid scrapped metal. People at Baird Associates saw a fertile product line for metal production analysis generally. The direct reader was all of these "things." Which is to say, it had aspects, properties, uses, and metaphorical meanings that gave it all these different meanings. It also, and significantly, had a thing-y-ness; it was not simply an idea.

8 Between Technology and Science

> Perhaps no device, in the entire range of mechanical
> inventions, has aided so much in developing and perfecting
> the steam-engine as the indicator.
>
> STEPHEN ROPER, *The Engineer's Handy-Book* (1885)

1. THE INDICATOR DIAGRAM

My central message in this book is that our material creations bear knowledge. Sometimes this knowledge has a theoretical or propositional counterpart. But sometimes it does not; the materials bear the knowledge independently of theory or in spite of bad theory. Here material devices — thing knowledge — lead theory. This situation is not uncommon. The development of the telescope preceded any decently accurate astronomical or optical theory, and the telescope had an enormous impact on astronomy. Recognizing this kind of interaction between thing knowledge and theory promotes a different and more productive picture of the role of technology, including that developed in industry, in the development of knowledge. The material products of technology are in many cases instances of thing knowledge, and this thing knowledge can lead to the development of more refined thing and theoretical knowledge. This chapter presents such a case. Recognizing an epistemological place for the material creations of technology, then, requires us to reconfigure our understanding and approach to the history of science and technology. Together, they provide an interwoven story of the development of our knowledge of the world.

The indicator diagram, or indicator, for short, is an instrument attached to the working cylinder of a heat engine. It produces a simultaneous trace of the pressure and volume inside the cylinder as the engine runs through its cycle. It can be used to show how much work is being extracted from the heat energy run through the engine (see fig. 8.1). James Watt and his assistant John Southern invented the indicator, probably during the early months of 1796 (Hills 1989, p. 92).

The indicator was developed within the context of the theory of a substantial latent and sensible heat, or caloric. Furthermore, not until well into the 1800s were the concepts of force, energy, and work settled. Nonetheless, the indicator provided perhaps the most important source of information for improving the steam engine. With its stable repetitive phenomenon, tracing out the pressure-volume changes in a steam engine's cycle, the indicator provided an empirical foundation for Émile Clapeyron's seminal contribution to thermodynamics.

The history of the indicator illustrates several important theses about the role of thing knowledge in scientific progress. The history shows how, in spite of the combination of a subsequently abandoned theory of heat and the absence of a clear theory of work, an important and lasting instrument could be made. Furthermore, the history shows how the stable phenomenon produced by the instrument provided important information despite the lack of relevant theoretical concepts with which to theoretically interpret the information. Finally, the history shows how the stable empirical phenomenon produced by an instrument—irrespective of how this phenomenon was interpreted at the time—provided the necessary empirical foundations for fundamental theoretical speculation. This history illustrates how scientific advance can be empirically grounded even when the theories used to understand the output of the instruments are either ill-formed or mistaken.

The main historical facts of this case are well documented. Watt, along with most of the scientific world at the time, subscribed to a substantive theory of heat. The concepts of force, work, and energy were not established at the time the indicator was invented. These erroneous and confused beliefs had implications for how Watt and others understood the extraction of motive power from steam. They also had implications for how Watt understood the indicator. Finally, the indicator provided an important explanatory and simultaneously empirical framework for the development of the new science of thermodynamics.

We should not infer from this history that the substantive theory of heat or the lack of an established theory of work caused Watt or others to fundamentally misunderstand the information provided by the indicator. Watt needed the indicator to better understand the relationships between pressure, the latent and sensible heats of steam, and the work produced by a steam engine. But Watt never discovered a satisfactory theory about these relationships. His seeking such a theory, however, did not cause him to understand the information supplied by the indicator as anything other than what we would now call the work produced by his engines. Watt used the term "duty." On the other hand, there was no theoretical framework

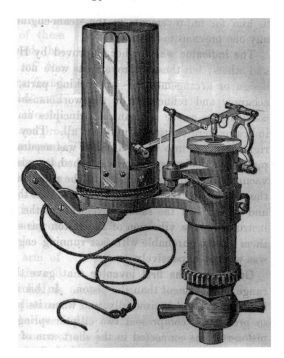

FIGURE 8.1 Thompson's improved indicator (Roper 1885, p. 251)

within which to embed this newly measured quantity, "work" or "duty." We cannot simply say that Watt's indicator measured a certain well-understood quantity—work—of a given physical system—the steam engine. Nonetheless, Watt's indicator did measure work as we now think of it, and indeed it may be that this instrument, along with Watt's persistent concern with "steam economy," helped to establish the central importance of the concept of work in the physical theory then developing. The indicator is one important example of theoretical advance being led by thing knowledge.

2. THE INDICATOR IN HINDSIGHT

As we see things now, the indicator gives a graphic display of the amount of work generated on each stroke of a heat engine.[1] The area enclosed by

1. Pressure is force per unit area, $P = F/A$, and hence force is pressure times area, $F = P \times A$. Work is the integral sum of force over a given distance, $W = \int F \, dx$. But $F = P \times A$, so $W = \int P \times A \, dx$. The area of a piston times the distance

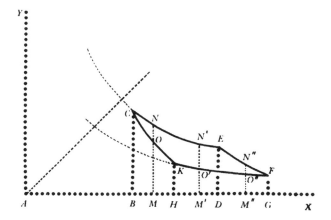

FIGURE 8.2 Émile Clapeyron's pressure-volume graph (from Mendoza 1960, p. 75). Reprinted by permission of Dover Publications, Inc.

the indicator diagram is the amount of work done on a cycle of the steam engine (fig. 8.2).

When the piston compresses the gas in a cylinder, work is done on the gas; when the gas expands in the cylinder, the gas does work on the piston. If more work is extracted when the gas expands than is spent compressing the gas, then the cycle yields a net production of usable work, or motive power. The area under the pressure-volume curve in the indicator diagram during the compression of the gas—under *F-K-C* in figure 8.2—measures the work required to compress the gas. The area under the curve during the expansion of the gas—under *C-E-F* in figure 8.2—measures the work done by the gas on the piston. The difference, which is the area enclosed by the indicator diagram curve, is the usable work extracted from the cycle of the engine.

Given such an understanding of work, force, pressure, and volume, the indicator seems a natural instrument to attach to a steam engine. Watt, however, did not have this concept of work to use. The indicator was important to Watt for two reasons. First, it provided a measure of an engine's performance that would be readily recognized in the steam engine market-

---

it moves is its change in volume, so $(A\ dx) = (dV)$. Consequently, the work done in moving a piston is the integral sum of the pressure through a given volume change, $W = \int P\ dV$. This is the area under the pressure-volume curve traced out by the indicator diagram.

place. Second, Watt believed that the pressure in the cylinder affected the ability of the latent and sensible heats in the steam to produce motive power. The indicator provided Watt with information about the pressure in the cylinder at all points during the steam engine cycle: "It was as if people could see what was actually happening to the steam inside the cylinder" (Hills 1989, p. 94). The indicator was, for Watt, a dynamic X-ray of the action of the steam in the cylinder.

3. EXPANSIVE WORKING

In 1782, Watt patented his principle of expansive working, although there is considerable evidence that he had conceived this idea as early as 1769 (Cardwell 1971, p. 52). Watt observed that he could "save steam" by refraining from admitting steam during the whole expansive phase of the engine cycle. He appended a table to his patent application showing pressures in the cylinder for each twentieth portion of the expansion stroke (fig. 8.3).

Steam was only admitted to the cylinder during the first quarter of the cycle. Then the valve was closed and no more steam was admitted. But the steam continued to expand at successively decreasing pressures until the piston was fully extended. Had steam been admitted during the entire expansion, the average pressure would have been 1. By summing all the pressures in the table and dividing by 20, Watt computed the average pressure obtained with expansive working. In this case, Watt computed an average pressure of $11.583/20 = 0.579$. While the average pressure when the steam was cut off was less than when the steam was admitted for the whole cycle, the amount of steam used was proportionally lower still. From only a quarter of the steam, Watt extracted more than half the average pressure. Expansive working is more "steam-efficient" than the then common practice of admitting steam throughout the expansion phase of the cycle.

The pressure-volume values that Watt used in this 1782 table were not obtained empirically. He assumed that pressure and volume were related according to Boyle's Law. Yet Watt knew that this law could not be supposed to be fully accurate, since it presupposed that the gas expanded at a constant temperature. Once again, as with Lawrence and the cyclotron (see chapter 3), the theory used in making an instrument was incorrect. While Watt knew Boyle's Law could not be accurate in this case, lacking any empirical data or any better theory, it was the best approximation he had. Indeed, as late as

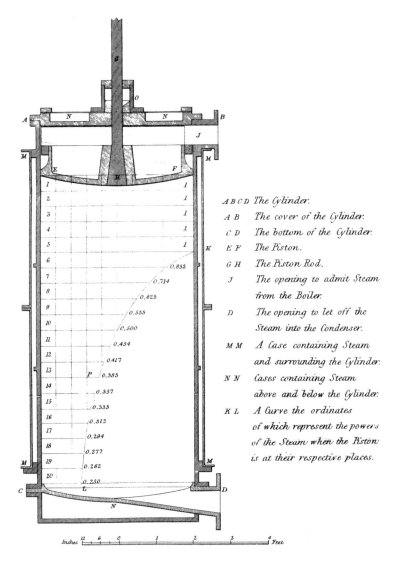

ABCD The Cylinder.
A B The cover of the Cylinder.
C D The bottom of the Cylinder.
E F The Piston.
G H The Piston Rod.
J The opening to admit Steam from the Boiler.
D The opening to let off the Steam into the Condenser.
M M A Case containing Steam and surrounding the Cylinder.
N N Cases containing Steam above and below the Cylinder.
K L A Curve the ordinates of which represent the powers of the Steam when the Piston is at their respective places.

FIGURE 8.3 Expansive working (from James Watt's 1792 patent application, reprinted in Hills 1989, p. 65). Reprinted by permission of Cambridge University Press.

1827 (forty-five years after Watt's expansive working patent), Davies Gilbert still used this incorrect approximation. In any case, Watt realized that he needed to be able to determine these pressure-volume values empirically, without the aid of the erroneous Boyle's Law. The indicator filled this need.

4. THE INDICATOR AND WORK

In an 1827 article, Gilbert reviewed the long-standing debate over how to measure work. He argued against both those who favored measuring work in terms of comparisons of inertia or momentum (mass $\times$ velocity) and those who favored measuring work in terms of *vis viva*, what we now call kinetic energy (mass $\times$ velocity^2):

> [N]either of these functions measures directly their [machine's] efficient power. The criterion of their efficiency is force multiplied by the space through which it acts ($f \times s$); and the effect which they produce, measured in the same way, has been denominated duty, a term first introduced by Mr. Watt, in ascertaining the comparative merit of steam engines. (Gilbert 1827, p. 26)

Later in the article, Gilbert showed how to use the integral calculus to determine the area under the pressure-volume curve and so to determine the duty or work performed by the engine—on the assumption of Boyle's Law. This is important, in part, because Gilbert must have performed similar computations during the 1790s while helping Jonathan Hornblower in a patent dispute against Watt and Boulton. It is for this reason that D. S. L. Cardwell credits Gilbert with being the first to understand the importance of the pressure-volume relationship (Cardwell 1971, p. 79).

Clearly, as early as 1796, Gilbert was on to the modern understanding of the work. Equally clearly, as late as 1827 in Britain, there was no established use for the concepts work, power, and energy. The indicator provided a measurement that is identical computationally to the modern concept of work. However, there was no theoretical context available in Britain at the beginning of the nineteenth century with which to understand this measurement as work as we now understand the concept. Cardwell warns of the confusion over the terms "work," "power," "moment of activity," "dynamical effect," and the like (Cardwell 1967). Peter Ewart, writing in 1813, pointed out that little progress had been made since Smeaton had written in the 1770s that "most approved writers had been liable to fall into errors in applying the doctrines of force to practical mechanics" (Ewart 1813, p. 107). Thus, Watt did not have available the theoretical concepts necessary to interpret the information supplied by the indicator diagram. As is clear from his expansive working patent, however, Watt did understand how the steam efficiency of his engines could be measured with the indicator. Indeed, in his 1813 paper, Ewart, at one time an employee of Watt and Boulton, promoted Watt's economically motivated measure of work as a measure of physical importance.

Gilbert assumed Boyle's Law in his calculations. He also mentioned several reasons why this assumption was not "strictly valid." Thus, while Gilbert perhaps had a clearer understanding of the physical importance of the average pressure exerted on a piston, he did not connect this with an empirical determination of the pressures in the cylinder at different points in the cycle. This needed an instrument.

The first detailed published description of the indicator occurs in an 1822 letter to the editor of the *Quarterly Journal of Science* signed "H. H.," which described the mechanical working of the instrument in some detail. As described, the indicator diagram consists of a board on which a sheet of paper can be mounted. The board sits on tracks, so that it can move laterally in response to the motion of the piston in and out of the cylinder. The lateral position of the board provides a measure of the volume in the cylinder. A pencil is attached to a spring-loaded pressure gauge attached to the cylinder. The vertical position of the pencil then provides a measure of the pressure in the cylinder. The line drawn by the pencil on the paper gives a simultaneous trace of the pressures and volumes attained inside the cylinder as the engine cycles. Andrew Jamieson and Stephen Roper provide nice reviews of the alternative methods for obtaining the pressure-volume trace that developed during the first half of the nineteenth century (Roper 1885, fourth part; Jamieson 1889, lecture 15).

The author of the *Quarterly Journal of Science* letter goes on to describe how to calculate the average pressure on the piston in a manner similar to Watt's expansive working patent calculation: "If this distance [the value on the pressure axis of the indicator diagram] be measured in eight or ten places, and an average taken, the simple proportion gives the pressure upon each square inch of the piston" (H. H. 1822, p. 92). Thus, instead of erroneously assuming that the gas would expand according to Boyle's Law, empirically observed pressure values could be used and greater confidence placed in the determination of the power.

The indicator provided what we now would call an "objective measure" of the action of the steam engine (see chapter 9). In contrast with the use of Boyle's Law, where we assign values based on—in fact, erroneous—theory, the indicator's information was taken directly from the source without need for interpretation by contentious theory:

> [I]t is only upon the unbiased results exhibited to our actual observation through the medium of inanimate matter, acting on known principles, that implicit confidence ought to be placed. The Indicator is an instrument of this kind; it exhibits to our view the successive changes of pressure which take place in a steam engine cylinder during each

stroke; and by also marking the duration of each particular pressure, it affords, with an elegant simplicity, a very near and correct approximation to the power exerted. (ibid., p. 91)

H. H. goes on to explain how, with the aid of the indicator, he discovered that the use of rape oil in place of neat's-foot oil caused excessive friction, slowing his steam engines and decreasing their power. The engineers who were in daily contact with his engines had failed to notice a 20 percent reduction in speed and consequent loss of power. The "inanimate" instrument, however, did not miss the change in engine operation (ibid., p. 91).

Gilbert's 1827 paper shows that the "known principles" mentioned in the passage above were not entirely understood in terms of physical theory. Nonetheless, those using the instrument were able to improve the performance of their engines. I suggest that the indicator operated "according to known principles" in the sense that the relation between efficiency and the area under the indicator diagram was easily recognized and applied, not that we had a well-understood conceptual framework with which to explain the operation of the indicator. The indicator provided a valid measurement—of exactly what, theoreticians were uncertain—but the measurement had a clear empirical meaning in terms of steam efficiency. And it was this meaning that engineers working with steam engines could understand and use to improve their engines.

Part of Watt's interest in the pressure-volume curve was motivated by his desire to compute the average, or "accumulated," pressure, and thereby the steam efficiency of his engines. However, this cannot have been the only or even the primary reason Watt developed the indicator. If this were so, little sense could be made of what little Watt published about the indicator. In order to appreciate Watt's underlying interest in the indicator, a short digression on how steam was understood to produce motive power is necessary.

5. ON LATENT HEAT AND THE MOTIVE POWER OF STEAM

In 1797, John Robison contributed an important article on the steam engine to the *Encyclopædia Britannica*. This article, along with various other scientific writings by Robison, was included in his posthumously published *System of Mechanical Philosophy* (1822). Watt edited the section of Robison's *System* dealing with the steam engine. From Watt's editorial insertions and editorial silences, we can get a good idea just what he thought was important about the indicator.

Before Robison discussed the steam engine, he discussed steam. Robison described Joseph Black's experimental discovery of latent heat: water at 212 degrees Fahrenheit can be heated with no discernible rise in the temperature. This additional "latent" heat combines with the water to form steam. Steam is a compound of latent heat and water:

> Observe, that during its [a steam bubble formed in boiling] passage up through the water, it is not changed or condensed; for the surrounding water is already so hot that the sensible or uncombined heat in it, is in equilibrium with that in the vapour, and therefore it is not disposed to absorb any of that heat which is combined as an ingredient of this vapour, *and gives it its elasticity.* (Robison 1822, 2: 11)

It is important to note that it is the latent heat that gives the steam its elasticity. Gases, and steam in particular, expand to fill the available space. In so doing, a gas can move a piston to further expand the space it occupies. The piston can also compress the gas into the cylinder. This is the elasticity of gases. From the point of view of both Watt and Robison, it was vital to understand how latent heat combined with the steam to give it its elasticity in order to understand how steam produced motion by expanding against a piston.

Virtually the first point Robison makes about the formation of steam is that its boiling point is lower at lower pressures. He discusses how pressure affects the boiling point and the relative content of latent and sensible heat in steam. He admits that it "is exceedingly difficult to make experiments of this kind. . . . It is, however, as we shall see by and by a subject of considerable practical importance in the mechanic arts" (ibid., p. 16). Robison's analysis of what was going on ultimately was seen to be unsatisfactory. Watt admits as much in his editorial comments. But the importance of the investigation is not questioned. Indeed, it is at this point in Robison's narrative that Watt inserts the footnote about the pulse glass mentioned in the first section of chapter 3.

While neither Watt nor Robison ever stated a theory that got the details right, their general approach to explaining the motive power of steam went something as follows. Motive power was derived from the elasticity of steam. This elasticity was understood to come from the combination of heat—understood as a substance—and water, which together produced the "compound" steam. Watt believed that the relative proportions of latent and sensible heat affected how much motive power the steam could produce. It is significant that Watt believed that there was a relationship between the pressure of the steam and its relative content of latent heat—and, hence, its ability to produce motive power. The need for the indicator was motivated in part by attempts to understand the conditions under which the steam was being maintained in the cylinder, and thus how motive power was produced by the steam.

Watt never achieved a fully satisfactory understanding of these relationships. At different points, he makes different and mutually contradictory statements. In 1765, he wrote in a letter to his first financial backer, John Roebuck: "That, in proportion as the sensible heat of steam increases, its latent [heat] diminishes, so, the steam engine working with pressures above 15 pounds must be more advantageous than below it; for not only the latent heat is diminished, but the steam is considerably expanded by the sensible heat, which is easily added" (quoted in Muirhead 1859, p. 161). However, he also investigated the following economizing scheme. Since water boils at lower temperatures at lower pressures, it would seem that less heat should be necessary to expand the water into steam and drive the engine. Thus, running the engine at low pressure should economize on the fuel necessary to run the engine.

Watt performed many experiments over forty years to try and better understand the relationship between the heat content and the pressure of steam, which are described in several places. They occupy a good portion of Watt's private *Notebook* on the researches he conducted between 1765 and 1814 (Robinson and McKie 1970, pp. 423–90). Watt published a description of some of his experiments in a long footnote at the beginning of Robison's section on steam (Robison 1822, 2: 5–11n). Watt also asked John Southern to perform experiments aimed at understanding the relationship between latent heat and pressure. Southern's work was published as a letter appended to Robison's article on the steam engine in his *System* (ibid., p. 168). Southern concluded that "it may be that this sum [of all sources of latent heat in the steam], together with the sensible heat, in different states of elasticity, may make a constant quantity" (ibid., p. 168). Watt added in a footnote: "I have for many years entertained a similar hypothesis: but I know of no experiment whereby the truth of it can be demonstrated conclusively" (ibid., p. 168n). The consequence of this law of constant heat would be that no economy could be achieved by operating the engine at low pressure—or at high pressure.

Cardwell insists that Robison is responsible for the persistent error of attributing Watt's discovery of the separate condenser, expansive working, and other improvements on the steam engine to his learning of Black's doctrine of latent heat (Cardwell 1971, p. 42). Robison does attribute considerable importance to Black's doctrine of latent heat in his description of how Watt came to invent the separate condenser. Watt takes issue with

Robison on this point, and in a long footnote relates his own version of how he came to this discovery (Robison 1822, 2: 113n). This is the source for the strength of Cardwell's claim. However, there can be little doubt from the construction of Robison's article, from Watt's editorial contributions to it, and from Watt's own experiments, that Watt placed great importance on understanding the nature of latent heat and its role in producing motive power from steam.

6. WATT AND ROBISON ON THE INDICATOR

The essential point is that Watt and Robison attributed the elasticity of steam to heat, which in combination with water makes steam. While they were unclear on the details, it seemed clear enough that heat, in its different forms—latent and sensible—acted differently. And, since the pressure affected the relative proportions of sensible and latent heat, it was important to have a detailed understanding of the pressure changes in the cylinder. This was why Watt wanted to "see inside the cylinder," and this is why the indicator was essential to better understand these relationships. Only read against this background do both Robison's and Watt's remarks about the indicator make sense.

After discussing experiments demonstrating that heat is the source of the elasticity of steam, and further experiments demonstrating the effect of pressure on the boiling point of water, Robison describes, in a schematic and rudimentary way, a device suitable for measuring pressure in the working cylinder of a steam engine at any point in the stroke. While Robison does not name the device, and his description is not detailed—unlike the description in the letter to the *Quarterly Journal of Science*—this is the first mention in print of what came to be known as the indicator. Robison writes: "We are informed that Messrs. Watt and Boulton have made this addition to some of their engines; and we are persuaded that, from the information which they have derived from it, they have been enabled to make the curious improvements from which they have acquired so much reputation and profit" (Robison 1822, 2: 95).

Although the indicator now serves as an instrument to measure the work output of an engine, this was not what Robison is referring to by "the information which they have derived from it." On the contrary, Robison prefaces his description of the instrument as follows: "It would be a most desirable thing to get an exact knowledge of the elasticity of the steam in the cylinder; and this is by no means difficult" (ibid., p. 95). The indicator served to help Watt and his associates understand the changes in the latent and sensible heat content—and hence the elasticity—of the steam in the cylinder. Its primary purpose was not the computation of the power produced by an engine.

At another point in his article, thirty-five pages after his description of the indicator, Robison describes Watt's principle of expansive working, showing how to compute the average, or, as Robison puts it, "the accumulated," pressure. By assuming that steam expands according to Boyle's Law, Robison obtained an analytically expressed function for the shape of the pressure-volume curve. Robison then computed the accumulated pressure by finding the area under this curve (ibid., pp. 127–30). In a footnote, Watt points out that the assumptions behind Robison's pressure-volume function have not been confirmed empirically (ibid., p. 130n). Neither Watt nor Robison mentions at any point that empirical values for pressure-volume relationship were available, thanks to the indicator.

In an appendix to Robison's article, Watt describes several important developments that Robison does not include. Among these, Watt includes a more detailed description of the indicator:

> The barometer being adapted only to ascertain the degree of exhaustion in the condenser where its variations were small, the vibrations of the mercury rendered it very difficult, if not impracticable, to ascertain the state of the exhaustion of the cylinder at the different periods of the stroke of the engine; it became therefore necessary to contrive an instrument for that purpose that should be less subject to vibration, and should show nearly the degree of exhaustion in the cylinder at all periods. The following instrument called the Indicator, is found to answer the end sufficiently. (ibid., p. 156)

Watt makes no reference here to the area of the indicator diagram, nor does he say anything about using the instrument to compute the work produced by the engine. The indicator was important to Watt because it told him what the "degree of exhaustion" was in the cylinder "at all periods."

It is perhaps important that Watt describes the output of the indicator as the "degree of exhaustion in the cylinder" and not the pressure on the piston. It is not the pressure being exerted by the steam on the piston that is important. Rather, it is just the reverse. It is the degree of exhaustion, which the piston's position causes the steam to be maintained at, that is important. This degree of exhaustion affects the relative contents of latent and sensible heats in the steam, and hence the ability of the steam to produce motive power.

Watt was motivated to develop the indicator by his belief that the pressure under which the steam was maintained affected its constitution—in terms of latent heat, sensible heat, and water. Moreover, the ability of the steam to produce motive power was somehow, although Watt did not know how, a function of the relative amounts of latent and sensible heat. The indicator provided important information about the conditions under which the steam was doing its work.

7. THE NEW SCIENCE OF THERMODYNAMICS

In his 1824 book *Réflexions sur la puissance motrice du feu et sur les machines propres à développer cette puissance* (Reflections on the Motive Power of Fire, and on Machines Fitted to Develop This Power) Sadi Carnot showed how to combine three important relationships to yield a powerful analysis of the possibilities for extracting work from heat (Mendoza 1960, pp. 1–69). Two of these are concerned with how the pressure and volume of a gas are related to its thermal properties. There is, in the first place, the pressure-volume relationship when the temperature of the gas is constant (isothermal compression and expansion), and, in the second place, the pressure-volume relationship when the heat content of the gas is constant (adiabatic compression and expansion). Finally, there is the relationship between pressure-volume changes and work, or motive power. By combining these relationships at their common point of the pressure-volume changes, Carnot could show how heat flow could produce work.

Carnot's genius was fundamentally theoretical. He managed to abstract away all of the irrelevant features of the heat engine and incorporate just those features essential for understanding how work can be extracted from heat flow. Thus, Carnot's work depended on certain theoretical assumptions. Of particular importance were, first, his assumption of a substantial (caloric) theory of heat—from which he came to the conclusion that heat flow, and not heat consumption, could produce work—and, second, his assumptions about the nature of adiabatic and isothermal relations in a gas. While there was little problem with Boyle's Law for isothermal expansion and compression, adiabatic expansion and compression were a subject of considerable confusion in 1824.

The indicator can empirically display the essence of Carnot's theory. On the one hand, it exhibits the work output in terms of pressure-volume changes. On the other hand, it exhibits the isothermal and adiabatic compression curves (assuming these conditions are met in the engine cylinder). Unfortunately, Carnot did not know of the indicator, but his fellow countryman Émile Clapeyron did (Cardwell 1971, p. 220). Ten years after Carnot's book, Clapeyron was able to use the diagram produced by an idealized heat engine and indicator to explain Carnot's theory of the heat engine both theoretically and empirically (Mendoza 1960, pp. 73–105).

Clapeyron could make use of the empirical nature of the indicator diagram to circumvent questionable assumptions about the exact nature of adiabatic compression and expansion. Clapeyron presents an idealized diagram that would be produced by an indicator attached to an ideal heat engine (see fig. 8.2).

Clapeyron determined the shape of curves *CE* and *FK* in this diagram from Boyle's Law. But there was no widely accepted law for adiabatic change. "[I]ts pressure decreases more rapidly *according to an unknown law*, which can be represented geometrically by a curve *EF*," Clapeyron writes (Mendoza 1960, p. 76; emphasis added). Since adiabatic compression and expansion behave according to an unknown law, the question arises, where did Clapeyron obtain the shape of this curve? The answer is that he has taken it—without attribution—from empirical diagrams produced by indicators (fig. 8.4).

The adiabatic curve is best seen in the chain-line, starting in the upper left-hand corner. Steam is admitted and the line is essentially horizontal. Then the valve is closed and the steam continues to expand, but at decreasing pressures. Here we have something approximating adiabatic expansion. It was from such empirical data—although almost certainly not from this particular indicator diagram—that Clapeyron would have been able to guess at the curve for the unknown law for adiabatic expansion.

Carnot found what Watt sought: the relationship between heat and work. There is something fundamentally important about Watt's two interests in the indicator. It does measure the work output of an engine, but it also shows (to the correctly prepared mind) how heat flow produces work. Watt never found a satisfactory theory for understanding how heat can produce work. But Watt did have the insight to know that the secret was hidden in the action of the indicator. Carnot found the "Rosetta stone" that allowed Clapeyron to understand the dual meaning of the indicator.

Carnot's and Clapeyron's analyses both made the mistake of assuming a substantial, caloric theory of heat. It took another sixteen years after Clapeyron's paper to sort out this erroneous idea—that heat, as a substance, is conserved—from the correct idea that energy is conserved. But the importance of the diagrams, initially produced empirically by the indi-

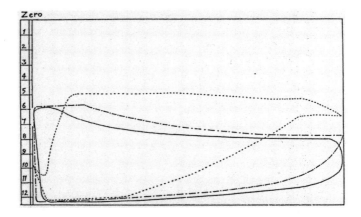

FIGURE 8.4 Graph from indicator diagram, c. 1803 (from Hills 1989, p. 93). Reprinted by permission of the Cambridge University Press.

cator and subsequently appropriated for use in the theoretical explanation of the relationship between heat and work, remained. Rudolf Clausius employed these diagrams to help state the second law of thermodynamics (Mendoza 1960, p. 118). Indeed, the initially empirical and subsequently theoretical diagram of the indicator remains the most common way to introduce the fundamental laws of thermodynamics. The reasons for this are, first, that it joins the fundamental concepts of thermodynamics—work and heat—in a simultaneous graphic display, and second, that it represents an empirical phenomenon observable in the indicator's actions with a steam engine. Thus, the fundamental conceptual relations of thermodynamics can be demonstrated simultaneously empirically and theoretically.

A subsequently discredited theory prompted Watt to seek to measure the pressure in the cylinder. The necessary conceptual framework was not at hand for understanding the meaning—in the modern sense—of the numbers produced by the indicator. Despite the theoretical confusion that surrounded the early development and use of the indicator, it clearly provided important and useful information, as the letter to the *Quarterly Journal of Science* and the epigraph to this chapter attest.

It is because of its empirical stability that the instrument could provide the background for fundamental speculations in the new science of thermodynamics. In modern terminology, the instrument is reliable—in that it provides consistent measurements—and the measurements it provides are valid—in that they do correspond to the amount of force applied through a given distance, or work. Watt would have said "duty." "Work"—

or "duty"—came to occupy a position of conceptual importance because of its relationship to the motive power extracted from engines. Clapeyron showed how to use the diagrammatic space of the indicator diagram to understand heat relationships by considering isothermal and adiabatic pressure-volume curves. Thus, the empirical regularity shown by the indicator could join the fundamental theoretical concepts of heat and work.

8. THING KNOWLEDGE, THEORETICAL PROGRESS

The indicator was developed by Watt and his associates in order to understand how to get the most from the steam used in his steam engines. One motivation for inventing the indicator diagram was Watt's belief that the pressure at which the steam was maintained affected its latent heat content and thereby affected its ability to produce motive power. Watt used the indicator to determine the conditions under which the steam was doing its work. Another motivation for the indicator diagram was Watt's need to determine the efficiency of his engines. In so doing, Watt helped to establish the importance of the concept of "duty," or "work." Despite the theoretical confusion surrounding the development and early use of the indicator, it was instrumental in promoting both material and theoretical progress.

The indicator exhibits, in a particularly clear way, the relevant properties of gases as they are compressed and expanded, heated and cooled, as they perform and absorb work. It encapsulates knowledge of this behavior of gases. As with the case discussed in chapter 4, two kinds of thing knowledge are synthetically joined in the indicator. In the first place, it presents a phenomenon, the behavior of pressure and volume in a steam engine cylinder as it goes through its cycle. The ability of the makers of the indicator to contrive this device and make it work regularly and reliably lay in how they encapsulated working knowledge of the steam engine in the instrument. At the same time, the indicator presents information. Initially, this information was understood in terms of "steam economy." The pressure and volume values taken from the indicator's behavior were understood in terms of measures of steam used and the average pressure obtained from this steam. Over the course of time, as our theoretical understanding of the concepts of work, force, and so on changed, the information provided by the indicator mutated. It became a measure of the work produced by the engine. The graphic space in which the indicator produced its diagrams encapsulated model knowledge. For Watt, it encapsulated model knowledge of steam economy. For Clapeyron and his successors, it encapsulated model knowledge of work.

What is crucial is that the indicator displays a phenomenon irrespective of the theories available for understanding that phenomenon. This allowed the indicator to survive the theoretical ignorance of its birth and promote both the material and the theoretical advances we now associate with it. This is also one way that scientific advance, at a theoretical level, can be empirically grounded despite the lack of a theory for properly understanding the signal supplied by the instrument doing the empirical grounding. The instrument presents a phenomenon; this ensures the reliability and validity of its signal, even when there is no way, or no way that is not contentious, to describe in words what the instrument is doing. That it is doing something, presenting working knowledge, is enough for it to lead to better material creations (better steam engines in the case at hand) and better theories (thermodynamics in the case at hand). This is why developing new instruments is a central goal for both technological and scientific progress. Theories come and go but a new instrumentally created phenomenon—working knowledge—endures. It can lead to better instruments—better thing knowledge—and sometimes such an enduring phenomenon can promote theoretical progress as well.

There is one final point to draw from this history. The case of the indicator provides a particularly compelling example of how knowledge—in this case thing knowledge—can flow from industry to fundamental science.[2] This is a key historiographic lesson to the material epistemology that I advocate. Knowledge moves between industry—technology, broadly speaking—and science in both directions and in both literary and material modalities. If we want to do internal history, a history of the epistemological factors that have played a role in how our knowledge of the world has developed and mutated, then we need to embrace thing knowledge. We need to embrace industry's epistemological role in the development of knowledge, both thing knowledge and theoretical knowledge.

Of course, this raises further questions: whether one wants to do internal history and whether one accepts a distinction between internal and external history. As a priori questions, I take no position on either. Because it is central to understanding knowledge, the key charge of an epistemologist, I am interested in internal history. Furthermore, I believe a distinction can

2. Brain and Wise 1999 follows the influence of the indicator diagram further to Helmholtz's work on muscle contraction.

be drawn here, although exactly how to do so is a delicate issue (D. Baird 1999). An impediment to writing internal history has been the (much-needed) rise in the study of experimentation by philosophers and historians—an impediment because experiment with a "life of its own" (Hacking 1983a, p. 150) does not directly contribute to theoretical *knowledge*. One of the goals of my materialist epistemology is to show how a focus on experiment, on the material, need not get in the way of internal history. The story of the indicator shows both that internal history needs to embrace thing knowledge and that, with the material epistemology articulated in this book, it can be done.

9 Instrumental Objectivity

[I]t is only upon the unbiased results exhibited to our actual observation through the medium of inanimate matter, acting on known principles, that implicit confidence ought to be placed.

> H. H., "Letter to the Editor: Account of a Steam-Engine Indicator"

1. MACHINE GRADING AND OBJECTIVITY

The Scholastic Aptitude Test (SAT), as developed and administered by the Educational Testing Service (ETS), is used to help implement a presumably merit-based admissions system for higher education in the United States. ETS's claim that the SAT "is an impartial and objective measure of student ability" (quoted in Crouse and Trusheim 1988, p. 5) is important. This claim to objectivity underwrites the SAT's claim to fairness. A significant component to claims for the objectivity of the SAT derives from the belief that individual exams can be accurately graded by machine. What is called "subjective human judgment" is seemingly not necessary.

Yet these claims to objectivity have not persuaded critics. In his preface to *The Reign of ETS*, Ralph Nader refers to the "patina of objectivity" that machine scoring provides (Nairn 1980, p. xi). In a scathing critique, David Owen writes: "When ETS refers to such tests as 'objective,' we seldom stop to think that the term can apply only to the mechanical grading process. There's nothing genuinely objective about a test like the SAT: it is written, compiled, keyed, and interpreted by highly subjective human beings" (Owen 1985, p. 33). Pursuing Banesh Hoffmann's (1962) line of criticism, Owen then takes several actual SAT questions and argues that it is misleading to suppose there is a single correct answer among the available choices (Owen 1985, ch. 3). Machine scoring guarantees neither that the answers the machine scores as correct are the correct answers nor that there is a unique correct answer among the available alternatives.

While Owen argues that SAT questions are not objective indicators of scholastic aptitude, he acknowledges that mechanical scoring is objective: "we seldom stop to think that the term can apply only to the mechanical grading process" (ibid., p. 33). ETS and its critics evidently agree that at least the machine-scoring part of the test is objective. In the epigraph to chapter 4, Ralph Müller presents a compelling notion of instrumental analysis. He sought methods where one would insert an unknown into an instrument, push a button, and get the answer—printed on paper if desired. For Müller, instrumental methods were objective methods. Instrumental methods of chemical analysis, like aptitude tests that can be scored by machine, present the actions of "inanimate matter" in which "implicit confidence ought to be placed" (see the epigraph to this chapter).

At the same time that Müller was articulating his "push-button" concept of instrumental objectivity for analytical chemists, Henry Chauncey was articulating a similar concept for psychometricians. From his position as the first president of ETS, Chauncey engineered the development and wide adoption of cognitive ability testing—most significantly, the SAT—as a means of decision making for admission to schools, jobs, the armed services, and so on. During the late 1940s, Chauncey worked with the Harvard psychologist Henry Murray to develop a test that would yield a more general profile of human personality than the SAT. In January 1950, he abandoned this collaboration, writing to his second-in-command at ETS:

> I personally am convinced that the laborious and subjective methods that he [Murray] uses are not going to result in . . . any effective measurement of personality traits. . . . I personally am not so much interested in obtaining an absolutely complete understanding of each individual as I am in identifying and measuring some important factors that will be useful on an actuarial basis in the prediction of success. (quoted in Lemann 1999, p. 89)

Chauncey wanted objective methods, by which he understood multiple-choice tests, graded by machines, to generate a profile of human personality. He was willing to sacrifice an "absolutely complete understanding" for a less precise outcome that would be "useful on an actuarial basis." He wanted Müller's push-button objectivity.

Objectivity is one of those concepts with generally positive connotations, but whose exact characterization proves elusive. According to the *American Heritage College Dictionary* (3d ed.), the adjective "objective" applies to that which has "actual existence or reality." "Objective observation" is "based on observable phenomena" and "uninfluenced by emotions or personal prejudices." Objectivity, it would seem, sits next to truth, or defines the right route to truth. What emerges in this chapter, however, shows a more complicated concept, a concept with a history serving various agendas through suitable shades of meaning and marriages of convenience with other concepts.

Instrumental objectivity has close ties to thing knowledge. When knowledge is borne by instruments, the actions of instruments can provide measurements that are not directly influenced by human judgment. If we see human judgment as subjective and prone to "human error" and bias, then we have a powerful moral and epistemological argument for the importance of instrumental objectivity. Müller's and Chauncey's instrumental methods of measurement are not simply cost-efficient and convenient ways to generate information about unknown chemicals or unknown intellects. They are fair and accurate. Chauncey's insistence on machine scoring, seen in the context of thing knowledge, simultaneously constitutes an epistemological and a moral demand for the objectivity of his tests. This chapter documents changes in the concept of objectivity that are tied to accepting the fact that instrumentation bears knowledge.

This is a fundamental cultural change. One can find instrumental objectivity nearly anywhere one looks in industrialized societies. Consider briefly two other examples. In 1990, then President George H. W. Bush signed legislation requiring the now familiar labels that appear on nearly all packaged foods in the United States.[1] We immediately know how many grams of fat—saturated, unsaturated, and total—each standardized serving contains. This information, brought to us by the chemical analysis of foodstuffs, promotes quick judgments about what to eat: "Seven grams of fat in that cereal? No thanks, I'll have the cereal with three grams of fat." It is as though each package of food was passed through an instrument and "the answer, printed on paper, is ours for the asking"—Müller's instrumental push-button objectivity.

Take a different example, fetal heart monitors (Hutson and Petrie 1986; Tallon 1994; Benfield 1995). Not too long ago, a fetus's progress during birth was followed with a simple stethoscope-like device called a fetoscope. These "low-tech" devices require the physical presence of the nurse, midwife, or doctor to operate. The fetoscope requires concentration, skill, patience, and a quiet environment (Benfield 1995, p. 6). Now, in many cases, a fetus's progress is followed by an electronic fetal heart monitor. These "high-tech" devices employ ultrasound technology to pick up data on the fetus's heart function. These data can be transformed into a variety of outputs, including "faux" heartbeat sounds, CRT representations of heart function, and paper printouts. Such a device can be set up so that it will only output an alarm when it "interprets" the data it picks up as a fetal

1. I am indebted to Nalini Bhushan and Stuart Rosenfeld for this example.

heart malfunction. So long as the device is properly attached to the pregnant mother, no person need be present along with mother and fetus to operate the device. Ultrasound imaging devices can present pictures of the fetus in utero. These, I have been told, are "the gold standard," a phrase that is perhaps too apt, for in addition to capturing the idea that ultrasound provides the best data on the state of the fetus, ultrasound is much more expensive (see also chapter 10 on MRI instrumentation).

2. THE IDEAL

Ultrasound, food labels, Chauncey's SAT, and Müller's instrumentation share a kind of objectivity. Information is gathered and digested by external devices—instruments—and represented in a way that promotes quick judgments. With ultrasound instrumentation, no human interpretation of fetoscope sounds is required; fetal heart monitors are not subject to misinterpretation because of a lack of skill, time, or a quiet enough room. With food labels we can—and many do—judge the quality of the food we eat from a matrix of ten or so numbers. I call this "instrumental objectivity," and I argue that the self-conscious adoption of thing knowledge—the instrumentation revolution—is central to the rise in importance of instrumental objectivity.

While ultrasound and food labels share a kind of objectivity, accuracy is another matter. Ultrasound images do provide valuable information about fetal development. However, there is no evidence that ultrasound heart monitors produce a more accurate account of the condition of a fetus's heart, and fetal heart monitors are subject to a variety of systematic sources of error (Tallon 1994, p. 187; Benfield 1995, p. 9). Moreover, no statistically significant difference in medical condition, as judged, for example, by APGAR scores, between babies delivered when a fetal heart monitor was in use and those delivered when a fetoscope was in use has been found (Benfield 1995, p. 11). It clearly is useful to have some key information about food content readily available, and yet there also is no doubt that healthy eating cannot be reduced to ten numbers. Already there is a major pitched battle over what foods get to be called "organic," presumably another dimension of healthy eating. At the same time, it is clear that many people will use these ten numbers or the "organic" label to "eat right."

Such examples could be multiplied manyfold. Think of measures of pesticides and other toxins in the water, or the numbers we use to assess the quality of teaching. The point is that we now have a model for an ideal kind of objective analysis—be it of steel alloy composition, scholastic aptitude, fetal heart condition, food quality, or whatever. We should be able to subject the object of analysis to some an instrument, the operation of which is relatively simple—ideally, push-button simple—and obtain "the answer." Of course, not everything can accommodate such an ideal, but as an ideal it serves to guide us as we develop and evaluate methods of analysis.

There are a variety of elements that make up this ideal. I argue that the two most central elements involve minimizing human judgment and cost-efficiency. Instrumental objective methods should be simple to perform—requiring minimal human judgment—and the results should be simple to interpret—again requiring minimal human judgment. Such simplicity typically comes with a cost; the instruments developed usually are expensive. But this expense can be compensated for by the ability of the instruments to perform many analyses in a given period of time. This can reduce the cost per analysis while simultaneously driving laboratories performing small numbers of analyses out of business. It homogenizes our thinking and concentrates power. It is significant that these two central elements are intertwined, because human judgment is relatively expensive: by allowing less highly trained personnel to perform analyses, objective instrumental methods decrease the labor cost of analysis.

In a nutshell, I argue that the self-conscious adoption of thing knowledge has helped promote an ideal of what objective analysis could and should be. This ideal, while variously interpreted and achieved in a very wide variety of contexts, has insinuated itself deeply into our thinking about and working in the world. Two key interdependent elements of this ideal are cost-efficiency and minimizing the role of human judgment.

The result is a profound change in the how the world "feels," in the "texture of the world" (on "texture" and "feel," see Hacking 1983b; Hacking 1987, p. 51). It is a qualitatively different experience to give birth with an array of electronic monitors. It is a qualitatively different experience to teach and be taught when student evaluations—"customer satisfaction survey instruments"—are used to evaluate teaching. It is a qualitatively different experience to make steel "by the numbers"—numbers produced by analytical instrumentation. Push-button instrumental objectivity has changed our world. In chapter 5, I used Hacking's notion of a "big revolution" to characterize the instrumentation revolution of the mid twentieth century—the advent of thing knowledge. Hacking claims that big revolutions are associated with a change in how the world feels. In this chapter, I consider how thing knowledge has changed how our world feels.

3. ANALYZING OBJECTIVITY

At its core, objectivity is supposed to be a guarantor of truth and freedom from ideology. At this most basic level of analysis, objectivity already concerns both results and methods of obtaining results. Thus, we may speak of an objective *result* because it is accurate and/or stated in a way we consider to be free of human bias; alternatively, we may speak of an objective *method* because it is specifically designed to avoid human bias in its application. Herein is a general problem. In evaluating a method, one confronts cases where the method is good, in that it will generally produce accurate results and only rarely an inaccurate one. So we can have objective methods that on occasion produce results that are not objective. The concept of objectivity is immediately susceptible to this seeming contradiction.

The conceptual analyst then requires distinctions: the result is objective in the sense that . . . ; the method is objective in the sense that . . . ; and so on. A special two-volume issue of *Annals of Scholarship* brought together fourteen articles by authors from a variety of disciplines to bring light to the various concepts of objectivity. Allan Megill, in his introduction, analyzed four basic senses of objectivity: absolute, disciplinary, dialectical, and procedural (1991). Instrumental objectivity does not easily fit into any of Megill's categories, although it comes closest to procedural objectivity. Megill writes: "Yet the governing metaphor of procedural objectivity is not visual, as in absolute objectivity: it does not offer us a 'view.' Nor does it stress action, as dialectical objectivity does. Rather, its governing metaphor is tactile, in the negative sense of 'hands off!' Its motto might well be 'untouched by human hands'" (Megill 1991, p. 310). Megill references Theodore Porter's work on objectivity in the service of statistics and public administration (Gigerenzer et al. 1989, ch. 7; Porter 1992; see also Porter 1995). As becomes evident below, there is a close relationship between statistics and instrumental objectivity.

This key epistemological concept has a history, of which I shall document a small part here. I most closely follow the work of Steve Shapin and Simon Schaffer (Shapin and Schaffer 1985) and Lorraine Daston (Daston 1988, 1991, 1992), and particularly Daston's joint work with Peter Galison (Daston and Galison 1992). These authors document a progressive removal of human judgment from—at least one kind of—objectivity. Shapin and Schaffer show how Robert Boyle sought to "let the air-pump speak"; the air pump's voice was to be preferred to the voices of people, with their various contentious metaphysical interests. Daston and Galison document how, through the nineteenth century, there was progressive removal of human judgment in the production of images used in science; mechanically produced images are more objective than those produced with the aid of human judgment and artistic skill.

I document further developments along this same trajectory. At the middle of this century, objective methods were identified with instrumental methods. At mid-century, the paradigm for analysis was to insert a sample of an unknown into a device, press a button, and have the device tell you what you wanted to know. Previously, a wide variety of "subjective" human judgments had been necessary. Has the reaction gone to completion? How does this fetal heart sound? How should we characterize this student's intellectual ability?

Conceptual analysis provides tidy descriptions free of vagueness and contradiction. But people rarely are so careful when they talk about their practices. For this reason, a concept may be used in quite inconsistent ways or in ways that conflate seemingly distinct concepts. Analytical chemists, for example, come to their work from a variety of institutional settings with a commensurate variety of concerns. Consequently, it may not be surprising that analytical chemistry, with its ties to industry, provides insight into how the concept of instrumental objectivity *in practice* ties together values frequently analyzed as distinct. These include values discussed under such headings as "de-skilling," "standardization," "black-boxing," and "cost-efficiency." Instrumental objectivity is not simply a matter of accuracy and truth. At the most basic level, as explained above, the reduction in the role of human judgment (a component of accuracy) is inextricably tied to reducing the labor costs of analysis by "de-skilling" the role of the analyst and "black-boxing" the instrument performing the analysis.

One could argue that, while it is true that the instruments developed during the 1940s and 1950s were more cost-efficient, required less skill to operate, and promoted standardization of data collection and presentation, this does not mean that they were more objective; that is a distinct question. Consequently, there is nothing to learn about the concept of objectivity from noting its—accidental—connection with these other values.

Such a point of view, however, misses a central historical point about the changing concept and practice of this kind of objectivity. I am concerned with understanding how the concept of objectivity has changed with the advent of thing knowledge. These new instrumental devices provide a "gold standard." Which devices do this? Those that remove—de-skill—

human judgment do so. Those that increase "analytical through-put" do so. Instruments that shift the expense burden away from people to hardware do so. Instruments that standardize the data do so. All of these values—and others, no doubt—must go together for the instrument to be a candidate for the "gold standard." Objective instrumentation, because it is instrumentation produced at a time when standardization and systemic interconnection are important, must accommodate all of these values. In short, it is our place in history that conflates objectivity with these other values. We may conceptually distinguish them, but doing so prevents us from understanding the concept and practice of instrumental objectivity.

I find many of the changes brought about by the advent of thing knowledge, including cost-efficiency, to be great achievements, a boon for all. The one serious concern I have is this: With the mechanization of objectivity, there has been an associated devaluing of human judgment as "merely subjective." Much human judgment, no doubt, is subjective, and very valuable and important for that. But much human judgment is objective—or should be understood as such—and it would be a great loss to devalue it.

4. "MODERN OBJECTIVITY IN ANALYSIS"

Perhaps the nicest statement of instrumental objectivity can be found in Walter Murphy's editor's column from the March 1948 issue of *Analytical Chemistry*. In the column, titled "Modern Objectivity in Analysis," Murphy presents and comments on H. V. Churchill's dinner address to the Third Annual Analytical Symposium of the Division of Analytical Chemistry.

Churchill was concerned about the proportion of material sampled when submitted to an instrumental analysis. At the time, remelting furnaces for the production of aluminum alloys had a capacity of 35,000 pounds. From this, a 60-gram sample was taken. When such a sample is submitted to spectrographic analysis, about 1 mg of material is consumed. Of the total electromagnetic radiation produced, about 30 billionths enters the spectrograph. Thus, Churchill concluded with a note of concern, the ratio of material producing sample data to the amount of material in the melt is about one in 45 quadrillion.

Murphy went on to describe Churchill's concerns as follows:

> Commenting on instrumental analysis, Mr. Churchill reminded his audience that most modern objective methods and instruments are methods and instruments for doing faster or in greater volume certain tasks

which can be done more slowly and in less volume by classical or traditional methods. Illustrating this point he reviewed a case history of one of the company's plants, where the analysis of aluminum alloys developed from the use of traditional or classical methods to a stage wherein the work was done spectrochemically—that is, by photographic spectroscopy—and finally is being done by the use of direct-reading spectrographs. The speaker reported the relative productivity of workers in these three stages of evolution has been in the ratio of 4:20:60. This is a 15-fold increase in productivity and speed in changing from subjective methods to those of increasing objectivity and with an increase in both precision and accuracy.

"Is it any wonder," said Mr. Churchill, "that some of us older chemists, who experienced some little difficulty in learning to weigh to tenths of milligrams or even as microchemists to weigh to micrograms, are a bit appalled by the brash temerity of these modern-day analytical chemists who go so far into infinitesimals? No wonder we must bolster our faith with the intricate formulas of statistical analysis, and little wonder we have an almost idolatrous faith in the laws of probability." (Murphy 1948a, p. 187)

There is a lot to unpack from this editorial. For starters, it is clear that both Churchill and Murphy identify "modern" objective methods with instrumental methods. The older, wet chemical methods are subjective.

We also learn these instrumental objective methods have yielded, in this case anyway, "a 15-fold increase in productivity and speed . . . with an increase in both precision and accuracy." It is immediately apparent that objective methods are tied up with economic ends; they involve the combination of productivity and accuracy. Churchill is worried that modern objective methods may sacrifice accuracy for productivity. The very fact that Churchill can worry that this instrumental notion of objectivity might sacrifice accuracy shows that accuracy is not essential to this concept of objectivity. This is remarkable, because separating the idea of accuracy from that of objectivity runs counter to the intuitive alignment of accuracy and objectivity. These changes tie instrumental objectivity more closely to productivity and loosen its connection with accuracy. While he grudgingly acknowledges the inevitability of the change to instrumental methods, Churchill is clearly nostalgic for older methods, perhaps for an older concept of objectivity that preserves a closer connection to accuracy.

It is also worth pointing out that these new instrumental objective methods rely on "statistical analysis . . . and an almost idolatrous faith in the laws of probability." Indeed, one of the analytical chemists at the University of South Carolina is largely concerned with improving analytical methods through a better use of statistics, currently a growth area in ana-lytical chemistry (Deming and Morgan 1987). This is interesting in its own right and even more so when we reflect on the manner in which develop-ments in statistics have had their own impact on the notion of objectivity (Porter 1986, 1992, 1995; Swijtink 1987). One of the features of the join-ing of physico-chemical—instrumental—methods with statistical analy-sis is the need to standardize. Standardization went hand in hand with the rise of statistical methods during the nineteenth century. Here is another value prominent in technology studies inserting itself into this modern no-tion of instrumental objectivity.

5. RALPH MÜLLER AS WITNESS

As noted in chapter 5, Ralph Müller began writing a regular column on in-strumentation for *Analytical Chemistry* in 1946. Müller's columns provide a detailed look at how objectivity got tied to thing knowledge. In the first place, we can find in them an explicit, articulated definition of modern ob-jective instrumental methods. In the second place, they show clearly how these developments were tied to industrial needs. And, finally, because of this connection, we can see how the technological values of black-boxing, standardization, and cost-efficiency were tied to this emerging notion of in-strumental objectivity. Müller serves as an excellent witness to changes in this notion of objectivity and the tensions that produced them.

Müller understood objective methods to be instrumental methods. Dis-cussing the use of photomultiplier tubes for the relief of eyestrain, Müller wrote: "Thus, whatever gains have been made in the mechanization of this optical procedure, such as objectivity and greater precision, the elimination of fatigue is not one of them" (Müller 1946c, p. 29A). Following Murphy's practice, "gains in . . . objectivity" referred to the use of devices external to the human to do things previously done by humans.

In this same column, Müller made a more general point about the "three Rs" of instrumentation: reading, 'riting, and 'rithmetic—indication, re-cording, and computation (see chapter 5, § 6, above). While Müller's "three Rs" provided a memorable way of thinking about instrumentation, one im-portant feature of instrumentation was left out: the use of servomecha-nisms to provide for feedback and control, both for better data gathering and for the control of materials. Müller devoted an equal portion of his "three Rs" column to servomechanisms (Müller 1946c, p. 29A). Here, instrumentation would directly intervene in its own calibration (see, e.g., chapter 7, § 9, above) and, ultimately, in the control of the materials on which measurements are being made. Müller's push-button objectivity required instruments with substitutes for "operator judgment." Instruments had to be able to calibrate themselves and interpret their data ('rithmetic!) (Müller 1947a, p. 23A). To the greatest extent possible, human involvement should be eliminated.

Despite strong reasons to develop integrated and automatic instrumentation, Müller encountered resistance. Doing so was not "real" science; at best it was applied physics:

> Recently we were taken to task by one of America's distinguished chemists for emphasizing these distinctions [between a direct-reading instrument and an instrument that provides data requiring further analysis]. "All a matter of applied physical chemistry," he explained patiently, "and therefore not particularly new." We are obtuse enough to feel that physicochemical techniques bear the same relationship to instrumental analysis as the violent oxidation of hydrocarbons does to the modern motor car. (Müller 1947a, p. 23A)

Müller's instrumental objectivity resided in the instrument, not in the principles of applied physical chemistry. The resistance Müller encountered here is tied to the classical notion that scientific knowledge is expressed in propositions, not things. Müller disagreed.

> The less sympathetic commentators on instrumentation will insist that the instrument of itself is of little importance, and what is important is the information which it provides and the proper scientific interpretation and application of the results. This is quite proper, in its way, but it has nothing to do with instrumentation. It is merely applying known principles of physics and physical chemistry, and little or nothing is learned about instrumentation. (ibid., p. 26A)

If data were all that was important, then perhaps instrumentation would not be an interesting topic on its own—except in the "instrumental sense" in which instruments produce data. However, there is a difference between knowledge understood in terms of principles and facts and knowledge understood as contrived things—Müller's instrumentation. Müller advocates the pursuit of better instrumentation as a end in itself for science—and not simply a practical end, but an epistemic end in itself. This is one way of understanding the thesis of thing knowledge.

Thing knowledge allows humans to be eliminated from the loop: automatic analysis. A 1988 text on this subject begins with the sentence "The

partial or complete replacement of human participation in laboratory processes is a growing trend that started in the 1960s and consolidated in the
next decade" (Valcárcel and Luque de Castro 1988, p. 1). Müller anticipated
this. His May 1946 column was concerned exclusively with automatic
analysis:

> We find numerous examples of distinct "bottlenecks" in analytical or
> control laboratories which have arisen from changes in manufacturing
> practice. The use of automatic controls and regulators has speeded up
> production in many cases to such an extent that the ordinary facilities
> for analysis or inspection are no longer adequate. . . . In such cases,
> automatic analysis becomes mandatory . . . A further advantage ulti-
> mately arises in this step because the "autoanalyzer" may just as well
> control the process itself. (Müller 1946e, p. 23A)

Müller continues by discussing the process of automatic analysis: "Each
final step would, of necessity, involve *objective* measurements." As he puts
it, "The primary considerations are speed, *adequate* precision, and an
equivalent for operator judgment" (ibid.; emphasis added). Objective instrumentation, as part of systems for automatic analysis and control, must
trade off cost-efficiency (in terms of initial costs, through-put, and operator expenses) against accuracy. Adequate precision, not the greatest precision available, is the trick.

While recognizing—and happily approving—the importance of the
economic concerns behind the development of much instrumentation,
Müller believed these values needed to be balanced. He sought academic research into "useless" instrumentation (Müller 1948, p. 21A; see also chapter 5, § 6, above). Left to industry alone, only immediately commercially
viable instruments would be developed. The result would be the predomi-
nance of economic values. Instrumental objectivity would have to be primarily profit making. Universities did not develop departments of instrumentation, however, and the "initiative and intelligent prosecution of
instrumental research" passed to industrial laboratories (Müller 1947a,
p. 26A).

Müller sought an amalgam of the academic and industrial. Yet the tensions between these two value systems—including the routine expectations of epistemic exchange (see chapter 10)—resisted. The entrenched
academic notion that the real goals of research are representation and truth
did not easily combine with the more thing-based goals of intervention and
the control of phenomena. Left to industry, instrumental objectivity had to
be tied to industrial values. Eric von Hippel found that 78 percent of the

sources for instrumental innovation in the 1980s came from the market for the instruments, not the makers themselves or universities, except insofar as they provided a market (Hippel 1988).

In November 1959, *Analytical Chemistry* ran an article by Van Zandt Williams, executive vice-president of Perkin-Elmer, a major analytical instrumentation company. Williams was concerned about the lack of cooperation between analytical chemists and instrument manufacturers. He emphasized the urgent need in industry for more efficient methods of analysis: "[T]he lack of chemical analytical instrumentation—particularly automatic, direct concentration readout, chemical analytical instrumentation—may well be a limitation on progress in the chemical industry today" (V. Z. Williams 1959, p. 25A). Progress was held up by a lack of cooperation between analytical chemist and instrument maker:

> One point of conflict is in the term "wide sales." The major factor limiting an instrument company's growth and profit potential is its development and engineering capacity. Within our own definitions, we aim to get $5 of profit before taxes for each instrument engineering dollar spent. . . . In general we cannot do a profitable business making instruments for only one company's needs, because the number would be too small to warrant the development expense. (ibid., p. 31A)

Instrument manufacturers didn't know what analytical chemists needed by way of instrumentation, and analytical chemists didn't know what instrument makers needed by way of profits. Significantly—and obviously—instrument makers had to make a profit on their instruments. This required them to pursue instrument development where a significant market was foreseeable—"wide sales." Müller's "useless" research, aimed at increasing our understanding of the world through instrumentation, was not the business of instrument makers or industrial analysts with specific analytical needs.

Müller's editorials teach us several lessons about the advent of instrumental objectivity. We learn how objectivity came to be understood instrumentally, and that the best instrumental objective methods were automatic methods. There was a strong economic need in industry for more efficient methods of analysis. Despite Müller's pleas, a science of instrumentation with its own academic departments did not develop in the university setting. In the commercial setting, economic values could not be separated from other desirable values in developing new analytical instruments. In short, instrumental objectivity came to incorporate values from the marketplace.

FIGURE 9.1 Baird Associates direct-reading spectrometer advertisement, inside, c. 1954. Reprinted by permission of Thermo-ARL, Inc.

6. PUSH-BUTTON SPECTROMETRY

The nicest possible summary of the transformation in instrumentation and objectivity can be found in a 1959 Baird-Atomic[2] advertisement that compares analytical methods—wet chemistry, spectrographic methods, and direct-reading spectrometry—with an iconic summary of each approach (fig. 9.1). As with any effective ad, the visual point is made quickly and clearly: wet chemical analysis takes more steps than spectrographic analysis, which itself takes more steps than spectrometric analysis using a direct-reading spectrometer. Furthermore, the steps involved are easier with spectrographic methods than with wet chemical analysis, and easier still with spectrometric methods.

A reading of the legend behind the icons reveals more. Three icons are involved, a finger pushing a button, a contented face, and an intensely concentrated face. For the finger and button, we are told, "Indicates an operation of push-button simplicity—human error minimized"; for the contented face, "Simple and highly routine human operation—little danger of human error"; for the intensely concentrated face, "Operation which requires skill, care or judgment—subject to human error" (Baird-Atomic 1959). Letting an instrument do the work will be easier and not subject to human error. There is no mention of the possibility of "instrumental error." The instrument provides the objective ideal.

The brochure is a single foldout two pages wide. The comparison of analytical methods runs across the inner two pages. The back page consists of a series of quotations from satisfied customers, all speaking to cost:

> "We saved 2000 man hours per month."
> ". . . in using the Direct Reader to cover 8 elements in each of 5 matrices for a little over a year we find we have been able to assign 2 chemists to other laboratory work, reduce the time of analysis 1300% and increase the quantity of analyses by 200%."
> ". . . actual money saved . . . $13,800 in laboratory costs alone based on former methods of analysis." (ibid.)

In the text inside the brochure, BA acknowledges that wet chemical methods are more versatile than spectrographic methods, which, in turn, are more versatile than spectrometric methods. But the decrease in versatility—

---

2. In 1954, following merger with Atomic Instruments Inc., Baird Associates changed its name to Baird-Atomic—still BA. See chapters 7 and 10 for more on BA's work developing spectrographic instruments.

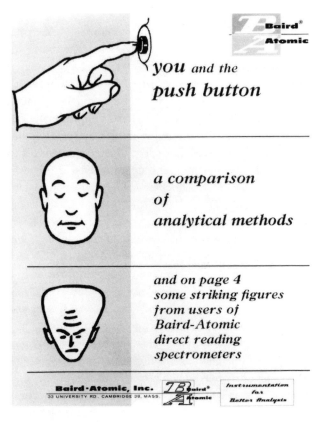

FIGURE 9.2 Baird Associates direct-reading spectrometer advertisement, front page, c. 1954. Reprinted by permission of Thermo-ARL, Inc.

if you can believe the advertising—is compensated for by the savings in money, person-power, and time.

The front page of the brochure provides, in many ways, the most interesting material (fig. 9.2). As an experiment, quickly read the page. What does it say?

The quick reading of the first line (below the corporate name) is "you push the button." But it does not say this; it says, "you and the push button." The effect, no doubt, is the result of the choice of type and the placement of the line break, along with the graphic. While it is impossible to say what was intended, it does carry a nice double meaning. On the one hand— the quick reading—we immediately learn that BA analytical instruments are easy to operate, push-button simple. On the other hand—the literal reading—we learn that a comparison is going to be drawn between you (a human) and the push button (the instrument). Given the text of the brochure, it is clear that you are subject to error, whereas the push button is not. This is BA's "Instrumentation for Better Analysis."

7. MACHINE OBJECTIVITY, EXPERT SUBJECTIVITY

At least during the late 1950s and early 1960s, marketing mileage in analytical instrumentation could be gained from the equation of machines with objectivity. Subjective methods were subject to human error, whereas operations of push-button simplicity minimized human error. Put in this context, the connection that the Educational Testing Service drew between machine scoring and objectivity is less surprising. Where various "noninstrumental" methods in chemical analysis may rightly have caused concern about error, such a concern is even more justified with cognitive tests that cannot be machine-scored. Essay tests are a well known and well studied case. Here, more than with chemical analysis, there is reason to mark a distinction between discriminations that can be done accurately by machine and those requiring human judgment.

Such a distinction is made, and the subjective/objective dichotomy is used to make it. The psychometrician Nicholas Longford, an ETS employee, presents an analysis of essay test grading in his *Models for Uncertainty in Educational Testing* (1995). He writes:

> Standardized educational tests have until recently been associated almost exclusively with multiple-choice items. . . . Scoring the test . . . can be done reliably by machine at a moderate cost. A serious criticism of this item format is the limited variety of items that can be administered and that certain aspects of skills and abilities cannot be tested by such items. . . . Certainly, problems that can be formulated as multiple-choice items are much rarer in real life; in many respects, it would be preferable to use items with realistic problems that require the examinees to construct their responses. (Longford 1995, p. 17)

Longford then notes that "[t]he principal problem with such *constructed-response* items is that they have to be graded by (human) experts" (Longford 1995, p. 17; his parentheses). Scores produced by "(human) experts" are subjective. Indeed, the title of Longford's next chapter is "Adjusting Subjectively Rated Scores" (ibid., ch. 3).

Longford presents an analysis of subjective scoring. With an essay test, for example, an examinee's performance—the essay written—provides information about grammar, clarity of expression, content, style, and so on.

Experts could read essays and judge them on these various dimensions. Then these verbal judgments could be translated into scores on an ordinal scale of, for example, 1 to 5. Unfortunately, experts disagree, and this disagreement "is a sure sign that the rating process is not perfect" (ibid., p. 18).

Longford analyzes the various ways in which "experts" disagree. He then develops statistical expressions that articulate the patterns in these disagreements. These statistical expressions can be used as a way both to measure the uncertainty in the experts' scores and to adjust the estimate of the "true score" of a given essay from expert scores.

How is the objective/subjective distinction used? Objective tests are just those that can be graded by machine. Even experts are subjective and not objective. At a superficial level of analysis, this is all that needs saying. With psychometric instruments, as with analytical instruments, objectivity lies in the ability of a machine to produce information with push-button simplicity at moderate cost. It is vital to realize that as a "concept in use" this superficial analysis is of prime importance. The marketing mileage BA got from "You and the push button" and the "patina" of disinterested objectivity that machine-graded tests provide ETS are significant. Consumers have bought this concept in use. Even critics such as Owen have bought it. And in so doing, the concept of objectivity becomes tied to machines and cost-efficiency.

But the SAT is not objective! "(Human) experts" build both psychometric and analytical instruments. They program the machine to grade certain responses "correct" and other responses "incorrect." They craft the systems that render information about the intellectual abilities of test takers. The situation calls for a deeper analysis.

8. RELIABILITY AND VALIDITY

Statisticians understand accuracy in terms of two other concepts, reliability and validity. Reliability concerns replication. Subjective essay scores are not reliable, because they vary; one essay graded by many different experts gets many different scores. On the other hand, at least among the experts at ETS, there is little or no variation among expert scores for the multiple-choice questions. Here is one prerequisite for programming a machine to score tests. We must be able to give the machine unambiguous instructions for how to score the questions. Reliability, then, must serve as one component of instrumental objectivity.

But reliability is not enough. There was near unanimity of opinion among "the experts" over the bewitching of the young women in seventeenth-century Salem, Massachusetts. We also need validity, insurance that the test actually measures a genuine piece of reality. Here matters get complicated. Psychometricians distinguish four facets of validity: content validity, construct validity, predictive validity, and concurrent validity.[3] These might best be understood as four different ways to argue for the underlying validity of a test (Murphy and Davidshofer 1991, p. 106).

Predictive and concurrent validity work by examining the correlation between test scores and some other measure(s). Thus, we are told by ETS that there is a moderately high correlation between SAT scores and performance during the first year of college—measured by grade point average. Here is a kind of "predictive argument" for the validity of the SAT. We also are told of a modest correlation between SAT scores and high school grade point average. Here is a kind of "concurrent argument" for the validity of the SAT.

We could develop a theory of the underlying trait that a test is supposed to measure. From this theory—this construct—we could make predictions on how test scores should vary, and if the test scores do vary in this way, we have an argument for the validity of the test based on its agreement with the theory. This is "construct validity." The SAT, for example, is supposed to measure an "aptitude," a basic, largely unchanging property of an individual that colloquially might be understood as the individual's capacity for intellectual work. Theoretically, this is a largely inborn, perhaps genetic, property. Thus, SAT scores for a given individual should not vary over time. Since this property is not attached to the acquiring of specific bodies of knowledge, it should not be possible to train for the test. If an individual's SAT scores were found both not to vary through time and not to respond to training, this would confirm the "construct validity" of the test. Evidence for both of these points has increasingly called this "construct" of the SAT into question.

Finally, there is "content validity." It stands to reason that a test that included only questions about the geography of Boston would be a poor test of knowledge of the history of philosophy. But what questions on the history of philosophy are necessary to measure knowledge of the history of philosophy? "Content validity" focuses on the degree to which test questions both are *about* the subject matter and *cover* the subject matter. To establish content validity, one systematically outlines the material that a test

---

3. See Lord and Novick 1968; Allen and Yen 1979; K. Murphy and Davidshofer 1991.

is supposed to cover. Then one can attempt to ensure that questions are included for all the items in the outline.

With a test on the history of philosophy, this is a difficult business. With scholastic aptitude, however, matters are worse, for it is disputable what skills do or ought to constitute scholastic aptitude. Few disagree about literacy or numeracy—although just how to test for all and only these abilities is a matter of debate. But what about the ability to speak in front of a group? What about the ability to manipulate objects by hand? What about patience? Arguably, each of these plays a role in various aspects of scholastic endeavor. Should tests of scholastic aptitude cover these areas? Can they? How such contentious questions get answered has a determinative impact on the estimation of content validity.

As a result, establishing content validity requires human judgment. In this sense, it is subjective. In their *Introduction to Measurement Theory*, Mary Allen and Wendy Yen write: "Content validity is established through a rational analysis of the content of a test, and its determination is based on individual subjective judgment" (1979, p. 95). As a consequence, content validity, they further contend, is subject to error: "Because content validity is based on subjective judgments, the determination of this type of validity is more subject to error than are other types of validity" (ibid., p. 96).

What, then, does this deeper analysis of test objectivity reveal? First, it reveals that replication is necessary for objectivity, and that replication is necessary for machine scoring. Thus, the ability to set up a machine to score tests does serve as an argument for one aspect of objectivity. Second, it reveals that questions of validity ultimately rest on human judgment, and human judgment is understood to be both subjective and prone to error. At the very least, it is an arena for vigorous debate.

9. OBJECTIVITY, INSTRUMENTS, PUBLIC POLICY, AND ECONOMICS

In the late 1980s, a National Commission on Testing and Public Policy was convened to examine the role of standardized testing in the United States. Its members included both representatives of the psychometric community and policymakers concerned with the issue. Bill Clinton, then governor of Arkansas, was a member. The report reaches a number of conclusions that include:

1. There is too much educational testing.

2. Tests are subject to insufficient public accountability.

3. Testing can undermine social policies.
4. Testing programs should be redirected from overreliance on multiple-choice tests toward alternative formats.
   (National Commission on Testing and Public Policy 1990, pp. x–xi)

Indeed, their most fundamental conclusion is stated in the title of their report, *From Gatekeeper to Gateway*. Testing, in their view, should help citizens find educational and vocational opportunities to best develop their talents. It should not block citizens from access to educational or vocational opportunities.

Yet this will require rethinking the ideal of instrumental objectivity. The model for instrumental objectivity has us ask an instrument to say whether some material—say a batch of steel alloy—meets specifications. It does not have us ask, how, given certain ascertained characteristics of some material, that material might best be used. That requires human judgment.

In a sobering analysis of the role of standardized testing in public policy formation, Lorraine McDonnell, writing for the RAND Corporation in 1994, notes that experts from the psychometric community and policymakers have divergent views about the appropriate uses of standardized student assessments. Psychometric experts are cautious and generally prefer to use assessment techniques to gain insight into school qualities and student abilities. Policymakers are enthusiastic, finding in standardized assessment an inexpensive objective means to hold schools and students accountable. McDonnell notes a trend away from simple multiple-choice tests, but she does not see a panacea here:

> The question arises, then, whether policymakers' enthusiasm for using student assessment as an instrument of education policy can be reconciled with experts' caution about its potential misuses. Will the move to alternative assessments and their policy applications repeat the recent experience with multiple choice tests, in which, over the last two decades, policymakers expanded the uses of multiple choice tests beyond their original, intended purposes, while testing experts documented the negative consequences on students and schools? The probable answer is yes. As long as policymakers see assessments as exerting a powerful leverage over school practice and, at the same time, are constrained by cost and other considerations, they will continue to use the same assessments for multiple purposes—some of which may have negative consequences for students, teachers and schools. (McDonnell 1994, p. viii)

McDonnell notes that cost is a prime driver here:

> Although new forms of assessment will cost more than older, multiple choice tests, policymakers view them as among the least expensive

strategies for reforming schools. A congressional staffer expressed this sentiment, "People settle on assessment as a cheap way to fix problems. One of the most prominent governors sees assessment as an important lever to change American education. . . . It's a lever for change without having to spend a lot of money." (ibid., p. 23)

Policymakers want—and have legislated and will continue to legislate—push-button instrumental objectivity. They have run with what Ralph Müller and Henry Chauncey provided. Chauncey sought objective methods, as opposed to "laborious and subjective methods." He sought methods of adequate precision that would be useful "on an actuarial basis." In the political arena, machine-scored methods of assessment can play to the connection between objectivity and fairness. Machines are politically neutral, are they not? Even experts have political biases, and so can offer, at best, only subjective opinions. The result, even in the face of analyses and recommendations such as those just mentioned urging caution and a move away from reliance on standardized testing, is more standardized testing in the educational arena and more instrumental push-button objectivity generally.

10 The Gift

> We also rightly speak of intuition or inspiration as
> a gift. As the artist works, some portion of his creation
> is bestowed upon him. . . . so that along with any true
> creation comes the uncanny sense that "I," the artist,
> did not make the work. "Not I, not I, but the wind that
> blows through me," says D. H. Lawrence.
>
> LEWIS HYDE, The Gift

1. ON THE SEEMING INEVITABILITY OF THE MARKET

The close of the nineteenth century was characterized by the rise of monopoly power over the then central industries of steel, oil, trains, and finance. The close of the twentieth century can similarly be seen as characterized by the rise of monopoly power. The struggle with monopoly is similar, with efficiencies of standardization and centralization pitted against efficiencies of the market and consumer choice. But now the central industries traffic in information, not steel, oil, trains, or finance, and this poses deeply troubling new questions.

Seth Shulman, in his polemic against the ownership of information, warns of "an ominous descent into a new Dark Age" (1999, p. 3). Shulman's concerns embrace the length and breadth of current high technology:

> Today doctors are claiming to own the medical procedures they once shared openly with colleagues. Software firms are winning monopolies on the basic building blocks of computer code needed to write new programs and using their ownership to stymie would-be competitors. Scientists at the nation's top universities and research institutes complain that collegial discourse has withered in the face of proprietary claims and secrecy among researchers. Drug companies are systematically gathering wild plants, insects, and microorganisms from the globe's far reaches and claiming exclusive dominion over the chemicals they contain. Even our own genetic makeup is being sold: of the portion of the human genome that has been mapped, roughly a third is already privately owned. (Shulman 1999, p. 3)

Critics of Shulman contest his dire claims. They argue that the patent system, through which the ownership claims Shulman objects to are being established, was designed explicitly to balance society's need for open disclosure with developers' needs to recoup expenses, thereby making development possible. In the rapidly advancing world of high technology, many of these disputes will be resolved through adjustments to how long a patent provides for exclusive ownership.

Beyond technical questions that might be resolved through changes in patent law, Shulman signals a new ethos in the communities where knowledge is generated. Knowledge itself is being treated as a commodity, sales of which can generate profits. This is a radical change with profound consequences, initially for the academy but ultimately for all areas of the social fabric. Deals struck between universities and private industry are the focal point for these struggles. In April 1999, the University of California at Berkeley negotiated an arrangement with Novartis Corporation. In exchange for $25 million, Novartis would have first right to negotiate licenses on roughly a third of the discoveries made in the Department of Plant and Microbial Biology, including the results of research supported by public funds (Press and Washburn 2000, pp. 39–40). Public universities, dealing with cutbacks in public funding and short of cash, need the funds private industry can provide. Private industry sees arrangements with universities as potentially valuable sources of competitive advantage in our knowledge-driven economy. But they need exclusivity and secrecy, in direct conflict with the central values underlying academic exchange.

In 1975, in a prophetic metaphor, Pierre Bourdieu described academic science in the following terms: "The 'pure' universe of even the 'purest' science is a social field like any other, with its distribution of power and its monopolies, its struggles and strategies, interests and profits" (Bourdieu 1975, p. 19). Bourdieu used the language of monopolies, struggles, strategies, interests, and profits as a metaphor. His aim was to expose the notion that "science progresses through the intrinsic strength of the true idea, and that the most 'powerful' are also the most 'competent'" (ibid., p. 40). In Bourdieu's view, this notion is a myth used to support those in a dominant position in science. But in the twenty-five years since Bourdieu published this article, we have witnessed the startling transformation of his metaphoric account into literal description.

Bourdieu's capitalist metaphor and the current capitalist reality in the "marketplace of ideas" seem inevitable. What alternative metaphors are there—indeed, *can* there be? Shulman speaks of a "conceptual commons" and points to the public library system and the national park system as models for shared goods (1999, ch. 11). While valuable and potentially practical, Shulman's analysis is not deep enough. Given an appropriate act of Congress, publicly owned goods still can be sold. They remain commodities. In this last chapter, I argue that we must understand our epistemic goods not simply as commodities. They are gifts. I argue that the telos of gift exchange, sharply different from the telos of commodity exchange, is necessary for knowledge making. In a recent article on the topic of gift economies, Bourdieu retains the capitalist metaphor but notes in closing:

> The purely speculative and typically scholastic questions of whether generosity and disinterestedness are possible should give way to the political question of the means that have to be implemented in order to create universes in which, as in gift economies, people have an interest in disinterestedness and generosity, or, rather, are durably disposed to respect these universally respected forms of respect for the universal. (Bourdieu 1997, p. 240)

The first step in the direction of respect for the universal is to better appreciate systems of exchange where this is part of the point, gift economies.

Our current struggles over alternatives to the seeming inevitability of commodity exchange are connected historically and conceptually to the advent of thing knowledge during the middle years of the twentieth century. Accepting things as bearers of knowledge creates the dilemma in which these struggles take place. The production and dissemination of things is much more expensive than the production and dissemination of ideas. Things are treated as commodities to support this expense. Ideas have been able to survive as something other than commodities, the expense of their production and dissemination covered in ways that insulate their creation from this expense.

But when things bear knowledge, the creation of this thing knowledge gets tied to the commodity market where these knowledgeable things are sold, thereby covering the expense of their creation. The previous two chapters testify to the kinds of difficulties that lie here. Watt's indicator diagram predated the advent of self-conscious thing knowledge, but it shows how thing knowledge developed in an industrial setting can prompt theoretical developments elsewhere. Watt felt that the indicator was of such value, however, that its operation was carefully kept secret, and although it was developed in the 1790s, it wasn't until 1822 that the first description of an indicator was published. Here is an example of the exclusivity and secrecy that Shulman complains has reached the academy. Objectivity's connection with analytical instrumentation finds this key bellwether of truth in bed with cost considerations. Thing knowledge challenges our tradition of treating knowledge exchange as a kind of gift exchange.

Lewis Hyde describes the struggle between gift and commodity economies as a struggle between those parts of our spirit that are personal and individual and those that "derive from nature, the group, the race, or the gods." He adds that "although these wider spirits are part of us, they are not 'ours'; they are endowments bestowed upon us" (Hyde 1979, p. 38):

> Every age must find its balance between the two, and in every age the domination of either one will bring with it the call for its opposite. For where, on the one hand, there is no way to assert identity against the mass, and no opportunity for private gain, we lose the well-advertised benefits of a market society—its particular freedoms, its particular kind of innovation, its individual and material variety, and so on. But where, on the other hand, the market alone rules, and particularly where its benefits derive from the conversion of gift property to commodities, the fruits of gift exchange are lost. At that point commerce becomes correctly associated with the fragmentation of community and the suppression of liveliness, fertility, and social feeling. (ibid., p. 38)

The advent of thing knowledge has altered this balance in favor of knowledge commodities, and this threatens the production of knowledge itself. I start with some contemporary stories from magnetic resonance imaging. I then return to an earlier instance of thing knowledge right at the cusp of the instrumentation revolution. Here we see the struggle between gift and commodity economy in raw form.

2. MAGNETIC RESONANCE IMAGING

In 1973, twenty-seven years after Felix Block's initial experimentation with nuclear magnetic resonance (NMR) (Block 1946; Block et al. 1946), Paul Lauterbur demonstrated that one could take advantage of the purely classical properties of the NMR phenomenon to form two-dimensional images (Lauterbur 1973).[1] While these first images represented local nuclear spin density, researchers already recognized that the rates of magnetization of the nuclei varied according to their local chemical and molecular environment. Today's magnetic resonance imaging (MRI) pictures are two-dimensional maps of these magnetization rates within slices of tissue.

Due to its extraordinary ability to form images of the inside of the body, based on passive recordings, and while avoiding exposure to hazards such

---

1. Material in this section is taken from Cohen and Baird 1999, a paper I wrote jointly with Mark Cohen, a scientist working on magnetic resonance imaging instrumentation and its use in understanding brain function. I am deeply indebted to him for the glimpse he has given me into this fascinating field of instrumental endeavor.

as ionizing radiation, MRI has become an immensely popular clinical tool. As of 1998, industry estimates suggest there are over 3,500 installed units in the United States alone. The capital investment in these instruments is enormous. The average installed instrument costs about 1.5 million dollars at delivery and is serviced by about $100,000 in upgrades each year (one of the largest manufacturers, General Electric, recommends, for example, that customers set aside an additional 10 percent of the instrument cost annually for upgrades). More than $5 billion has been spent on installations, and $350 million is spent yearly on upgrades. Why? Because for an incredible number of diseases, MRI is considered the definitive diagnosis—the "gold standard"—justifying a cost per use of $500–$1,000.

MRI equipment encapsulates a tremendous amount of knowledge, from knowledge of nuclear induction to knowledge of body chemistry and structure. Putting this knowledge to work in the instrument provides medical clinicians with a powerful tool for diagnosing human illness.

People from a wide variety of professional settings have to engage one another to make MRI a clinical reality. Physicists have to develop the conceptual tools that provide insight into nuclear induction. Experimenters and instrument makers have to make the devices that can produce these interactions. Instrument-manufacturing firms have to make and market the instruments. Clinicians and their patients have to use them. There is no common understanding of these instruments shared by all of the various people who interact with MRI instrumentation. In Peter Galison's sense, trading zones are established to facilitate the exchange of information, skills, and devices (Galison 1997). The languages used to communicate in these trading zones do not capture any particular group's full understanding of MRI satisfactorily. Physicians focus on the clinical meanings of the images produced; instrument makers focus on the phenomena created by interactions between "specimen" and instrument, and on the algorithms for rendering images from data.

It is in the slippage in communication brought on by this distribution of labor and the consequent specialized understandings of the instrumentation that difficulties can arise. When these difficulties occur in the context of a profit-seeking MRI industry, we can see at a practical level how the struggle between gift and commodity economies affects our lives. Here are several instances.

The Gibbs Ringing Artifact

In the vast majority of cases, MRI is performed in Fourier space (Lauterbur 1973, 1981; Kumar et al. 1975). When the raw data that make up an image

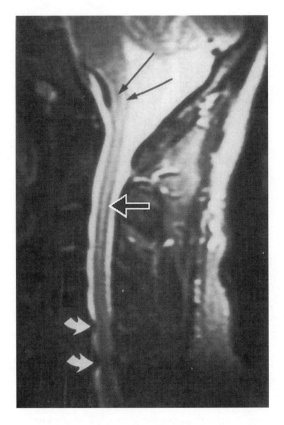

FIGURE 10.1 Magnetic resonance image, Gibbs ringing artifact (from Bronskill et al. 1988). Reprinted by permission of the Radiological Society of North America.

are sampled incompletely—which they must be, because "true" raw data have to be infinite in Fourier time series—a characteristic artifact, known as "Gibbs ringing," occurs at abrupt intensity discontinuities. This artifact appears as a dark band parallel to, but slightly displaced from, a lighter region resulting from a large intensity gradient. Such artifacts are well known to the physicists and engineers who work on MRI instrumentation, as are optimization procedures for their mitigation (Henkelman and Bronskill 1987).

There was a period of about three years (1987–90) when it became fashionable for physicians to reduce the long imaging times by using aniso-tropically shaped (i.e., non-square) imaging pixels in studies of the spine. As it turned out, this resulted in a prominent dark line appearing within the spinal cord. The dark line was a Gibbs ringing artifact.

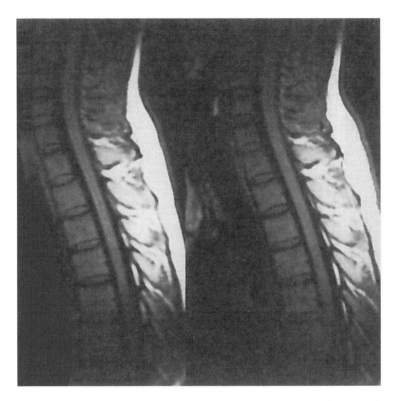

FIGURE 10.2 Magnetic resonance image, Gibbs ringing artifact amelioration (from Bronskill et al. 1988). Reprinted by permission of the Radiological Society of North America.

The clinical MR image in figure 10.1 shows the presence of an artifact caused by Fourier truncation. This appears as a bright line in the center of the spinal cord (outline arrow). Not knowing the mathematics used to transform the instrument signal into an image, clinicians unfortunately interpreted this artifact as a fluid-filled lesion called a "syrinx," requiring aggressive medical treatment. The white arrows in figure 10.1 indicate the clinical condition of cervical spondylosis, at a point where, curiously, the artifact does not appear. (The thin black arrows point to yet another artifact.)

Ultimately, the artifact was detected and explained by M. J. Bronskill (1988), whose knowledge bridged medicine and physics. In figure 10.2, a pair of MR images shows amelioration of the artifact. On the left, the syrinx-link artifact appears as a dark line in the middle of the spinal cord (just to the right of the spinal column). On the right, this dark line has largely been removed. Unfortunately, the artifact was not detected until after many patients had been misdiagnosed and (mis)treated. Once the nature of the artifact was recognized, and its implications appreciated, other researchers later identified it as the cause of misdiagnosis of other disorders, for example, spinal cord atrophy (Yousem et al. 1990).

Fat and Water Signal Difference

Here is another example. Since the very early days of spectroscopy using NMR, it has been known that the resonance frequency of fat differs from that of water. Because MRI using the Lauterbur method capitalizes on the resonance frequency of the signal to determine spatial location, a so-called chemical shift difference between fat and water results in a spatial displacement of fat and water signals. From the very earliest days of practical medical instrument design (1981 or 1982), minimization of the "chemical shift difference" artifact has been an important goal. Instrument engineers took this artifact to be a major design constraint that ultimately would limit the effective signal-to-noise ratio and perhaps resolution of the instrument (Hoult and Richards 1976; Hoult et al. 1986; Henkelman and Bronskill 1987).

Surprisingly, given the care with which instrument engineers had worked on the chemical shift difference, a highly visible error surfaced in 1990. General Electric noted a flaw in some of its most commonly used data acquisition programs, known as a "pulse sequence." Generally, two or more radio frequency pulses are used to form the signal that makes up an MR image. In order to avoid or minimize an artifact known as a stimulated echo, the instruments produced by GE had since at least 1985 applied each of the two image-forming pulses to a different spatial location—one for aqueous tissue and another for lipid (fat-containing) tissue. The result was an image with a depleted fat signal. From the theoretician's perspective, this was a serious error.

When the flaw was recognized, GE fixed the software and sent the new version to users of its MRI equipment, along with a clear description of the problem. Now a marketing problem arose. Having become used to the presentation provided by the original flawed software, many physicians disliked the new corrected software. Not only were images on individual patients made with the new software incommensurate with the prior images, but also the physicians were more familiar with and better able to interpret images from the original software. In a textbook, only-in-America response, GE decided to offer both variants. By pressing a button labeled

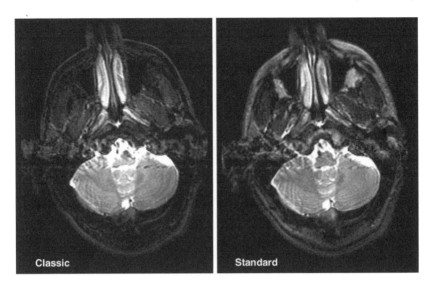

FIGURE 10.3 Magnetic resonance image, classic v. standard MR images. Reprinted by permission of Mark S. Cohen.

"Classic" clinicians could make the instrument use the older, flawed, software. The GE software manual includes a section titled "The Classic Difference," which gives instructions for switching between systems (General Electric Medical Systems 1993).

The difference in the appearance of "classic" and "standard" images is quite dramatic. The scans in figure 10.3 compare images acquired before (left) and after (right) the software modification and are quite different. Fortunately, this led only to modest health care errors—the effects were limited to a slightly reduced diagnostic sensitivity, and, over time, radiologists have become familiar with images made by the new software.

Back Pain

A much more challenging, and vastly more expensive, failure of communication between instrument engineer and medical clinician relating to MR images is now being played out. Back pain is currently the single most important medical condition leading to lost work time in this country. The economic consequences of back pain are staggering, and yet we have only the vaguest sense of its causes (Gawande 1998).

When clinical MRI first appeared, its applications were mostly inside the head, where the skull has always rendered the brain nearly invisible to X-ray methods. Although the brain has remained a major focus of clinical

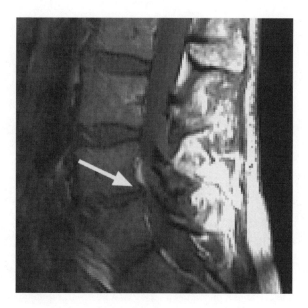

FIGURE 10.4 Magnetic resonance image, intervertebral spinal disc bulges. Reprinted by permission of Mark S. Cohen.

applications, by 1986, MR imaging of the spine consumed about 50 percent of scanner time, the brain about 35 percent, and the rest of the body about 15 percent. MR images of the spine were showing a tremendous incidence of disk prolapse; the disks that separate and cushion the bones of the spine were bulging into the space that should be occupied by the spinal cord and nerves. The conventional wisdom with respect to pain at the time was that inflammation of the spinal nerves would lead to pain. The image in figure 10.4 shows a small (<3 mm) bulge (arrow) of an intervertebral disc into the thecal sac, which encloses the spinal cord. It was thought that such bulges compressed the spinal nerves where they exit the cord, causing chronic back pain.

Seeing the intense interest from the referring physicians (and lawyers), MR imaging centers pushed hard for manufacturers to develop improved tools to study the spine. Physicians complained vigorously that the manufacturers were dragging their feet on this pressing medical problem. The demand became so great that the large instrument vendors—enormous companies like General Electric, Philips, and Siemens—lost significant sales to small startup companies that were able to bring one such tool—called a "surface coil"—to market more quickly. A complete spine exam would cost insurance companies (or the unfortunate patient) about $1,000, and such exams were performed at the rate of more than 10,000 per day.

Once the disease was identified, the need for therapy began. The spine, unfortunately, is a terribly difficult site for surgery. The bones are large, in many cases deeply buried in muscle tissue, and the putative disease site (the disk) can only be reached after going around the spinal cord and nerves. Nevertheless, the surgeons press on. Alas, the patients do not experience consistent or substantial relief, even after repeated surgeries. It turns out that the visible "abnormalities" shown in the MR images are not correlated with the pain (Annertz et al. 1996; Savage et al. 1997; Rankine et al. 1998). Patients who refused surgical treatment, or who were treated "conservatively" (i.e., nonsurgically), showed a remarkable effect: disk prolapse came and went without any intervention!

This is a case of a clinical artifact. The instrument did not "lie" about the disks. We misunderstood the meaning of disk prolapse. Since we did not have prior experience seeing this phenomenon, and since it "stood to reason" that disk prolapse would cause the reported pain, images were taken to show a diagnostically significant situation, when it was diagnostically insignificant—normal body behavior.

Not surprisingly, the demand for spinal MRI has dropped. This most likely is due to decreasing fiscal reimbursements from the third-party HMO payers. But, in large part, this probably is secondary to the inability of the therapeutic establishment to take significant advantage of the MRI findings.

3. THE MARKET AND THE INSTRUMENT

MRI instrumentation provides a focus for professionals from many different settings with many different interests. The instruments are expensive and the companies that make and market them reasonably enough want to make a profit on their product. Imaging centers that buy these expensive instruments also reasonably want a return on their investment. Patients, of course, want relief from their ailments. Here is a case where different groups of professionals, all pursuing their own interests, can produce undesirable consequences. The invisible hand can fumble.

The first example emphasizes the fact that the space in which clinicians work and interact with MRI instrumentation differs from the space in which MRI instrument engineers work. They share the MR image. It is the pidgin of their trading zone, to use Galison's word (1997). But the image has diagnostic meaning for the clinician that it does not have for the engineer. Conversely, for the engineer, the image represents a complicated algorithm, incorporating a variety of trade-offs in dealing with the kind of signal NMR provides. There is a clear need for persons who bridge instrument engineering and clinical uses of MRI instrumentation. It was because of Bronskill's unique position that the Gibbs ringing artifact was discovered in spinal MR images.

But who is going to pay for this bridging work? Given the relatively limited number of instrument makers and the large number of users with installed instruments, it seems most likely that this work will fall on the manufacturers. And for this reason, it seems very likely that marketing will get mixed in with this bridging work. Indeed, it was a bit of marketing genius that resolved clinician dissatisfaction with the new, "corrected," MRI software by offering "MRI Classic."

These examples show how significant marketing pressure has had an impact on the development and use of the instrument. In the case of back pain, despite an enthusiastic pursuit of what appeared to be a promising clinical application of MRI, we misunderstood the meaning of the images. The instrument has nonetheless acquired tremendous capital momentum. The massive installed base alone is a significant incentive to find diagnostic uses for MRI equipment on the part of both the manufacturers and clinicians who must sell diagnostic images in order to pay for their instruments.

The instrument and the diagnostic images it produces are commodities. This has a significant impact on the nature of the trading done in the variety of trading zones that center on MRI instrumentation. In order to appreciate the significance of this point, I now turn to a discussion of an alternative form of exchange, gift economies.

4. GIFT ECONOMIES

Much of the literature on gift economies flows from the seminal work of Marcel Mauss, first published in French in 1925 (Mauss 1990). Predating Mauss, Ralph Waldo Emerson had written an influential essay on gifts in the mid nineteenth century (Emerson 1876), and, albeit from a different tradition, Friedrich Nietzsche's *Thus Spoke Zarathustra* (Nietzsche 1982) is centrally concerned with gift economies (Shapiro 1991). The structuralist Claude Lévi-Strauss expanded on Mauss's analysis (Lévi-Strauss 1969), and the literature on gifts has continued to increase (see, e.g., Zelizer and

Rotman 1979; Caplow 1982, ch. 10; Gregory 1982; Cheal 1988; Carrier 1995; Schrift 1997; Godelier 1999).

Lewis Hyde presents a theory of gifts and gift exchange in his marvelous book *The Gift: Imagination and the Erotic Life of Property* (1979). He argues that artists and their works must live in a world of gifts and gift exchange: "[W]orks of art exist simultaneously in two 'economies,' a market economy and a gift economy. Only one of these is essential, however: a work of art can survive without the market, but where there is no gift there is no art" (Hyde 1979, p. xi). Existence in a gift economy is necessary for the inspiration from which art flows (ibid., ch. 8).

So it is with knowledge as well. Gift economies are necessary for knowledge creation, production, and dissemination. Consider the fact that typically academics are not paid by the piece—although just this kind of tradition is challenged by the move toward ownership of ideas. Academic articles are written and published, but typically, no fee is paid to their authors. The articles are intellectual gifts given in return for receiving the intellectual gifts of others.

Gift economies function in a wide variety of circumstances. While each has its own specificity, several generalities describe the range of gift practices. Here I mention those that are key to understanding gift economies generally, but that relate specifically to my concern with thing knowledge.

Social Ties

The fundamental difference between gift and commodity economies is expressed in the curious subtitle of Hyde's book: *Imagination and the Erotic Life of Property*. Gift economies serve to bind people together. They create and maintain social groups. All the various rules or expectations that govern gift exchange serve this end. "The gift, to be true, must be the flowing of the giver unto me, correspondent to my flowing unto him," according to Emerson (1876, p. 163). Seen in a wider social context, gift economies establish social boundaries; one must give to the group in order to be part of the group and receive the groups' gifts in return: property bonding people together—hence, the erotic life of property.

Commodity economies work against bonding. The rules and expectations that govern commodity exchange serve to define and delimit mutual responsibility and future obligation between the parties involved. Ideal commodity exchanges occur when the parties involved understand at the outset just what each must give and can expect to receive, and when the interaction is to be concluded.

In a sense, commodity exchanges aim to establish mutually beneficial *conclusions* of interactions. Gift exchanges aim to *initiate and maintain* interactions. In stark contrast to commodity exchanges, gifts cannot have a dollar-measurable value. Such a value would allow a gift recipient to close the interaction; a gift of equal value could be returned, leaving neither party obligated to the other. No further interaction would be necessary. Assigned dollar values work against social bonding.

Gifts Are Personal

Gifts cannot be produced by toil alone, nor by taking some object "off the shelf." An artist cannot make art without having his or her own artistic gifts—understanding, talent, and skill bequeathed to the artist at birth and by upbringing and participation in an artistic gift economy. Objects that are gifts need something of the giver. Emerson again: "Rings and other jewels are not gifts, but apologies for gifts. The only gift is a portion of thyself. Thou must bleed for me" (1876, p. 161). An extreme sentiment, perhaps, but it does capture a distinction commonly understood between a "pro forma" and a "real," or "personal," gift.

Herein lies a central piece to the argument that creative endeavors, be they artistic or epistemic, rely on a gift economy. Edison may well have said that invention is 99 percent perspiration and 1 percent inspiration, but it would be foolish to deny that Edison was a gifted inventor. The various skills, bequeathed at birth and developed through his upbringing and his dedication to his craft were gifts that he brought to his inventive activity; inspiration—even if only 1 percent—remains necessary. One can see recent corporate attempts to promote "intrapreneurial" inventive activity as a way to put the necessary personal element into invention while still operating in a profit-based commodity market.

Gifts Must Move

Gift economies require a cycle of giving. The racist expression "Indian giver" has its source in this aspect of gift giving. In his 1764 history of the Massachusetts colony, Thomas Hutchinson said: "An Indian gift is a proverbial expression signifying a present for which an equivalent return is expected" (quoted in Hyde 1979, p. 3). Hyde goes on to describe how the Massachusetts Indians may have shared a peace pipe with the Puritan settlers, leaving the pipe with the newcomers. But the Indians expected the pipe to be returned or, better, recycled and given to others as part of the socially binding cycle of giving and peacemaking. "The Indian giver (or the original one, at any rate) understood a cardinal property of the gift: whatever we have been given is supposed to be given away again, not kept," Hyde writes. "Or if it is kept, something of similar value should move on in its stead" (ibid., p. 4).

Herein is one sense of the often-quoted aphorism that a great scientist may see further only because he or she stands on the shoulders of giants. Someone who learns what science has to teach but does not give back to scientific culture is not a scientist. In the section "On the Gift-Giving Virtue" of *Zarathustra*, Nietzsche wrote, "One repays a teacher badly if one always remains nothing but a pupil. And why do you not want to pluck at my wreath?" (1982, p. 190). In taking an intellectual gift, one incurs a debt to contribute an intellectual gift in return, passing along or recycling the gift.

"Stewardship" is a better term than "ownership" for one's relationship to gifts received. For a time, one becomes the keeper of something whose value lies in its movement among those in a gift community. Accumulation, then, provides another stark contrast between gift and commodity economies. Businesses aim to accumulate capital in the form of profits. This capital can then be used in various ways at the discretion of the business managers. Gifts, on the contrary, cannot be accumulated like profits; they must be plowed back into the cycle of gift giving. Gifts received must be given away, or they cease to be gifts and the recipient of the gift ceases to belong to the gift group.

Obligation

This erotic life of property is a life of bonding or ensnaring people. Here is an essential duality of gift economies. Gifts given and gifts received call up the joy of human connection, but also the suffering of obligation: bonding and ensnaring. Nietzsche described the gift-giving virtue as the "lust to rule" (Nietzsche 1982, p. 301; Shapiro 1991, p. 17). Just as commodity economies establish status hierarchies based on how much is accumulated, gift economies establish hierarchies through how much one gives. Much literature, following early anthropological work, has characterized gift economies as highly oppressive because of this feature (Lévi-Strauss 1969; Mauss 1990).

5. FOUNDING A COMPANY IN GIFT / COMMODITY CONFLICT

MRI instrumentation has developed in a context where there is little question that these instruments are commodities. What else could they be? The development of commercial grating spectrographs during the 1930s, 1940s, and 1950s presents a different picture. Here at the advent of our conceptualization of thing knowledge, we can see a struggle between gift and commodity economies.

Baird Associates (BA), the company founded by my father, Walter S. Baird, John Sterner, and Harry Kelly, has been discussed at several points in earlier chapters. Jason Saunderson's direct-reading spectrometer, described in chapter 4, was ultimately licensed to BA for manufacture, marketing, and sale. BA was one of the instrumentation firms that took part in the scientific instrumentation revolution described in chapter 5. Chapter 7, on the thing-y-ness of things, follows the trajectory of spectrographic instrumentation developed and sold by BA. And, finally, advertising by Baird-Atomic, BA's subsequent corporate name, is used in chapter 9 to illustrate the connection between objectivity and instrumentation. It is perhaps fitting, then, to close the book with a discussion of the founding of BA.[2]

At the beginning of 1936, John Sterner and Walter Baird were working at the Watertown Arsenal in Watertown, Massachusetts. Baird had just finished his doctorate in electrical engineering at Johns Hopkins. Sterner was working on a Ph.D. in spectroscopy at MIT. Harry Kelly had just finished his spectroscopy Ph.D. at MIT and was working at American Thermos in Norwalk, Connecticut.

One of the principal functions of the Arsenal was the analysis of metals used in guns and ordinance. Sterner worked in the spectroscopy lab; Baird worked in the X-ray diffraction lab. In the process of this work, it became clear to them that chemical analysis could be done more easily with instruments such as the spectrograph and X-ray diffraction tube than by the traditional "wet" methods. In 1936, such instrumental analysis was, however, limited to a few academic and government laboratories with the expertise and funds to build the necessary instruments themselves.

On July 21, 1936, Henry Aughey of the Du Pont company saw a demonstration of Baird's X-ray diffraction apparatus. A month later (July 31, 1936), he wrote and asked Baird how he could get a tube of his own. With this "order" from Du Pont, Baird quit work at the Arsenal to devote himself full-time to building an X-ray tube for Du Pont. Sterner and Kelly kept their jobs in order to provide capital for the new partnership.

BA's budget for the last half of 1936 showed a shortfall of $1,582 — and

2. More detail on the early history of Baird Associates can be found in D. Baird 1991.

this took into account Kelly's and Sterner's salaries. Baird accordingly wrote his father, George C. Baird, in 1937:

> Dear Pop— . . . The essential purpose of the company (partnership) is to design and develop apparatus for industrial laboratories—X-ray apparatus, spectrographic etc. At the same time it is our purpose to set up a laboratory here to be used for demonstration work and for consulting. We have spent most of our time recently getting together our own laboratory and have now either finished or partly finished an X-ray tube, high vacuum and evaporation outfits and a grating spectrograph. The X-ray equipment is a salable article. So far also we have promoted a vacuum gage which a local instrument maker is manufacturing and selling. From this we collect a royalty. Our general policy is to carry on this sort of thing—develop and try out a piece of equipment—turn it over to some established concern for production. The money we need is for the carry-over period between development and sale of an article. We have sufficient to take care of running expenses. Our credit is good. I have a very good chance to get the order for a grating spectrograph next month—a $1,500 job—this requires some outlay for machine work, etc., so we need the money right away. We are after $1000 and can offer 10% for a year. . . . We can assure payment. . . . Business is booming—industry is now ready for the equipment we are putting out—lack of capital only prevents us from being ready for it. . . . I state again that we need the money right now.

Baird's father's reply came two days later. He would provide $50, not $1,000. With this and some other money in hand, Baird purchased the partnership's first grating from Johns Hopkins.

The three partners in BA were not inclined initially to undertake the manufacturing and marketing of their products. They conceived of BA as a "think/do-tank" aimed at producing designs and prototypes for useful analytical instruments, and this continued to be the stated purpose of the firm at least through the end of 1938. It is spelled out in a mission statement written in the form of a series of questions and answers:

3. Q. Purpose?
   A. 1. To bridge the gap between the conception of new methods of physical measurement and their practical applications.
      2. To build up a laboratory for the analysis and solution of special industrial physical problems . . .

7. Q. What is involved in the policy of the company as stated above in the first part of the answer to Question 3?
   A. 1. Development of simple, rugged, accurate, generally usable instruments to make the measurements under consideration.

2. Finding a market for and constructing a limited number of these instruments.
3. Educating the public to the realization of the importance of the measurements involved and/or the suitability of the specific instruments for making those measurements . . .

9. Q. Can this development be financed in part by orders from industrial companies and universities received prior to detailed development?
   A. The Baird Associates have found that such has been the case in the majority of instruments developed to date . . .

14. Q. What is the company's attitude toward the manufacture of instruments developed?
   A. We do not wish to become a manufacturing organization except where production is on a very small scale or where inadequacy of available manufacturing facilities makes such a course seem necessary and advisable.

15. Q. How then can the company make profits?
   A. From professional services rendered, limited manufacturing activities, and royalties on any larger scale production which might ensue. (Baird Associates 1938, pp. 1–4)

The idea of a think/do-tank aimed at creating instruments nicely distinguished the scientific or gift economy contribution from the manufacturing or commodity economy contribution in the production of instruments. Financial demands, however, continued to push these two contributions together. Contrary to their optimistic assessment here, it was difficult to finance the research and development of new instruments with "orders from industrial companies and universities received prior to detailed development."

Here is one important moral about scientific instrument making. It is not generally profitable to separate the research and development of an instrument from its manufacture. It is tempting to make such a separation, because it is tempting to regard research and development as epistemically privileged; this is where new thing knowledge is created. Manufacture is involved with more pragmatic issues of knowledge diffusion, matters typically handled in a commodity economy. But because of the need for operating capital, this distinction was not viable. BA originally had in mind to establish an environment for something like university research where the goal would be a prototype instrument, not a published paper. Commodity economics worked against this aim.

6. GRATINGS AND GIFTS

In his February 8, 1936, diary entry, W. S. Baird noted: "Harrison of Tech seems to have pretty conclusive evidence in which he shows that the spectrograph is a lot more handy device to use than the X-ray." On November 17, 1936, Sterner wrote to Kelly:

> Walter is contemplating taking the tube to Duponts and trying to sell them a camera at the same time. Also trying to get hold of a grating from Hopkins. It sounds like a good idea to me. What do you think? . . . Through the Arsenal a possibility of selling a grating has come up. Of course it is very vague, but indications point toward a very lucrative business in grating spectrographs if we can get one set up in our lab. to expt. with. I have made several good contacts regarding possible customers on that score. But we must have one built. Walter seems to feel that he can go down and come back with some sort of a grating.

This was where my grandfather's $50 was spent. My father came back with "some sort of a grating."

Through Sterner's connection, BA was party to work in George Harrison's MIT spectroscopy lab (see chapter 5, § 8, above). This was very important, because the MIT lab was pursuing advanced research in spectrographic analysis, in improving the instruments for spectrographic analysis, and in finding markets for spectrographic analysis. Harrison's summer conferences helped to take spectrographs out of isolated academic and government laboratories and bring them to a wide array of private-sector concerns where spectrographic instruments could help analytical research. In the beginning, this was all done on an academic gift economy model. Personal connections were developed through these conferences. Ideas for instruments and applications were shared. A new community was built through this give-and-take gifting of knowledge.

By the late 1930s, the most serious problem holding back the production of grating spectrographs was the availability of gratings. A 1968 review of the development of spectrograph design tells us, "Between the world wars a good grating could only be obtained by personal contact between the head of a research group and the few possible sources of supply, and such a grating was a highly prized possession" (Learner 1968, p. 540). Gratings were exchanged as intellectual gifts, and my father's being able to come back from Hopkins with a grating was not a given, but a gift.

From his graduate work at Hopkins, Baird knew the people responsible for producing the gratings. This personal contact was important, as too were BA's intentions. R. W. Wood was particular about the people to whom he would sell gratings. During a trip to Hopkins to try and get some gratings from Wood, Baird wrote Sterner as follows:

> Wood showed me correspondence from Bausch & Lomb. They have written for a price on 25 plane gratings (per year) which they intend to use in a Littrow mounting for chemical analysis. They demand ghost free gratings with little scattered light. They seem to know little about chemical analysis, and the lens necessary introduces the same dispersion troubles now dogging the prism model. R. W. snorts at the above order—says that B&L wants to make 80% on their instruments and he doesn't like it.

The BA spectrograph, designed for a concave grating, not a plane grating, held greater promise of being capable of quantitative spectrographic analysis. The instrument would be enclosed in a transportable light-tight cabinet. Confining the optical elements to a small cabinet had the additional benefit of making precise control of the temperature simpler. It would be a genuine contribution to science. Finally, Wood trusted Baird's intentions: BA was in it not for the money but to contribute to science.

These negotiations display all of the features of a gift economy. BA—to be more precise, Baird, Sterner, and Kelly—had the qualifications to be members of the scientific gift community. Their aim was to give something back to science: a transportable spectrograph suitable for quantitative analysis—something science did not then have. Baird approached Wood on a personal level, which he was able to do because of his graduate study at Hopkins. Wood accepted that profit was not BA's primary motive, that it did not aim to become a major instrument-manufacturing firm.

In 1939, BA traded one of its spectrographs to Johns Hopkins. On delivery, there was a disagreement over the number of gratings BA was to receive in return for its instrument. Wood had "not been tamed as yet, but am beating on him," Baird wrote Sterner. "Dieke is on my side but the practical politics need careful handling. . . . The sad part is that since RW's retirement, his salary comes partially from the grating department, so this barter is cash out of his pocket." In 1975, Baird remembered the trade as follows:

> I had a big argument with one R. W. Wood about whether I got three gratings or four gratings. I wanted the gratings, and I gave him the

1-meter spectrograph. However, when we got right down into the final nitty gritty argument, it turns out that he said you get three, and I said I want four. We both understood that you can't cut a grating in half, so I ended up with three. (Baird 1975, ch. 11, p. 4)

My father often told this story, and I know that when he spoke of cutting a grating in half, he was alluding to the biblical story in which King Solomon determined which of two women was the mother of a baby. When the king threatened to cut the baby in half, the true mother relinquished her claim in order to save her child's life. In the 1930s, gratings, like babies, were gifts. The grating in question was Wood's to give or not; it was not a commodity whose price could be set by "fair negotiations." BA did not get the fourth grating.

While Wood officially was in charge of the ruling engines, Wilbur Perry was the technician who ruled the gratings and kept the ruling engines in proper running order. Baird was on good terms with Perry. At one point, he writes that he "managed to save [for Baird] one of the 30,000 line gratings so Wood didn't find it." Throughout the 1930s and 1940s, Perry did his best to provide BA with good gratings when they were needed. Some of his postcards to BA:

1939: Dear Walter, I trust you have received the grating which was sent from here Aug 1st. This grating seemed to be a good looking one. . . .

July 1941: Dear Walter, I am working on your two gratings now and should finish one by the 19th. . . . I plan to rule a 3 meter for you every time that the machine is free to keep a supply on hand.

November 1941: Dear Walter, . . . There was no mistake about ruling it with 30,000 instead of 15,000 because I needed a surface to locate my aluminum film troubles. Treat it well.

1945: Dear Walter, . . . The order from Baird Associates for 18 gratings nearly floored R. W., because he very promptly brought it down to me and informed me at the time that it should keep me busy for some time to come.

Through this contact, BA could depend on a reliable supply of what were the best gratings in the world.

7. FROM GIVING TO SELLING

BA rushed to get the first spectrograph finished so that it could be displayed at the 1937 MIT Spectroscopy Conference, July 19–22, 1937 (Baird Associates 1950). The instrument was not sold until 1940 (see below). But it did

A Custom Built Grating Spectrograph

Baird Associates

30 Palmer Street   *Cambridge, Massachusetts*

FIGURE 10.5 Baird Associates three-meter spectrometer advertisement, c. 1938. Reprinted by permission of Thermo-ARL, Inc.

induce the U.S. Bureau of Mines to order an instrument of its own. That instrument was built by BA and delivered, after many delays, in April 1938. BA's profit over the direct costs of its manufacture was $1,260. But there were many indirect costs associated with setting up a laboratory and manufacturing facility (Baird Associates 1937; Walsh 1988, p. 1338) (see fig. 10.5).

While the spectrograph was sold at a loss, the sale was nonetheless important. This spectrograph helped to demonstrate the advantages of gratings over prisms. On the basis of eighteen months' experience with the BA spectrograph, Morris Slavin of the Bureau of Mines argued in favor of grating spectrographs at the 1939 MIT summer conference (Slavin 1940). Thus, while BA did not profit financially, it did profit in gift terms. Through its gift of a good grating spectrograph to the developing community of instrumental analysts, BA helped establish this way of doing analysis.

Through the remainder of the 1930s, BA sold seven more grating spectrographs. While sales started slowly, they picked up in the 1940s: fifty-four spectrographs were sold through the 1940s, and the line continued in production well into the 1960s. The price dropped in 1938 and 1939 from $2,610 to about $2,175, but thereafter it rose steadily. By 1940, the price of a three-meter spectrograph had risen to $3,700 (Baird Corporation n.d.). BA's financial officer during the 1950s wrote: "When the instrument was housed in a wooden case and employed an open (dangerous) electrode stand, the margin was reasonably good, but ever since it was all enclosed in steel costs have been too high to show a net profit" (Chamberlain 1958, p. 12). Given the nature of the market, BA could not expect a large volume of sales. Unfortunately, a small number of sales drives up the proportion of indirect research costs that each instrument has to bear. Small numbers drive down profitability. Once several instruments had been placed in use, however, BA did make some money on accessories and supplies for these instruments.

With the advent of World War II, BA sales volume picked up substantially (see table 10.1; the numbers are *not* in millions of dollars). While there was growth prior to 1942, after 1942, business nearly tripled. A *Fortune* magazine article featuring Baird Associates put it this way:

> Spectrochemistry, old in principle, was used only in advanced-research laboratories until about ten years ago. Researchers, who often built their own instruments, were seldom interested in devising routine methods for analyzing standard chemical substances. And the chemists who ran the industrial control laboratories were cool toward academic

TABLE 10.1 Baird Associates Balance Sheet, 1936–1946 (in dollars)

Year	Total Net Sales	Gross Profit (Loss)	Earnings before Taxes
1936	$230	$34	($41)
1937	726	(1,084)	(1,460)
1938	6,036	204	(592)
1939	10,126	2,740	749
1940	27,486	3,593	2,200
1941	49,129	16,930	11,600
1942	128,889	32,278	23,038
1943	203,498	47,956	29,469
1944[a]	140,922	50,850	43,332
1945	387,558	45,472	30,301
1946	353,645	72,103	32,603

SOURCE: Baird Associates 1953.
[a] Eight months only.

techniques that obtained answers by measuring the wave length of invisible ultraviolet and infrared light.

When the war came along many control laboratories were caught flat-footed. Time-consuming methods of nineteenth-century chemistry finally had to be dropped in favor of spectrochemistry. ("Instrument Makers of Cambridge," 1948, p. 133)

The demand for rapid analyses, particularly of metals such as those used at the Watertown Arsenal, brought industry to spectrochemical methods and the necessary instruments. The capital to finance this move from nineteenth-century wet techniques to instrumental techniques came from the government as part of the financing of the war. By the time the war was over, a new tradition in chemical analysis had been established, which depended on expensive instrumentation supplied by companies such as BA.

World War II also marked another, more local, transition. By the late 1940s, the BA spectrograph was a commodity, and an expensive one at that—in 1953, the unit sold for $12,500 (Baird Associates 1953). War funding and the shared goal of defeating fascist aggression cushioned the transition from gift to commodity. All the "competing" instrument makers shared this central goal. Funding was abundant. So initially treating the instruments as commodities did not damage their epistemic gift status and the epistemic community BA entered into in the 1930s.

The first spectrograph BA built, the one that had been on display at the 1937 MIT conference, was sold in 1940 to New England Spectrochemical to raise capital for the firm.[3] Writing in his diary on January 20, 1940, Baird lamented the sale:

> Our first spectrograph now has a new home. I am not too well pleased with its new owners for I am sure they will not treat Specky with the proper degree of affection. I could hardly expect them to. To me that instrument represents nearly a week's work without sleep. It also represents the feeling that went into this business—something which money cannot buy. We sold it because we need money and Specky represented most of our capital. We also sold it knowing we could replace it with a more perfect instrument. It was Specky's imperfections which endeared "her" to us for I know every inch, every screw. We may build many an instrument but that one has a soul where all the others have only bodies.

Specky was BA's gift to instrumental analysis. Specky was the direct result of its makers' intimate familiarity with optics, spectrochemical analysis, and mechanical design. The knowledge built into Specky gave its users a direct appreciation for some of nature's possibilities and simultaneously allowed them to perform new feats of measurement. At the same time, Specky represented capital that was badly needed to keep BA financially alive. The Janus-faced first spectrograph was thus simultaneously a gift and a commodity.

BA survived, but it did not thrive financially. Still, it did thrive in the academic gift economy. During the 1940s and 1950s BA was known primarily as a research group. First-rate scientists were attracted to BA because they could maintain membership in the academic gift economy. Baird reflected on the company's record in 1975 in an unpublished memoir:

> [C]ertain things could have been done better. They could have been done with more of an idea with respect to money. But here was a period that was absolutely exciting in terms of . . . producing new and interesting stuff. . . . More than that, I guess my alumni from that period [BA employees from the 1930s, 1940s, and 1950s] are probably more interesting and more important than almost anything I know right now. . . . I guess the difference, looking backwards, is that I was much more interested in science and the improvement of science and what science could do than I was interested in making money. Now that may sound kind of peculiar but, nevertheless, I think if you go back over

3. This instrument now is at the Smithsonian's Museum of History and Technology.

all these years and look at all of our annual reports, you will find that somehow each year we ended with a little bit of plus and a hell of a lot of excitement. (Baird 1975, ch. 10, pp. 2–3)

The trick was to promote this excitement while making sure that each year ended up "with a little bit of plus."

8. THE GIFT

Pierre Bourdieu presents science in terms of capitalist metaphors in order to counter "the irenic image of the 'scientific community', as described by scientific hagiography" (Bourdieu 1975, p. 19). He seeks to create more critical space between those who create scientific knowledge and those who study the creation of science and technology, who have subsequently come to be called science and technology scholars. He argues against "the notion of a sort of 'kingdom of ends' knowing no other laws than that of the perfect competition of ideas, a contest infallibly decided by the intrinsic strength of the true idea" (ibid., p. 19).

The recent fracas known as "the science wars" testifies to the success of the movement Bourdieu helped initiate. We now have detailed studies of the argumentation and politics that make up the daily lives of scientists and engineers. No one now sees the development of science and technology as a "perfect competition of ideas." Why are there "science wars" then? On what basis can someone take up the standard against this evidently realistic portrayal of the development of science and technology?

Many scientists and engineers find the descriptions of "their work" by science and technology studies scholars (in a general and not necessarily personal sense) grossly inaccurate. Since in many cases such descriptions are not complimentary, and since these same scientists and engineers are interested parties, their reluctance to accept and rejoice in the descriptions presented by science and technology scholars is not surprising. But more is at issue here. It is the mythology of science and technology—"the notion of a sort of 'kingdom of ends' knowing no other laws than that of the perfect competition of ideas"—that has been challenged. If all is simply struggle for position, for "epistemic capital" held and deployed by "epistemic robber barons," then the "hell of a lot of excitement" that took place at Baird Associates in the 1930s, 1940s, and 1950s makes little sense. Baird and his partners weren't simply trying to gain market share, either in capitalist or in epistemic terms. In "producing new and interesting stuff," they were finding out about the world. This was exciting. They were—or at least they believed they were—contributing to humankind's knowledge. This was their "kingdom of ends."

Understanding knowledge in terms of gift exchange serves this kingdom of ends. The primary feature of gift economies, as opposed to commodity economies, is the creation of community. In the case of making knowledge, gift exchange creates the community that contributes to that kingdom of ends that can best be characterized by our learning about our world. It is participation in a community that believes in such a kingdom of ends that justifies the struggles both with nature—the week my father went without sleep building Specky—and with other members of the community for recognition and reward, as documented by science and technology scholars.

Knowledge is a gift. It is a miracle that we can make knowledge and that we can take knowledge made by our predecessors and make new knowledge with it. To be able to "stand on the shoulders of giants," to join this community, is not an entitlement. We need to do what we can to preserve this community so that we can continue to engage in the excitement of knowledge making. Thing knowledge makes this task more difficult, but, in our contemporary high-tech "thing-knowledge world," more vital. This will be a defining struggle during the twenty-first century.

References

Allen, M. J., and W. M. Yen. 1979. *Introduction to Measurement Theory.* Monterey, Calif.: Brooks/Cole.

Anderson, R. G. W., J. A. Bennett, and W. F. Ryan, eds. 1993. *Making Instruments Count: Essays on Historical Scientific Instruments Presented to Gerard L'Estrange Turner.* Aldershot, Hants; Brookfield, Vt.: Variorum.

Annertz, M., H. Wingstrand, et al. 1996. "MR Imaging as the Primary Modality for Neuroradiologic Evaluation of the Lumbar Spine: Effects on Cost and Number of Examinations." *Acta Radiologica* 37, no. 3, pt. 1: 373–80.

Aristotle. 1984. *The Complete Works of Aristotle: The Revised Oxford Translation.* Edited by Jonathan Barnes. Princeton: Princeton University Press.

Ashmore, Malcolm. 1993. "The Theatre of the Blind: Starring a Promethean Prankster, a Phoney Phenomenon, a Prism, a Rocket, and a Piece of Wood." *Social Studies of Science* 23: 67–106.

Audi, R. 1998. *Epistemology: A Contemporary Introduction to the Theory of Knowledge.* London: Routledge.

Ayer, A. J. 1974. "Truth, Verification and Verisimilitude." In *The Philosophy of Karl Popper,* edited by P. A. Schilpp, pp. 684–91. La Salle, Ill.: Open Court.

Baird Associates. 1937. "Financial Statement." Cambridge, Mass.: Baird Associates.

———. 1938. "Statement of Organization and Aims." Cambridge, Mass.: Baird Associates.

———. 1950. *Better Analysis,* 1: 1–12. Cambridge, Mass.: Baird Associates.

———. 1953. Untitled. Cambridge, Mass.: Baird Associates.

———. 1956. *Spectromet: Direct Reading Analysis on the Plant Floor.* Advertising Bulletin #42. Cambridge, Mass.: Baird Associates.

Baird-Atomic. 1959. *A Comparison of Analytical Methods.* Advertising Brochure. Cambridge, Mass.: Baird-Atomic.

Baird Corporation. N.d. *Installations of Optical Emission Instruments.* Bedford, Mass.: Baird Corporation.

Baird, D. 1983. "Conceptions of Scientific Law and Progress in Science." In *The*

Limits of Lawfulness: Studies on the Scope and Nature of Scientific Knowledge, edited by N. Rescher, pp. 33–41. Lanham, Md.: University Press of America.

———. 1987. "Exploratory Factor Analysis, Instruments and the Logic of Discovery." *British Journal for the Philosophy of Science* 38: 319–37.

———. 1991. "Baird Associates Commercial Three-Meter Grating Spectrograph and the Transformation of Analytical Chemistry." *Rittenhouse* 5, no. 3: 65–80.

———. 1999. "Internal History and the Philosophy of Experiment: An Essay Review of *The Creation of Scientific Effects* by Jed Z. Buchwald; *Experiment and the Making of Meaning* by David Gooding; [and] *The Mangle of Practice* by Andrew Pickering." *Perspectives on Science* 7, no. 3: 383–406.

Baird, D., and T. Faust. 1990. "Scientific Instruments, Scientific Progress and the Cyclotron." *British Journal for the Philosophy of Science* 41: 147–75.

Baird, D., and A. Nordmann. 1994. "Facts-Well-Put." *British Journal for the Philosophy of Science* 45: 37–77.

Baird, W. S. 1975. Memoirs. MS in the possession of Davis Baird.

———. 1979. Acceptance Speech: 1979 Scientific Apparatus Makers Association Award. MS in the possession of Davis Baird.

Baly, E. C. C. 1927. *Spectroscopy.* London: Longmans, Green.

Bedini, S. A. 1994. "In Pursuit of Provenance: The George Graham Proto-Orreries." In *Learning, Language and Invention: Essays Presented to Francis Maddison,* edited by W. D. Hackmann and A. J. Turner, pp. 54–77. Astrolabica, no. 6. Brookfield, Vt.: Ashgate; Paris: Société internationale de l'Astrolabe; Aldershot, Hants: Variorum.

Benfield, R. 1995. "Nursing Science: Considering a Philosophy of Instrumentation." MS.

Bennett, J. A. 1984. *The Celebrated Phaenomena of Colours: The Early History of the Spectroscope.* Cambridge: Whipple Museum of the History of Science.

Black, J. 1803. *Lectures on the Elements of Chemistry.* 2 vols. Edinburgh: W. Creech.

Block, F. 1946. "Nuclear Induction." *Physical Review* 70: 460–74.

Block, F., W. W. Hansen, et al. 1946. "The Nuclear Induction Experiment." *Physical Review* 70: 474–85.

Bonjour, L. 1985. *The Structure of Empirical Knowledge.* Cambridge, Mass.: Harvard University Press.

Bourdieu, P. 1975. "The Specificity of the Scientific Field and the Social Conditions of the Progress of Reason." *Social Science Information* 14, no. 6: 19–47.

———. 1997. "Marginalia—Some Additional Notes on the Gift." In *The Logic of the Gift,* edited by A. D. Schrift, pp. 231–41. New York: Routledge.

Boyle, R. 1660. *New Experiments Physico-Mechanicall, Touching The Spring of the Air, and its Effects, (Made, for the most part, in a New Pneumatical Engine).* Oxford: T. Robinson.

————. 1809. "New Pneumatical Experiments about Respiration." In *Philosophical Transactions of the Royal Society,* edited by C. Hutton, G. Shaw, and R. Pearson (abridged), 1: 473–89. London: Baldwin.

Brain, R. M., and M. N. Wise. 1999. "Muscles and Engines: Indicator Diagrams and Helmholtz's Graphical Methods." In *The Science Studies Reader,* edited by M. Biagioli, pp. 51–66. New York: Routledge.

Bronowski, J. 1981. "Honest Jim and the Tinker Toy Model." In *The Double Helix: A Personal Account of the Discovery of the Structure of DNA.* Edited by G. Stent. New York: Norton.

Bronskill, M. J., E. R. McVeigh, et al. 1988. "Syrinx-like Artifacts on MR Images of the Spinal Cord." *Radiology* 166, no. 2: 485–88.

Brush, S. 1988. *The History of Modern Science: A Guide to the Second Scientific Revolution, 1800–1950.* Ames: Iowa State University Press.

Bucciarelli, L. L. 1994. *Designing Engineers.* Cambridge, Mass.: MIT Press.

————. 2000. "Object and Social Artifact in Engineering Design." In *The Empirical Turn in the Philosophy of Technology,* edited by P. A. Kroes and A. W. M. Meijers, pp. 67–80. Research in Philosophy and Technology, ser. ed., C. Mitcham, vol. 20. Amsterdam: JAI-Elsevier, 2001.

Buchwald, J. Z. 1985. *From Maxwell to Microphysics.* Chicago: University of Chicago Press.

————. 1994. *The Creation of Scientific Effects.* Chicago: University of Chicago Press.

————. 1998. "Reflections on Hertz and the Hertzian Dipole." In *Heinrich Hertz: Classical Physicist, Modern Philosopher,* edited by D. Baird, R. I. G. Hughes, and A. Nordmann, pp. 269–80. Dordrecht: Kluwer.

Busch, W. 1986. *Joseph Wright of Derby: Das Experiment mit der Luftpumpe. Eine Heilige Allianz zwischen Wissenschaft und Religion.* Frankfurt a / M: Fischer Taschenbuch.

Caplow, T. 1982. *Middletown Families: Fifty Years of Change and Continuity.* Minneapolis: University of Minnesota Press.

Cardwell, D. S. L. 1967. "Some Factors in the Early Development of the Concepts of Power, Work and Energy." *British Journal for the History of Science* 3, no. 11: 209–24.

————. 1971. *From Watt to Clausius: The Rise of Thermodynamics in the Early Industrial Age.* London: Heinemann Educational Books.

Carnot, Sadi. 1824. *Réflexions sur la puissance motrice du feu et sur les machines propres à développer cette puissance.* Paris: Bachelier.

Carpenter, R. O. B., E. DuBois, et al. 1947. "Direct-Reading Spectrometer for Ferrous Analysis." *Journal of the Optical Society of America* 37: 707–13.

Carrier, J. G. 1995. *Gifts and Commodities: Exchange and Western Capitalism since 1700.* New York: Routledge Chapman & Hall.

Cartwright, N. 1983. *How the Laws of Physics Lie.* Oxford: Oxford University Press.

Chamberlain, F. 1958. *Baird-Atomic, Inc.: Principal Products, Past and Present (1936–1957).* Cambridge, Mass.: Baird-Atomic.

Cheal, D. 1988. *The Gift Economy.* New York: Routledge Chapman & Hall.

Clarke, B. L. 1947. "What Is Analysis?" *Industrial and Engineering Chemistry, Analytical Edition* 19, no. 11: 822.

Cockcroft, J. D., and E. T. S. Walton. 1932. "Experiments with High Velocity Positive Ions, II: The Disintegration of Elements by High Velocity Protons." *Proceedings of the Royal Society* A 137: 229–42.

Cohen, I. B. 1985. *Revolution in Science.* Cambridge, Mass.: Harvard University Press.

Cohen, M., and D. Baird. 1999. "Why Trade?" *Perspectives on Science* 7, no. 2: 231–54.

Collins, H., and M. Kusch. 1998. *The Shape of Actions.* Cambridge, Mass.: MIT Press.

Conant, J. B. 1950. *Robert Boyle's Experiments in Pneumatics.* Cambridge, Mass.: Harvard University Press.

Conant, J. B., and L. K. Nash, eds. 1957. *Harvard Case Studies in Experimental Science.* Cambridge, Mass.: Harvard University Press.

Crick, F. 1988. *What Mad Pursuit: A Personal View of Scientific Discovery.* New York: Basic Books.

Crouse, J., and D. Trusheim. 1988. *The Case against the SAT.* Chicago: University of Chicago Press.

Daniell, J. F. 1820a. "On a New Hygrometer, Which Measures the Force and Weight of Aqueous Vapor in Atmosphere, and the Corresponding Degree of Evaporation." *Quarterly Journal of Science* 8: 298–336.

———. 1820b. "On the New Hygrometer." *Quarterly Journal of Science* 9: 128–37.

———. 1823. *Meteorological Essays.* London: T. & G. Underwood.

Darwin, E. [1791] 1978. *The Botanic Garden.* New York: Garland.

Daston, L. 1988. "The Factual Sensibility." *Isis* 79: 452–67.

———. 1991. "Baconian Facts, Academic Civility, and the Prehistory of Objectivity." *Annals of Scholarship* 8, no. 3: 337–63.

———. 1992. "Objectivity and the Escape from Perspective." *Social Studies of Science* 22: 597–618.

Daston, L., and P. Galison. 1992. "The Image of Objectivity." *Representations* 40 (Fall 1992): 81–128.

Davenport, W. R. 1929. *Biography of Thomas Davenport: The "Brandon Blacksmith," Inventor of the Electric Motor.* Montpelier, Vt.: Vermont Historical Society.

Davis, N. P. 1968. *Lawrence and Oppenheimer.* New York: Simon & Schuster.

Deming, S., and S. Morgan. 1987. *Experimental Design: A Chemometric Approach.* Amsterdam: Elsevier.

Dieke, G. H., and H. M. Crosswhite. 1945. "Direct Intensity Measurements of Spectrum Lines with Photo-Multiplier Tubes." *Journal of the Optical Society of America* 35: 471–80.

Donkin, S. B. 1937. "The Society of Civil Engineers (Smeatonians)." *Transactions of the Newcomen Society for the Study of the History of Engineering and Technology* 17: 51–71.

Dow Chemical Company. 1946. "Mechanical Brain for Magnesium Analysis." *Dow Diamond,* 2–5.

Duffendack, O. S., and W. E. Morris. (1942). "An Investigation of the Properties and Applications of the Geiger-Muller Photoelectron Counter." *Journal of the Optical Society of America* 32: 8–24.

Dym, C. 1994. *Engineering Design: A Synthesis of Views.* Cambridge: Cambridge University Press.

Elkins, J. 1999. *What Painting Is.* New York: Routledge.

Emerson, R. W. 1876. *Essays, Second Series.* Boston: Houghton Mifflin.

Ewart, P. 1813. "On the Measure of Moving Force." *Memoirs and Proceedings of the Manchester Literary and Philosophical Society* 7: 105–258.

Ewing, G. 1969. *Instrumental Methods of Chemical Analysis.* New York: McGraw-Hill.

———. 1976. "Analytical Chemistry: The Past 100 Years." *Chemical and Engineering News,* April 6.

Faraday, M. 1821a. "Historical Sketch of Electro-Magnetism." *Annals of Philosophy* 18: 195–200, 274–90.

———. 1821b. "On Some New Electromagnetical Motions, and on the Theory of Magnetism." *Quarterly Journal of Science* 12: 74–96.

———. 1822a. "Description of an Electro-Magnetical Apparatus for the Exhibition of Rotatory Motion." *Quarterly Journal of Science* 12: 283–85.

———. 1822b. "Electro-Magnetic Rotations Apparatus." *Quarterly Journal of Science* 12: 186.

———. 1822c. "Historical Sketch of Electro-Magnetism." *Annals of Philosophy* 19: 107–21.

———. 1822d. "Note on New Electro-Magnetical Motions." *Quarterly Journal of Science* 12: 416–21.

———. 1844. *Experimental Researches in Electricity.* London: Richard & John Edward Taylor.

———. 1971. *The Selected Correspondence of Michael Faraday,* vol. 1, *1812–1848.* Cambridge: Cambridge University Press.

Ferguson, J. 1809. *Astronomy Explained.* London: J. Johnson.

Fischer, R. B. 1956. "Trends in Analytical Chemistry—1955." *Analytical Chemistry* 27, no. 12: 9A–15A.

———. 1965. "Trends in Analytical Chemistry—1965." *Analytical Chemistry* 37, no. 12: 27A–34A.

Francoeur, E. 1997. "The Forgotten Tool: The Design and Use of Molecular Models." *Social Studies of Science* 27, no. 1: 7–40.

Franklin, A. 1986. *The Neglect of Experiment.* Cambridge: Cambridge University Press.

———. 1990. *Experiment: Right or Wrong.* Cambridge: Cambridge University Press.

Franklin, B. 1941. *Benjamin Franklin's Experiments: A New Edition of Frank-lin's Experiments and Observations on Electricity*. Cambridge, Mass.: Harvard University Press.

―――. 1972. *The Papers of Benjamin Franklin*. New Haven, Conn.: Yale University Press.

Franks, Felix. 1983. *Polywater*. Cambridge, Mass.: MIT Press.

Friedel, R., P. Israel, and B. S. Finn. 1987. *Edison's Electric Light: Biography of an Invention*. New Brunswick, N.J.: Rutgers University Press.

Galison, P. 1987. *How Experiments End*. Chicago: University of Chicago Press.

―――. 1997. *Image and Logic: A Material Culture of Microphysics*. Chicago: University of Chicago Press.

Gawande, A. 1998. "The Pain Perplex." *New Yorker*, September 21, 1998, pp. 86–94.

Gee, B. 1991. "Electromagnetic Engines: Pre-technology and Development Immediately Following Faraday's Discovery of Electromagnetic Rotations." *History of Technology* 13: 41–72.

General Electric Medical Systems. 1993. *Scanning: Signa Advantage 5.4 Operating Documentation, GE Medical Systems*.

Gerlach, W., and E. Schweitzer. 1931. *Foundations and Methods of Chemical Analysis by the Emission Spectrum*. London: Adam Hilger.

Giere, R. 1988. *Explaining Science: A Cognitive Approach*. Chicago: University of Chicago Press.

Gigerenzer, G., Z. Swijtink, et al., eds. 1989. *The Empire of Chance: How Probability Changed Science and Everyday Life*. Cambridge: Cambridge University Press.

Gilbert, D. 1827. "On the Expediency of Assigning Specific Names to All Such Functions of Simple Elements as Represent Definite Physical Properties: With a Suggestion of a New Term in Mechanics; Illustrated by an Investigation of the Machine Moved by Recoil, and Also by Some Observations on the Steam Engine." *Philosophical Transactions of the Royal Society* 117, no. 1: 25–38.

Gleick, J. 1993. *Genius: The Life and Science of Richard Feynman*. New York: Pantheon Books.

Godelier, M. 1999. *The Enigma of the Gift*. Chicago: University of Chicago Press.

Goldman, A. 1986. *Epistemology and Cognition*. Cambridge, Mass.: Harvard University Press.

Gooding, D. 1990. *Experiment and the Making of Meaning*. Dordrecht: Kluwer.

Goodman, N. 1968. *Languages of Art: An Approach to a Theory of Symbols*. New York: Bobbs-Merrill.

―――. 1983. *Fact, Fiction and Forecast*. Cambridge, Mass.: Harvard University Press.

Gregory, C. A. 1982. *Gifts and Commodities*. New York: Academic Press.

Haack, S. 1979. "Epistemology *with* a Knowing Subject." *Review of Metaphysics* 33, no. 2: 309–35.

———. 1991. "What is 'the Problem of the Empirical Basis', and Does Johnny Wideawake Solve It?" *British Journal for the Philosophy of Science* 42, no. 3: 369–89.

———. 1993. *Evidence and Inquiry: Toward Reconstruction in Epistemology.* Oxford: Blackwell.

Hacking, I., 1983a. *Representing and Intervening.* Cambridge: Cambridge University Press.

———. 1983b. "Was There a Probabilistic Revolution 1800–1930?" In *Probability since 1800: Interdisciplinary Studies of Scientific Development,* edited by M. Heidelberger, L. Krüger, and R. Rheinwald, pp. 487–506. Bielefeld, Germany: B. K. Verlag GmbH.

———. 1987. "Was There a Probabilistic Revolution 1800–1930?" In *The Probabilistic Revolution,* vol. 1: *Ideas in History,* edited by L. Krüger, L. Daston, and M. Heidelberger, 1: 45–55. Cambridge, Mass.: MIT Press.

———. 1992. "The Self-Vindication of the Laboratory Sciences." In *Science as Practice and Culture,* edited by A. Pickering, pp. 29–64. Chicago: University of Chicago Press.

Hacking, I., ed. 1981. *Scientific Revolutions.* Oxford Readings in Philosophy. Oxford: Oxford University Press.

Hallett, L. T. 1947. "The Analyst's Column." *Industrial and Engineering Chemistry, Analytical Edition* 19, no. 10: 15A.

———. 1948. "The Analyst's Column." *Analytical Chemistry* 20, no. 10: 25A.

Hankins, T., and R. Silverman, eds. 1995. *Instruments and the Imagination.* Princeton, N.J.: Princeton University Press.

Harrison, G. R. 1938a. "A Comparison of Prism and Grating Instruments for Spectrographic Analysis of Materials." In *Spectroscopy in Science and Industry: Proceedings of the Fifth Summer Conference on Spectroscopy and its Applications,* edited by G. R. Harrison, pp. 31–37. New York: Wiley.

———, ed. 1938b. *Proceedings of the Fifth Summer Conference on Spectroscopy and Its Applications.* New York: Wiley.

———. 1939a. "New Tables of the 100,000 Principal Spectrum Lines of the Chemical Elements between 10,000 Å and 2,000 Å." In [MIT], *Massachusetts Institute of Technology Wavelength Tables, with Intensities in Arc, Spark, or Discharge Tube,* measured and compiled under the direction of G. R. Harrison, pp. 118–24. New York: Wiley.

———, ed. 1939b. *Proceedings of the Sixth Summer Conference on Spectroscopy and Its Applications.* New York: Wiley.

———, ed. 1940. *Proceedings of the Seventh Summer Conference on Spectroscopy and Its Applications.* New York: Wiley.

Harrison, G. R., R. C. Lord, and J. R. Loofbourow. 1948. *Practical Spectroscopy.* New York: Prentice-Hall.

Hasler, M. F. 1938. "The Practice of Arc Spectrochemistry with a Grating Spectrograph." In *Proceedings of the Fifth Summer Conference on Spectroscopy and Its Applications*, edited by G. R. Harrison, pp. 43–46. New York: Wiley.

Hasler, M. F., and H. W. Dietert. 1944. "Direct Reading Instrument for Spectrochemical Analysis." *Journal of the Optical Society of America* 34: 751–58.

Hasler, M. F., R. W. Lindhurst, et al. (1948). "The Quantometer: A Direct Reading Instrument for Spectrochemical Analysis." *Journal of the Optical Society of America* 38: 789–99.

Heidegger, M. 1977. *The Question Concerning Technology and Other Essays.* New York: Harper & Row.

Henkelman, R., and M. Bronskill. 1987. "Artifacts in Magnetic Resonance Imaging." *Reviews of Magnetic Resonance in Medicine* 2, no. 1: 1–126.

Hesse, M. 1963. *Models and Analogies in Science.* London: Sheed & Ward.

H. H. 1822. "Letter to the Editor: Account of a Steam-Engine Indicator." *Quarterly Journal of Science, Literature and the Arts* 13: 91–95.

Hills, R. L. 1989. *Power from Steam: A History of the Stationary Steam Engine.* Cambridge: Cambridge University Press.

Hindle, B. 1981. *Emulation and Invention.* New York: Norton.

Hindle, B., and S. Lubar. 1986. *Engines of Change: The American Industrial Revolution 1790–1860.* Washington, D.C.: Smithsonian Institution Press.

Hippel, E. von. 1988. *The Sources of Innovation.* Oxford: Oxford University Press.

Hoffmann, B. 1962. *The Tyranny of Testing.* New York: Crowell-Collier Press.

Hoffmann, R. 1995. *The Same and Not the Same.* New York: Columbia University Press.

Hoult, D., C.-N. Chen, et al. (1986). "The Field Dependence of NMR Imaging II. Arguments Concerning an Optimal Field Strength." *Magnetic Resonance Medicine* 3: 730–46.

Hoult, D., and R. Richards. 1976. "The Signal to Noise Ratio of the Nuclear Magnetic Resonance Experiment." *Journal of Magnetic Resonance* 24: 71–85.

Hughes, R. I. G. 1997. "Models and Representation." *Philosophy of Science* 64 (Proceedings): S325–S336.

Hughes, T. P. 1998. *Rescuing Prometheus.* New York: Pantheon Books.

Hutson, J. M., and R. H. Petrie. 1986. "Possible Limitations of Fetal Monitoring." *Clinical Obstetrics and Gynecology* 29, no. 1: 104–13.

Hyde, L. 1979. *The Gift: Imagination and the Erotic Life of Property.* New York: Vintage Books.

Ihde, A. 1984. *The Development of Modern Chemistry.* New York: Dover.

Ihde, D. 1991. *Instrumental Realism.* Evanston, Ill.: Northwestern University Press.

Industrial and Engineering Chemistry, Analytical Edition 11, no. 10 (1939): 563–82.

"Instrument Makers of Cambridge." *Fortune* 33, no. 6 (December 1948): 136–41.

James, William. [1890] 1955. *The Principles of Psychology*. New York: Dover.

Jamieson, A. 1889. *A Text-book on Steam and Steam-Engines*. London: Charles Griffin.

Juaristi, E. 1991. *Introduction to Stereochemistry and Conformational Analysis*. New York: Wiley.

Judson, H. F. 1979. *The Eighth Day of Creation*. New York: Simon & Schuster.

Keyes, D. B. 1947. "The Importance of the Analytical Research Chemist in Industry." *Industrial and Engineering Chemistry, Analytical Edition* 19, no. 8: 507.

King, H. C., and J. R. Millburn. 1978. *Geared to the Stars: The Evolution of Planetariums, Orreries, and Astronomical Clocks*. Toronto: University of Toronto Press.

King, W. J. 1963. "The Development of Electrical Technology in the Nineteenth Century." In Smithsonian Institution, *Contributions from the Museum of History and Technology*, 19–30: 231–407.

Kirchhoff, G., and R. Bunsen. 1860a. "Chemical Analysis by Spectrum Observations, 1." *Philosophical Magazine* 20: 89–109.

———. 1860b. "Chemische Analyze durch Spectralbeobachtungen, 1." *Annalen der Physik und Chemie* 111: 160–89.

———. 1861a. "Chemical Analysis by Spectrum Observations, 2." *Philosophical Magazine* 22: 329–510.

———. 1861b. "Chemische Analyze durch Spectralbeobachtungen, 2." *Annalen der Physik und Chemie* 113: 337–425.

Kolthoff, I. 1973. "Development of Analytical Chemistry as a Science." *Analytical Chemistry* 45.

Kroes, P. 1996. "Technical and Contextual Constraints in Design: An Essay on Determinants on Technological Change." In COST A4, vol. 5: *The Role of Design in the Shaping of Technology*, edited by J. Perrin and D. Vinck, pp. 43–76.

———. 1998. "Technological Explanations: The Relation between Structure and Function of Technological Objects." *Techné: Journal of the Society for Philosophy and Technology* 3, no. 3, http://scholar.lib.vt.edu/ejournals/SPT/v3n3/html/KROES.

———. 2000. "Technical Functions as Dispositions: A Critical Assessment." *Techné: Journal of the Society for Philosophy and Technology* 5, no. 3, http://scholar.lib.vt.edu/ejournals/SPT/v3n3/html/KROES.html.

Krüger, L., L. J. Daston, et al., eds. 1987. *The Probabilistic Revolution*. 2 vols. Cambridge, Mass.: Harvard University Press.

Kuhn, T. S. [1962] 1970, 1996. *The Structure of Scientific Revolutions*. 2d ed., enl., 1970. 3d ed. 1996 Chicago: University of Chicago Press.

———. 1977. "The Function of Measurement in Modern Physical Science." In id., *The Essential Tension: Selected Studies in Scientific Tradition and Change*, pp. 178–224. Chicago: University of Chicago Press.

Kumar, A., D. Welti, et al. 1975. "NMR Fourier Zeugmatography." *Journal of Magnetic Resonance* 18: 69–83.

Kurie, F. N. D. 1938. "Present-Day Design and Technique of the Cyclotron." *Journal of Applied Physics* 9: 691–701.

Lacey, W. N. 1924. *A Course of Instruction in Instrumental Methods of Chemical Analysis.* New York: Macmillan.

Laitinen, H., and W. Harris. 1975. *Chemical Analysis: An Advanced Text and Reference.* New York: McGraw-Hill.

Laitinen, H. A., and G. W. Ewing, eds. 1977. *A History of Analytical Chemistry.* Washington, D.C.: American Chemical Society, Division of Analytical Chemistry.

Lakatos, I. 1970. "Falsification and the Methodology of Scientific Research Programmes." In *Criticism and the Growth of Knowledge,* edited by I. Lakatos and A. Musgrave, pp. 91–197. Cambridge: Cambridge University Press.

———. 1978. *The Methodology of Scientific Research Programmes.* Vol. 1 of *Philosophical Papers.* Cambridge: Cambridge University Press.

Lakatos, I., and A. Musgrave, eds. 1970. *Criticism and the Growth of Knowledge.* Cambridge: Cambridge University Press.

Latour, B. 1987. *Science in Action: How to Follow Scientists and Engineers through Society.* Cambridge, Mass.: Harvard University Press.

———. 1999. *Pandora's Hope: Essays on the Reality of Science Studies.* Cambridge, Mass.: Harvard University Press.

Latour, B., and S. Woolgar. 1979. *Laboratory Life.* Beverly Hills, Calif.: Sage.

Laudan, L. 1977. *Progress and Its Problems.* Berkeley: University of California Press.

Lauterbur, P. C. 1973. "Image Formation by Induced Local Interactions: Examples Employing Nuclear Magnetic Resonance." *Nature* 242: 190–91.

———. 1981. "NMR Zeugmatographic Imaging by True Three-Dimensional Reconstruction." *Journal of Computer Tomography* 5: 285.

Lawrence, E. O. 1952. "The Evolution of the Cyclotron." In *Les Prix Nobel en 1951.* Stockholm: Nobelstifting.

Lawrence, E. O., and D. Cooksey. 1936. "On the Apparatus for the Multiple Acceleration of Light Ions to High Speeds." *Physical Review* 50: 1131–40.

Lawrence, E. O., and N. E. Edlefsen. 1930. "On the Production of High Speed Protons." *Science* 72: 376–77.

Lawrence, E. O., and M. S. Livingston. 1932. "The Production of High Speed Light Ions without the Use of High Voltages." *Physical Review* 40: 19–35.

———. 1934. "The Multiple Acceleration of Ions to Very High Speeds." *Physical Review* 45: 608–12.

Lawrence, E. O., M. S. Livingston, et al. 1932. "The Disintegration of Lithium by Swiftly Moving Protons." *Physical Review* 42: 150–51.

Lawrence, E. O., and D. Sloan. 1931. "The Production of High Speed Canal Rays without the Use of High Voltages." *Proceedings of the National Academy of Sciences* 17: 64–70.

Learner, R. C. M. 1968. "Spectrograph Design, 1918–68." *Journal of Scientific Instruments*, 2d ser., 1: 589–94.

Lemann, N. 1999. *The Big Test: The Secret History of the American Meritocracy.* New York: Farrar, Straus & Giroux.

Lévi-Strauss, C. 1969. *The Elementary Structures of Kinship.* Boston: Beacon Press.

Liebhafsky, H. A. 1962. "Modern Analytical Chemistry: A Subjective View." *Analytical Chemistry* 34, no. 7: 23A–33A.

Lingane, J. J. 1948. "The Role of the Analyst." *Analytical Chemistry* 20, no. 1: 1–3.

Livingston, M. S. 1931. "The Production of High-Velocity Hydrogen Ions without the Use of High Voltages." Ph.D. thesis, University of California, Berkeley.

———. 1933. "The Attainment of High Vacua in Large Metal Chambers." *Physical Review* 43: 214.

———. 1936. "The Magnetic Resonance Accelerator." *Review of Scientific Instruments* 7: 55–68.

———. 1944. "The Cyclotron II." *Journal of Applied Physics* 15: 128–147.

———. 1969. *Particle Accelerators: A Brief History.* Cambridge, Mass.: Harvard University Press.

———. 1985. "History of the Cyclotron, I." In *History of Physics: Readings from Physics Today, Number Two,* edited by S. R. Weart and M. Phillips, 255–60. New York: American Institute of Physics.

Livingston, M. S., and J. P. Blewett. 1962. *Particle Accelerators.* New York: McGraw-Hill.

Livingston, M. S., and E. O. Lawrence. 1933. "The Production of 4,800,000 Volt Hydrogen Ions." *Physical Review* 43: 212.

Longford, N. 1995. *Models for Uncertainty in Educational Testing.* New York: Springer-Verlag.

Lord, F., and M. Novick. 1968. *Statistical Theories of Mental Test Scores.* Reading, Mass.: Addison-Wesley.

Mahoney, M. 1999. Reading a Machine. Princeton University, http://www.princeton.edu/~hos/h398/readmach/modelt.html.

[MIT] Massachusetts Institute of Technology. Spectroscopy Laboratory. 1939. *Massachusetts Institute of Technology Wavelength Tables with Intensities in Arc, Spark, or Discharge Tube of More Than 100,000 Spectrum Lines, Most Strongly Emitted by the Atomic Elements under Normal Conditions of Excitation between 10,000 Å and 2000 Å Arranged in Order of Decreasing Wavelengths.* Measured and compiled under the direction of George R. Harrison by staff members of the Spectroscopy Laboratory of the Massachusetts Institute of Technology, assisted by the Works Progress Administration. [Cambridge, Mass.:] Technology Press, Massachusetts Institute of Technology; New York: Wiley.

Matheson, L. A., and J. L. Saunderson. 1952. "Optical and Electrical Properties of Polystyrene." In *Styrene: Its Polymers, Copolymers and Derivatives,* edited by R. H. Boundy, R. F. Boyer, and S. Stoesser, pp. 517–73. New York: Reinhold.

Mauss, M. [1925] 1990. *The Gift: The Form and Reason for Exchange in Archaic Societies.* New York: Norton.

Maxwell, J. C. 1876. "General Considerations Concerning Scientific Apparatus." In *Special Loan Collection of Scientific Apparatus,* pp. 1–21. London: South Kensington Museum Handbooks.

McCrone, W. C. 1948. "The Role of the Analyst." *Analytical Chemistry* 20, no. 1: 2–4.

McDonnell, L. M. 1994. *Policymakers' Views of Student Assessment.* Santa Monica, Calif.: RAND.

McMillan, E. M. 1959. "Particle Accelerators." In *Experimental Nuclear Physics,* edited by E. Segrè, 3: 639–785. New York: Wiley.

———. 1979. "Early History of Particle Accelerators." In *Nuclear Physics in Retrospect: Proceedings of a Symposium on the 1930's,* edited by R. H. Stuewer, pp. 113–55. Minneapolis: University of Minnesota Press.

———. 1985. "History of the Cyclotron." In *History of Physics: Readings from Physics Today, Number Two,* edited by S. R. Weart and M. Phillips, pp. 261–70. New York: American Institute of Physics.

Meggers, W. F., and B. F. Scribner. 1938. *Index to the Literature on Spectrochemical Analysis, 1920–1939.* Philadelphia: American Society for Testing Materials.

Megill, A. 1991. "Four Senses of Objectivity." *Annals of Scholarship* 8, nos. 1–2: 301–20.

Mellon, M. G. 1952. "Fisher Award Address: A Century of Colormetry." *Analytical Chemistry* 24, no. 6: 924–31.

Melville, S. H. 1962. "The Effect of Instrument Development on the Progress of Chemistry." *Transactions of the Society of Instrument Technology:* 216–18.

Mendoza, E., ed. 1960. *"Reflections on the Motive Power of Fire," by Sadi Carnot; and Other Papers on the Second Law of Thermodynamics, by É. Clapeyron and R. Clausius.* New York: Dover Publications.

Middleton, W. E. K. 1969. *Invention of the Meteorological Instruments.* Baltimore: Johns Hopkins Press.

Millburn, J. R. 1976. *Benjamin Martin: Author, Instrument-Maker, and "Country Showman."* Leyden: Noordhoff International Publishing.

Millburn, J. R., and H. C. King. 1988. *Wheelwright of the Heavens: The Life and Work of James Ferguson, FRS.* London: Vade-Mecum Press.

Mitcham, C. 1994. *Thinking Through Technology.* Chicago: University of Chicago Press.

Moore, J. H., C. C. Davis, and M. A. Coplan. 1983. *Building Scientific Apparatus: A Practical Guide to Design and Construction.* Reading, Mass.: Addison-Wesley.

Morris, P., ed. 2001. *From Classical to Modern Chemistry: The Instrumental Revolution.* London: National Museum of Science and Industry.

Morrison, M. 1998. "Modelling Nature: Between Physics and the Physical World." *Philosophia Naturalis* 35, no. 1: 65–85.

Muirhead, J. P. 1859. *The Life of James Watt with Selections from His Correspondence.* London: John Murray.

Müller, R. 1940. "American Apparatus, Instruments, and Instrumentation." *Industrial and Engineering Chemistry, Analytical Edition* 12, no. 10: 571–630.

———. 1941. "Instrumental Methods of Chemical Analysis." *Industrial and Engineering Chemistry, Analytical Edition* 13, no. 10: 667–754.

———. 1946a. "Instrumentation in Analysis." *Industrial and Engineering Chemistry, Analytical Edition* 18, no. 1: 21A–22A.

———. 1946b. "Instrumentation in Analysis." *Industrial and Engineering Chemistry, Analytical Edition* 18, no. 2: 25A–26A.

———. 1946c. "Instrumentation in Analysis." *Industrial and Engineering Chemistry, Analytical Edition* 18, no. 3: 29A–30A.

———. 1946d. "Instrumentation in Analysis." *Industrial and Engineering Chemistry, Analytical Edition* 18, no. 4: 24A–26A.

———. 1946e. "Instrumentation in Analysis." *Industrial and Engineering Chemistry, Analytical Edition* 18, no. 5: 23A–24A.

———. 1946f. "Instrumentation in Analysis." *Industrial and Engineering Chemistry, Analytical Edition* 18, no. 10: 25A.

———. 1947a. "Instrumentation." *Industrial and Engineering Chemistry, Analytical Edition* 19, no. 1: 23A–24A.

———. 1947b. "Instrumentation." *Industrial and Engineering Chemistry, Analytical Edition* 19, no. 5: 25A–26A.

———. 1947c. "Instrumentation in Analysis." *Industrial and Engineering Chemistry, Analytical Edition* 19, no. 7: 19A–20A.

———. 1947d. "Instrumentation." *Industrial and Engineering Chemistry, Analytical Edition* 19, no. 9: 26A–27A.

———. 1948. "Instrumentation." *Analytical Chemistry* 20, no. 6: 21A–22A.

———. 1949. "Instrumentation in Analysis." *Analytical Chemistry* 21, no. 6: 23A.

Murphy, K., and C. Davidshofer. 1991. *Psychological Testing: Principles and Applications.* Englewood Cliffs, N.J.: Prentice-Hall.

Murphy, W. J. 1947a. "The Profession of Analytical Chemist." *Industrial and Engineering Chemistry, Analytical Edition* 19, no. 3: 145.

———. 1947b. "The Analytical Chemist: Dispenser of Analyses or Analytical Advisor?" *Industrial and Engineering Chemistry, Analytical Edition* 19, no. 5: 289.

———. 1947c. "The Analytical Chemist." *Industrial and Engineering Chemistry, Analytical Edition* 19, no. 6: 361–63.

———. 1947d. "We Have Arrived!" *Industrial and Engineering Chemistry, Analytical Edition* 19, no. 12: 1131.

———. 1947e. "Fisher Award." *Industrial and Engineering Chemistry, Analytical Edition* 19, no. 10: 699.

———. 1948a. "Modern Objectivity in Analysis." *Analytical Chemistry* 20, no. 3: 187.

———. 1948b. "The Merck Fellowship in Analytical Chemistry." *Analytical Chemistry* 20, no. 10: 885.

Murphy, W. J., L. T. Hallett, et al. 1946. "Editorial Policies: Scope of the Analytical Edition." *Industrial and Engineering Chemistry, Analytical Edition* 18, no. 4: 217–18.

Muter, J. 1906. *A Short Manual of Analytical Chemistry.* Philadelphia: P. Blakiston's Son.

Nairn, A. 1980. *The Reign of ETS: The Corporation That Makes Up Minds.* Washington, D.C.: Ralph Nader.

National Commission on Testing and Public Policy. 1990. *From Gatekeeper to Gateway: Transforming Testing in America.* Chestnut Hill, Mass.: National Commission on Testing and Public Policy.

Nelson, C. E. 1952. Citation for the Willard H. Dow Memorial Award for Research in Magnesium for the year 1952. Midland, Mich.: Dow Chemical Company.

Nietzsche, F. 1982. *Thus Spoke Zarathustra.* In *The Portable Nietzsche,* edited by W. Kaufmann. New York: Penguin Books.

Nordmann, A. 1994. "Der Wissenschaftler als Medium der Natur." In *Die Erfindung der Natur,* edited by K. Orchard and J. Zimmermann, pp. 60–66. Freiburg: Rombach.

Noyes, W. A. 1911. *The Elements of Qualitative Analysis.* New York: Holt.

Olby, R. 1974. *The Path to the Double Helix.* Seattle: University of Washington Press.

Olsen, J. C. 1916. *Quantitative Chemical Analysis.* New York: D. Van Nostrand.

Ostwald, W. 1895. *The Scientific Foundations of Analytical Chemistry.* Translated by George M'Gowan. London: Macmillan.

Owen, D. 1985. *None of the Above: Behind the Myth of Scholastic Aptitude.* Boston: Houghton Mifflin.

Pacey, A. 1974. *The Maze of Ingenuity.* Cambridge, Mass.: MIT Press.

Pais, A. 1986. *Inward Bound: Of Matter and Forces in the Physical World.* New York: Oxford University Press.

Paul, W. 1979. "Early Days in the Development of Accelerators." In *Aesthetics and Science: Proceedings of the International Symposium in Honor of Robert R. Wilson,* pp. 25–71. Batavia, Ill.: Fermi National Accelerator Laboratory.

Peirce, C. S. 1931–35, 1958. *The Collected Papers of Charles Sanders Peirce.* Edited by C. Hartshorne and P. Weiss. 8 vols. Cambridge, Mass.: Harvard University Press.

Pickering, A. 1995. *The Mangle of Practice: Time, Agency and Science.* Chicago: University of Chicago Press.

Pitt, J. 1999. *Thinking about Technology.* New York: Seven Bridges Press.

Pitt, J., and E. Lugo, eds. *The Technology of Discovery and the Discovery of*

Technology: Proceedings of the 1991 Annual Conference of the Society for Philosophy and Technology. Blacksburg, Va.: Society for Philosophy and Technology.

Pittsburgh Conference. 1971. "The Pittsburgh Conference on Analytical Chemistry and Applied Spectroscopy." *Applied Spectroscopy* 25, no. 1: 121–52.

———. 1999. *Pittcon '99 Book of Abstracts.* Pittsburgh: Pittsburgh Conference.

Polanyi, M. 1966. *The Tacit Dimension.* Garden City, N.Y.: Doubleday.

Popper, K. 1959. *The Logic of Scientific Discovery.* London: Hutchinson. Originally published as *Logik der Forschung* (Vienna: J. Springer, 1935).

———. [1962] 1969. *Conjectures and Refutations: The Growth of Scientific Knowledge.* 3d ed. London: Routledge & Kegan Paul.

———. 1972. *Objective Knowledge: An Evolutionary Approach.* Oxford: Oxford University Press.

Porter, T. 1986. *The Rise of Statistical Thinking: 1820–1900.* Princeton, N.J.: Princeton University Press.

———. 1992. "Objectivity as Standardization: the Rhetoric of Impersonality in Measurement, Statistics, and Cost-Benefit Analysis." *Annals of Scholarship* 9, no. 2: 19–59.

———. 1995. *Trust in Numbers: The Pursuit of Objectivity in Science and Public Life.* Princeton, N.J.: Princeton University Press.

Press, E., and J. Washburn. 2000. "The Kept University." *Atlantic Monthly,* 285, no. 3: 39–54.

Price, D. J. de Solla. 1964. "Automata and the Origins of Mechanism and Mechanistic Philosophy." *Technology and Culture* 5, no. 1: 9–23.

———. 1980. "Philosophical Mechanism and Mechanical Philosophy: Some Notes toward a Philosophy of Scientific Instruments." *Annali dell'Istituto e Museo di Storia della Scienza di Firenze* 5: 75–85.

———. 1982. "Scientists and their Tools." In *Frontiers of Science: On the Brink of Tomorrow,* edited by D. d. S. Price, pp. 1–23. Washington, D.C.: National Geographic Special Publications.

———. 1984. "Notes towards a Philosophy of the Science / Technology Interaction." In *The Nature of Technological Knowledge: Are Models of Scientific Change Relevant?* edited by R. Laudan, pp. 105–14. Dordrecht: D. Reidel.

Priestley, J. 1775. *The History and Present State of Electricity, with Original Experiments.* London: Bathurst.

———. 1817–31. *Lectures on History and General Policy.* Vol. 24 of *The Theological and Miscellaneous Works of Joseph Priestley.* Edited by J. T. Rutt. 25 vols. London: G. Smallfield.

Quinton, A. J. 1966. "The Foundations of Knowledge." In *British Analytical Philosophy,* edited by B. Williams and A. Montefiore, pp. 55–86. London: Routledge & Kegan Paul.

Radder, H. 1988. *The Material Realization of Science.* Assen, Netherlands: Van Gorcum.

Rajchman, J. A., and R. L. Snyder. 1940. "An Electrically-Focused Multiplier Phototube." *Electronics* 13 (December): 20–23ff.

Rank, D. H., R. J. Pfister, et al. 1942. "Photoelectric Detection and Intensity Measurement in Raman Spectra." *Journal of the Optical Society of America* 32: 390–96.

Rankine, J. J., K. P. Gill, et al. 1998. "The Therapeutic Impact of Lumbar Spine MRI on Patients with Low Back and Leg Pain." *Clinical Radiology* 53, no. 9: 688–93.

Reid, D. B. 1839. *Elements of Chemistry*. Edinburgh: Machlachlan, Stewart.

Reynolds, T. 1983. *Stronger than a Hundred Men: A History of the Vertical Water Wheel*. Baltimore: Johns Hopkins University Press.

R. L. 1958. "Businessman-Scientist." *Johns Hopkins Magazine* 9: 11–22.

Robinson, E., and D. McKie. 1970. *Partners in Science: Letters of James Watt and Joseph Black*. Cambridge, Mass.: Harvard University Press.

Robison, J. 1822. *A System of Mechanical Philosophy*. 4 vols. Edinburgh: J. Murray.

Roper, S. 1885. *Engineer's Handy-Book*. Bridgeport, Conn.: Frederick Keppy.

Rose, M. E. 1938. "Focusing and Maximum Energy of Ions in the Cyclotron." *Physical Review* 53: 392–408.

Rosenberg, N. 1982. *Inside the Black Box: Technology and Economics*. Cambridge: Cambridge University Press.

Rothbart, D., and S. Slayden. 1994. "The Epistemology of a Spectrometer." *Philosophy of Science* 61, no. 1: 25–38.

Rowland, H. A. 1882. "Preliminary Notice of the Results Accomplished in the Manufacture and Theory of Gratings for Optical Purposes." *Philosophical Magazine* 13: 469–74.

———. 1883. "Concave Gratings for Optical Purposes." *American Journal of Science* 26: 87–98.

———. 1902. *The Physical Papers of Henry Augustus Rowland, Johns Hopkins University, 1876–1901; Collected for Publication by a Committee of the Faculty of the University*. Baltimore: Johns Hopkins Press.

Salleron, J. 1858–64. *Notice sur les instruments de précision, construits par J. Salleron*. 3 vols. Paris: 1, rue du Pont-de-Lodi (24, rue Pavée, au Marais).

Saunders, A. P. 1908. "A Note on the Experiment of the Cyrophorus." *Journal of Chemistry* 12: 279–82.

Saunderson, J. L. 1947. "Spectrochemical Analysis of Metals and Alloys by Direct Intensity Measurement Methods." In *Electronic Methods of Inspection of Metals: A Series of Seven Educational Lectures on Electronic Methods of Inspection of Metals Presented to Members of the A.S.M. during the Twenty-eighth National Metal Congress and Exposition, Atlantic City, November 18 to 22, 1946*, pp. 16–53. Cleveland: American Society for Metals.

Saunderson, J., V. J. Caldecourt, and E. W. Peterson. 1945. "A Photoelectric Instrument for Direct Spectrochemical Analysis." *Journal of the Optical Society of America* 35: 681–97.

Saunderson, J. L., and E. DuBois, inventors; Baird-Atomic, Inc., assignee. 1958. June 10. Automatic Means for Aligning Spectroscopic Components. U.S. patent 2,837,959.

Saunderson, J. L., and T. M. Hess. 1946. "Commercial Use of Direct Reading Spectrochemical Analysis of Magnesium Alloys." *Metal Progress* 49: 947–55.

Savage, R. A., G. H. Whitehouse, et al. 1997. "The Relationship between the Magnetic Resonance Imaging Appearance of the Lumbar Spine and Low Back Pain, Age and Occupation in Males." *European Spine Journal* 6, no. 2: 106–14.

Sawyer, R. A. 1944. *Experimental Spectroscopy.* New York: Prentice-Hall.

Sawyer, R. A., and H. B. Vincent. 1939. "Characteristics of Spectroscopic Light Sources." In *Proceedings of the Sixth Summer Conference on Spectroscopy and Its Applications,* edited by G. R. Harrison, pp. 54–59. New York: Wiley.

Schaffer, S. 1994. "Machine Philosophy: Demonstration Devices in Georgian Mechanics." *Osiris* 9: 157–82.

Schenk, G. H., R. B. Hahn, et al. 1977. *Quantitative Analytical Chemistry: Principles and Life Science Applications.* Boston: Allyn & Bacon.

Schiffer, M. 1994. "The Blacksmith's Motor." *Invention and Technology* 9, no. 3: 64.

Schrift, A., ed. 1997. *The Logic of the Gift.* New York: Routledge.

Science 110, no. 2858. 1949.

Shapin, S., and S. Shaffer. 1985. *Leviathan and the Air-Pump.* Princeton, N.J.: Princeton University Press.

Shapiro, G. 1991. *Alcyone: Nietzsche on Gifts, Noise, and Women.* Albany: State University of New York Press.

Shinn, T., and B. Joerges, eds. 2001. *Instrumentation: Between Science, State and Industry.* Sociology of the Sciences, vol. 22. Dordrecht: Kluwer.

Shulman, S. 1999. *Owning the Future.* Boston: Houghton Mifflin.

Sibum, O. 1994. "Working Experiments: Bodies, Machines and Heat Values." In *The Physics of Empire,* edited by R. Staley, pp. 29–56. Cambridge: Cambridge University Press.

———. 1995. "Reworking the Mechanical Value of Heat." *Studies in History and Philosophy of Science* 26: 73–106.

Skempton, A. W., ed. 1981. *John Smeaton, F.R.S.* London: Thomas Telford.

Skoog, D. A., and D. M. West. 1971. *Principles of Instrumental Analysis.* New York: Holt, Rinehart & Winston.

———. 1976 [1963]. *Fundamentals of Analytical Chemistry.* New York: Holt, Rinehart & Winston.

Slavin, M. 1940. "Prism versus Grating for Spectrochemical Analysis." In *Proceedings of the Seventh Summer Conference on Spectroscopy and Its Applications,* edited by G. R. Harrison, pp. 51–58. New York: Wiley.

———. 1978. *Atomic Absorption Spectroscopy.* New York: Wiley.

Smeaton, J. 1809a. "An Experimental Enquiry concerning the Natural Powers of Water and Wind to turn Mills and other Machines, depending on Circular Motion." In *Philosophical Transactions of the Royal Society of London from Their Commencement in 1665 to the year 1800, Abridged with notes and illustrations*, edited by C. Hutton, G. Shaw, and R. Pearson, 11: 338–70. London: C. & R. Baldwin.

———. 1809b. "An Experimental Examination of the Quantity and Proportion of Mechanic Power Necessary to be employed in giving Different Degrees of Velocity of Heavy Bodies from a State of Rest." In *Philosophical Transactions of the Royal Society of London from Their Commencement in 1665 to the year 1800, Abridged with notes and illustrations*, edited by C. Hutton, G. Shaw, and R. Pearson, 14: 72–84. London: C. & R. Baldwin.

———. 1809c. "New Fundamental Experiments on the Collision of Bodies." In *Philosophical Transactions of the Royal Society of London from Their Commencement in 1665 to the year 1800, Abridged with notes and illustrations*, edited by C. Hutton, G. Shaw and R. Pearson, 15: 295–305. London: C. & R. Baldwin.

Smiles, S. 1862. *Lives of the Engineers, with an Account of Their Principal Works: Comprising also a History of Inland Communication in Britain*. 3 vols. London: John Murray.

Smith, G. M. 1921. *Quantitative Chemical Analysis*. New York: Macmillan.

Snow, C. P. 1963. *The Two Cultures and a Second Look*. Cambridge: Cambridge University Press.

Sobel, D. 1995. *Longitude*. New York: Walker.

Staubermann, K. 1998. "Controlling Vision: The Photometry of Karl Friedrich Zöllner. History and Philosophy of Science." Ph.D. diss., University of Cambridge.

Strobel, H. A., and W. R. Heineman. [1960] 1989. *Chemical Instrumentation: A Systematic Approach*. 3d ed. New York: Wiley.

Strong, F. C. 1947. "Trends in Quantitative Analysis." *Industrial and Engineering Chemistry, Analytical Edition* 19, no. 12: 968–71.

Strong, J. 1936a. "Effect of Evaporated Films on Energy Distribution in Grating Spectra." *Physical Review* 49: 291–96.

———. 1936b. "The Evaporation Process and its Application to the Aluminizing of Large Telescope Mirrors." *Astrophysical Journal* 83: 401–23.

———. 1984. "Rowland's Diffraction-Grating Art." In *Henry Rowland and Astronomical Spectroscopy*, edited by R. C. Henry, D. H. DeVorkin, and P. Beer, pp. 137–41. Oxford: Pergamon Press.

Suckling, C. J., K. E. Suckling, et al. 1978. *Chemistry through Models: Concepts and Applications of Modelling in Chemical Science, Technology and Industry*. Cambridge: Cambridge University Press.

Suppe, F., ed. 1977. *The Structure of Scientific Theories*. Urbana: University of Illinois Press.

Suppes, P. 1961. "A Comparison of the Meaning and Use of Models in Mathematics and the Empirical Sciences." In *The Concept and Role of the Model in Mathematics and Natural and Social Science,* edited by H. Freudenthal, pp. 163–77. Dordrecht: D. Reidel.

———. 1962. "Models of Data." In *Logic, Methodology and Philosophy of Science: Proceedings of the 1960 International Congress,* edited by E. Nagel, P. Suppes, and A. Tarski, pp. 252–61. Stanford, Calif.: Stanford University Press.

———. 1967. "What Is a Scientific Theory?" In *Philosophy of Science Today,* edited by S. Morgenbesser, pp. 55–67. New York: Basic Books.

Swijtink, Z. 1987. "The Objectification of Observation: Measurement and Statistical Methods in the Nineteenth Century." In *The Probabilistic Revolution,* vol. 1: *Ideas in History,* edited by L. Krüger, L. Daston, and M. Heidelberger, 1: 261–85. Cambridge, Mass.: MIT Press.

Sydenham, P. H. 1979. *Measuring Instruments: Tools of Knowledge and Control.* Stevenage, UK: Peter Peregrinus.

Tallon, R. W. 1994. "Technology Assessment: Electronic Fetal Monitoring." *Midwives Chronicle and Nursing Notes,* May, pp. 186–88.

Taub, L. 1998. "Orrery." In *Instruments of Science: An Historical Encyclopedia,* edited by D. J. Warner and R. Bud, 1: 429–30. New York: Garland.

Taylor, J. K. 1985. "The Impact of Instrumentation on Analytical Chemistry." In *The History and Preservation of Chemical Instrumentation,* edited by J. Stock and M. Orna, pp. 1–17. Dordrecht: D. Reidel.

Taylor, L. R., R. B. Papp, and B. D. Pollard. 1994. *Instrumental Methods for Determining Elements.* New York: VCH Publishers.

Tenner, E. 1996. *Why Things Bite Back.* New York: Knopf.

Turing, A. M. [1950] 1981. "Computing Machinery and Intelligence." In *The Mind's I: Fantasies and Reflections on Self and Soul,* edited by D. R. Hofstadter and D. Dennett, 53–68. New York: Basic Books.

Turner, G. L. E. 1983. *Nineteenth-Century Scientific Instruments.* London: Sotheby Publications; Berkeley: University of California Press.

Twyman, F. 1941. *The Spectrochemical Analysis of Metals and Alloys.* Brooklyn: Chemical Publishing Co.

Valcárcel, M., and M. D. Luque de Castro. 1988. *Automatic Methods of Analysis.* Amsterdam: Elsevier Science Publishers.

Van Fraassen, B. C. 1980. *The Scientific Image.* New York: Oxford University Press.

Van Helden, A., and T. Hankins, eds. 1994. *Instruments.* Special issue of *Osiris.* Chicago: University of Chicago Press.

Van Nostrand's Scientific Encyclopedia. 1983. Edited by D. M. Considine. 6th ed. New York: Van Nostrand Reinhold.

Vance, E. R. 1947. "Direct-Reading Device Provides Rapid Steel Analysis." *Steel,* September 22.

———. 1949. "Melting Control with the Direct Reading Spectrometer." *Journal of Metals* 1 (October): 28–30.

Vincenti, W. 1990. *What Engineers Know and How They Know It: Analytical Studies from Aeronautical History*. Baltimore: Johns Hopkins University Press.

Walker, J. T. 1939. "The Spectrograph as an Aid in Criminal Investigation." In *Proceedings of the Sixth Summer Conference on Spectroscopy and Its Applications*, edited by G. R. Harrison, pp. 1–5. New York: Wiley.

Wallace, A. F. C. 1978. *Rockdale: The Growth of an American Village in the Early Industrial Revolution*. New York: Knopf.

Walsh, D. F. 1988. "The History of Baird Corporation: A Broad Perspective on the Progress of Industrial Spectroscopy." *Applied Spectroscopy* 42: 1336–50.

Warner, D. 1994. "Terrestrial Magnetism: For the Glory of God and the Benefit of Mankind." In *Instruments*, edited by A. van Helden and T. Hankins, 9: 67–84. Special issue of *Osiris*. Chicago: University of Chicago Press.

Watson, J. [1968] 1981. *The Double Helix: A Personal Account of the Discovery of the Structure of DNA*. Edited by G. S. Stent. New York: Norton.

Watson, J., and F. Crick. 1953. "Molecular Structure of Nucleic Acids." *Nature* 171: 737.

Weart, S., ed. 1976. *Selected Papers of Great American Physicists: The Bicentennial Commemorative Volume of The American Physical Society 1976*. New York: American Institute of Physics.

White, F. 1961. *American Industrial Research Laboratories*. Washington, D.C.: Public Affairs Press.

Wideröe, R. 1928. "Über ein Neues Prinzip zur Herstellung hoher Spannungen [On a New Principle in Generating High Voltages]." *Archiv für Elektrotechnik* 21: 387–406.

Williams, C. 1948. "The Role of the Analyst." *Analytical Chemistry* 20, no. 1: 2.

Williams, L. P. 1964. *Michael Faraday: A Biography*. New York: Basic Books.

Williams, V. Z. 1959. "Cooperation between Analytical Chemist and Instrument Maker." *Analytical Chemistry* 31, no. 11: 25A–33A.

Wilson, E. B. 1952. *An Introduction to Scientific Research*. New York: McGraw-Hill.

Wilson, P. 1955. "The Waterwheels of John Smeaton." *Transactions of the Newcomen Society for the Study of the History of Engineering and Technology* 30: 25–48.

Wilson, R. R. 1938. "Magnetic and Electrostatic Focusing in the Cyclotron." *Physical Review* 53: 408–420.

———. 1941. "A Vacuum-Tight Sliding Seal." *Review of Scientific Instruments* 12: 91–93.

Wise, N. 1979. "The Mutual Embrace of Electricity and Magnetism." *Science* 203 (March 30): 1310–18.

———, ed. 1995. *The Values of Precision*. Princeton, N.J.: Princeton University Press.

Wollaston, W. H. 1812. "On a Method of Freezing at a Distance." *Philosophical Transactions of the Royal Society* 103: 71–74.

———. 1813. "On a Method of Freezing at a Distance." *Annals of Philosophy* 2: 230.

Wood, R. W. 1911. *Physical Optics.* New York: Macmillan.

———. 1912. "Diffraction Gratings with Controlled Groove Form and Abnormal Distribution of Intensity." *Philosophical Magazine* 23: 310–17.

———. 1935. "Anomalous Diffraction Gratings." *Physical Review* 48: 928–36.

———. 1944. "Improved Diffraction Gratings and Replicas." *Journal of the Optical Society of America* 34: 509–16.

Wright, E. C. 1938. "The Early Smeatonians." *Transactions of the Newcomen Society for the Study of the History of Engineering and Technology* 18: 101–10.

Wright, J. 1999. *Vision, Venture and Volunteers: Fifty Years of History of the Pittsburgh Conference on Analytical Chemistry and Applied Spectroscopy.* Philadelphia: Chemical Heritage Foundation.

Yousem, D. M., P. A. Janick, et al. 1990. "Pseudoatrophy of the Cervical Portion of the Spinal Cord on MR Images: A Manifestation of the Truncation Artifact." *American Journal of Roentgenology* 154, no. 5: 1069–73.

Zelizer, V., and A. Rotman. 1979. *Morals and Markets: The Development of Life Insurance in the United States.* New York: Columbia University Press.

Zworykin, V. K., and J. A. Rajchman. 1939. "The Electrostatic Electron Multiplier." *Proceedings of the Institute of Radio Engineers* 27: 558–66.

Index

Compositor:	G & S Typesetters, Inc.
Text:	10/13 Aldus
Display:	Aldus
Indexer:	Andrew Joron
Printer and binder:	Thomson-Shore, Inc.